Getting Started with the Graph Query Language (GQL)

A complete guide to designing, querying, and managing graph databases with GQL

Ricky Sun

Jason Zhang

Yuri Simione

Getting Started with the Graph Query Language (GQL)

Copyright © 2025 Packt Publishing

Portfolio Director: Sunith Shetty
Relationship Lead: Teny Thomas
Project Manager: Shashank Desai
Content Engineer: Saba Umme Salma
Technical Editors: Seemanjay Ameriya and Aniket Shetty
Copy Editor: Safis Editing
Indexer: Rekha Nair
Production Designer: Shantanu Zagade

First published: August 2025

Production reference: 2031225

Published by Packt Publishing Ltd.
Grosvenor House
11 St Paul's Square
Birmingham
B3 1RB, UK.

ISBN 978-1-83620-401-5
www.packtpub.com

Contributors

About the authors

Ricky Sun is a serial entrepreneur and an expert in high-performance storage and computing systems. He is also the author of several technology books. Ricky began his career in Silicon Valley, working with his professor a year before graduating from Santa Clara University. Over the past 20+ years, he has experienced three mergers and acquisitions. Ultipa is his fourth venture. Ricky previously served as CTO of EMC Asia R&D Center, managing director of EMC Labs China, and chief architect of Splashtop, a pre-IPO unicorn start-up. He was also the CEO of Allhistory, a knowledge graph-powered causality search engine, now part of Human, a publicly traded online education services company. Ricky is also the author of *The Essential Criteria of Graph Databases*.

Jason Zhang holds a master's degree in computer science from SUPINFO, Paris, and has over 10 years of IT experience. He has worked for start-ups and is currently the director of engineering at Ultipa and CTO at Ultipa HK. In his role, Jason has contributed to the design and implementation of Ultipa's property graph database, recognized as one of the most performant and innovative in the market. He leads the implementation of Ultipa Graph and adds support for the GQL standard.

Yuri Simione holds a master's degree in computer science from the University of Pisa, Italy. He has nearly 30 years of IT experience. He has worked with large enterprises such as Xerox and EMC (now Dell EMC), specializing in managing unstructured information projects with products such as OpenText Documentum and Adobe Experience Manager. In 2014, Yuri recognized the potential of graph databases for handling unstructured data and shifted his focus to this technology and the semantic knowledge graphs market. He currently serves as VP of partnerships and alliances at Ultipa, a leading graph database and graph analytics vendor.

About the reviewers

Keith Hare has worked with JCC Consulting, Inc. since 1985, first as a senior consultant and then, since 2019, as president. At JCC Consulting, he has worked on high-performance, high-availability database applications in multiple companies and multiple industries, focusing on database administration, performance tuning, and data replication.

Keith has participated in both US and international standards processes for the database languages SQL and GQL since 1988 and has served as the convenor of the international committee ISO/IEC JTC1 SC32 WG3 Database Languages since 2005.

Pearl Cao brings over a decade of experience in the IT industry, having worked across a wide range of sectors. Currently serving as senior content strategist at Ultipa, she leads all technical writing initiatives for the company. Pearl spearheaded the development of Ultipa GQL's official documentation, training programs, and certification systems, playing a central role in shaping how users and partners engage with Ultipa's technology. Her work bridges the gap between complex graph database concepts and clear, actionable content for both technical and business audiences.

Table of Contents

Chapter 3: Getting Started with GQL   65

Chapter 4: GQL Basics 83

Preface

Over the past several decades, the world of data has evolved dramatically—from the structured era of relational databases to the expansive realms of big data and fast data. Today, we are entering a new phase: the age of deep and connected data. As data volumes grow and analytics become increasingly interdependent, traditional database systems are being reimagined. Graph technology has emerged as a powerful solution, offering new possibilities for modeling and querying complex relationships.

Before the standardization of **Graph Query Language** (**GQL**), the graph database landscape was fragmented. Popular query languages such as Cypher (Neo4j), Gremlin (Apache TinkerPop), GSQL (TigerGraph), UQL (Ultipa), and AQL (ArangoDB) each introduced unique features tailored to specific platforms. While these innovations advanced the field, they also created challenges for users—requiring time and effort to learn multiple proprietary syntaxes.

The introduction of GQL (ISO/IEC 39075) marks a pivotal moment in database history. As the second standardized database query language—following SQL's release in 1986 (ANSI) and 1987 (ISO)—GQL provides a unified, vendor-neutral syntax for querying graph databases. This standardization fosters interoperability, reduces learning curves, and accelerates adoption across industries.

This book begins with the evolution of graph databases and query languages, setting the stage for a comprehensive understanding of GQL. You'll explore its syntax, structure, data types, and clauses, and gain hands-on experience through practical examples. As you progress, you'll learn how to write efficient queries, optimize performance, and apply GQL to real-world scenarios such as fraud detection.

By the end of this journey, you'll have a solid grasp of GQL, be equipped to implement a graph-based solution with GQL, and gain insight into the future direction of graph technology and its growing role in data ecosystems.

Who this book is for

As GQL emerges as a new standard for querying graph databases, its relevance is expanding across nearly every industry. This book is designed for a wide range of professionals who work with data and seek to harness the power of graph-based systems. Whether you're a developer, engineer, data analyst, **database administrator (DBA)**, data engineer, or data scientist, you'll find valuable insights and practical guidance in these pages. GQL opens new possibilities for modeling and analyzing complex, interconnected data. As such, this book serves as both an introduction and a deep dive into the language, helping readers of all backgrounds understand and apply GQL effectively in real-world scenarios.

Note: Some features covered in this book may not work as expected with the current versions of GQL Playground and the cloud. These features are planned for future releases. The book includes them to provide a comprehensive guide to GQL and its evolving capabilities.

What this book covers

Chapter 1, Evolution Towards Graph Databases, traces the journey from relational databases to NoSQL, and ultimately to the emergence of GQL, which promises to redefine how we query and manage complex, interconnected data in the digital age.

Chapter 2, Key Concepts of GQL, introduces the key concepts of GQL and graph theory. The foundational knowledge covered here will enhance your understanding of the remaining sections of the book.

Chapter 3, Getting Started with GQL, takes you on a journey to acquiring practical experience in interacting with graph data using GQL. You will learn how to formulate and execute GQL queries against a graph database, which is essential for querying, manipulating, and analyzing graph-structured data.

Chapter 4, GQL Basics, explores the fundamentals of GQL, uncovering the power of GQL statements and learning how to match data and return results tailored to your needs.

Chapter 5, Exploring Expressions and Operators, explores expressions and operators to be able to filter nodes and relationships, compute metrics over graph structures, construct dynamic labels, and transform properties on the fly.

Chapter 6, Working with GQL Functions, introduces a variety of essential functions for effective data manipulation and analysis.

Chapter 7, Delve into Advanced Clauses, delves into more advanced usages of GQL that allow for more sophisticated graph queries and operations.

Chapter 8, Configuring Sessions, delves into session management, exploring the creation, modification, and termination of sessions. This chapter presents a detailed overview of the session context, commands for setting session parameters, and resetting and closing sessions.

Chapter 9, Graph Transactions, delves into the specifics of initiating transactions using the TRANSACTION commands, detailing the syntax, usage, and conditions.

Chapter 10, Conformance to the GQL Standard, overviews conformance to the GQL standard, including required capabilities, optional features, and implementation-defined and implementation-dependent elements.

Chapter 11, Beyond GQL, explores GQL extensions provided by Ultipa Graph Database, including operations such as additional options to create a graph, constraints, and index operations, as well as access controls.

Chapter 12, A Case Study – Anti-Fraud, provides hands-on practice by tackling a common issue with GQL, identifying suspicious transactions in bank accounts.

Chapter 13, The Evolving Landscape of GQL, explores local Terraform automation processes and implementing a CI/CD pipeline to apply Terraform configuration automatically.

Chapter 14, Glossary and Resources, provides definitions of key terms and a comprehensive list of required and optional GQL features, along with additional resources for further learning.

Download the example code files

The code bundle for the book is hosted on GitHub at https://github.com/PacktPublishing/Getting-Started-with-the-Graph-Query-Language-GQL. We also have other code bundles from our rich catalog of books and videos available at https://github.com/PacktPublishing. Check them out!

Download the color images

We also provide a PDF file that has color images of the screenshots/diagrams used in this book. You can download it here: https://packt.link/gbp/9781836204015.

Conventions used

There are a number of text conventions used throughout this book.

CodeInText: Indicates code words in text, database table names, folder names, filenames, file extensions, pathnames, dummy URLs, user input, and Twitter/X handles. For example: "TRAIL mode excludes paths that contain duplicate edges, such as the a->b->a->b path, where the edge a->b is traversed more than once."

A block of code is set as follows:

```
GQL:
INSERT (a:Node {_id: 'a'}),
       (b:Node {_id: 'b'}),
       (c:Node {_id: 'c'}),
       (i:Node {_id: 'i'}),
       (j:Node {_id: 'j'}),
       (b)-[:Edge]->(a),
       (a)-[:Edge]->(c),
       (c)-[:Edge]->(i),
       (i)-[:Edge]->(j)
```

When we wish to draw your attention to a particular part of a code block, the relevant lines or items are set in bold:

```
GQL:
FOR id in ["a", "b", "z"]
OPTIONAL CALL {
    MATCH (start {_id: id })
    MATCH (start)-(end)
    RETURN COLLECT_LIST(end._id) as neigbours
}
LET neigbours = COALESCE(neigbours, [])
RETURN id, neigbours
```

Bold: Indicates a new term, an important word, or words that you see on the screen. For instance, words in menus or dialog boxes appear in the text like this. For example: "In this case, the results are generated by computing the **Cartesian product** of the result sets from the individual patterns."

Warnings or important notes appear like this.

Tips and tricks appear like this.

Get in touch

Feedback from our readers is always welcome.

General feedback: If you have questions about any aspect of this book or have any general feedback, please email us at customercare@packt.com and mention the book's title in the subject of your message.

Errata: Although we have taken every care to ensure the accuracy of our content, mistakes do happen. If you have found a mistake in this book, we would be grateful if you reported this to us. Please visit http://www.packt.com/submit-errata, click **Submit Errata**, and fill in the form.

Piracy: If you come across any illegal copies of our works in any form on the internet, we would be grateful if you would provide us with the location address or website name. Please contact us at copyright@packt.com with a link to the material.

If you are interested in becoming an author: If there is a topic that you have expertise in and you are interested in either writing or contributing to a book, please visit http://authors.packt.com/.

Share your thoughts

Once you've read *Getting Started with the Graph Query Language (GQL)*, we'd love to hear your thoughts! Scan the QR code below to go straight to the Amazon review page for this book and share your feedback.

https://packt.link/r/1836204019

Your review is important to us and the tech community and will help us make sure we're delivering excellent quality content.

Free Benefits with Your Book

This book comes with free benefits to support your learning. Activate them now for instant access (see the "*How to Unlock*" section for instructions).

Here's a quick overview of what you can instantly unlock with your purchase:

PDF and ePub Copies   **Next-Gen Web-Based Reader**

Free PDF and ePub versions

Next-Gen Reader

Access a DRM-free PDF copy of this book to read anywhere, on any device.

Use a DRM-free ePub version with your favorite e-reader.

Multi-device progress sync: Pick up where you left off, on any device.

Highlighting and notetaking: Capture ideas and turn reading into lasting knowledge.

Bookmarking: Save and revisit key sections whenever you need them.

Dark mode: Reduce eye strain by switching to dark or sepia themes.

How to Unlock

Scan the QR code (or go to packtpub.com/unlock). Search for this book by name, confirm the edition, and then follow the steps on the page.

Note: Keep your invoice handy. Purchases made directly from Packt don't require one.

1

Evolution Towards Graph Databases

In today's data-driven world, the way we store, manage, and query data has evolved significantly. As businesses and organizations handle more complex, interconnected datasets, traditional database models are being stretched to their limits. Graph databases, in particular, have gained traction due to their ability to model relationships in ways that relational databases cannot. According to a recent report by Gartner, the graph database market is expected to grow at a **compound annual growth rate (CAGR)** of 28.1%, reflecting its increasing adoption across industries such as finance, healthcare, and social media.

This chapter explores the evolution of database query languages, right from the early innovations that laid the foundation for modern database systems. We'll trace the journey from relational databases to NoSQL, and ultimately to the emergence of **Graph Query Language (GQL)**, which promises to redefine how we query and manage complex, interconnected data in the digital age.

Free Benefits with Your Book

Your purchase includes a free PDF copy of this book along with other exclusive benefits. Check the *Free Benefits with Your Book* section in the *Preface* to unlock them instantly and maximize your learning experience.

History of database query languages

Before electronic databases, data management was manual. Records were maintained in physical forms such as ledgers, filing cabinets, and card catalogs. Until the mid-20th century, this was the primary approach to data management. This method, while systematic, was labor-intensive and prone to human errors.

Discussions on database technology often begin with the 1950s and 1960s, particularly with the introduction of magnetic tapes and disks. These developments paved the way for navigational data models and, eventually, relational models. While these discussions are valuable, they sometimes overlook deeper historical perspectives.

Before magnetic tapes, punched cards were widely used, particularly for the 1890 U.S. Census. The company behind these tabulating systems later evolved into IBM Corporation, one of the first major technological conglomerates. I vividly recall my father attending college courses on modern computing, where key experiments involved operating IBM punch-card computers—decades before personal computers emerged in the 1980s.

Examining punched card systems reveals a connection to the operation of looms, one of humanity's earliest sophisticated machines. Looms, which possibly originated in China and spread globally, have been found in various forms, including in remote African and South American villages.

Across the 3,000 to 5,000 years of recorded history, there have been many inventions for memory-aiding, messaging, scheduling, or recording data, ranging from tally sticks to quipu (khipu). While tally sticks were once thought to be a European invention, Marco Polo, after his extensive travels in China, reported that they were widely used there to track daily transactions.

On the other hand, when quipu was first discovered by Spanish colonists, it was believed to be an Inca invention. However, if the colonists had paid more attention to the pronunciation of *khipu*, they would have noticed that it means *recording book* in ancient Chinese. This suggests that quipu was a popular method for recording data and information long before written languages were developed.

Why focus on these pre-database inventions? Understanding these historical innovations through a graph-thinking lens helps illustrate how interconnected these concepts are and underscores the importance of recognizing these connections. Embracing this perspective allows us to better understand and master modern technologies, such as graph databases and graph query languages.

Early computer-based data management

The advent of electronic computers marked the beginning of computerized data storage. World Wars I and II drove major advancements in computing technology, notably the German Enigma machine and the Polish and Allied forces deciphering its encrypted messages, which contained top-secret information from Nazi Germany. When mechanical machines proved inadequate for the required computing power—such as in brute-force decryption—electronic and much more powerful alternatives were invented. Consequently, the earliest computers were developed during and before the end of World War II.

Early computers such as the ENIAC (1946) and UNIVAC (1951) were used for calculations and data processing. The Bureau of the Census and military and defense departments quickly adopted them to optimize troop deployment and arrange the most cost-effective logistics. These efforts laid the foundation for modern global supply chains, network analytics, and social behavior network studies.

The concept of systematic data management, or databases, became feasible with the rapid advancement of electronic computers and storage media, such as magnetic disks. Initially, most of these computers operated in isolation; the development of computer networks lagged significantly behind telecommunication networks for over a century.

The development of database technologies is centered around how data modeling is conducted, and the general perception is that there have been three phases so far:

- *Phase 1*: Navigational data modeling
- *Phase 2*: Relational (or SQL) data modeling
- *Phase 3*: Not-only-SQL (or post-relational, or GQL) data modeling

Let's briefly examine the three development phases so that we have a clear understanding of why GQL or the graphical way of data modeling and processing was invented.

Navigational data modeling

Before navigational data modeling (or navigational databases), the access of data on punched-cards or magnetic-tapes was sequential. Hence, this was very counter-productive. To improve speed, systems introduced *references*, which were similar to pointers, that allowed users to navigate data more efficiently. This led to the development of two data navigation models:

- Hierarchical model (or tree-like model)
- Network model

The hierarchical model was first developed by IBM in the 1960s on top of their mainframe computers, while the network model, though conceptually more comprehensive, was never widely adopted beyond the mainframe era. Both models were quickly displaced by the relational model in the 1970s.

One key reason for this shift was that navigational database programming is intrinsically procedural, focusing on instructing the computer systems with steps on how to access the desired data record. This approach had two major drawbacks:

- Strong data dependency
- Low usability due to programming complexity

Relational data modeling

The relational model, unlike the navigational model, is intrinsically declarative. This means instructing the system what data to retrieve, which means better data independence and program usability.

Another key reason for the shift from navigational databases/models was their limited search capabilities, as data records were stored using linked lists. This limitation led Edgar F. Codd, while working at IBM's San Jose, California Labs, to invent tables as a replacement for linked lists. His groundbreaking work culminated in the highly influential 1970 paper titled *A Relational Model of Data for Large Shared Data Banks*. This seminal paper inspired a host of relational databases, including IBM's *System R* (1974), UC Berkeley's *INGRES* (1974, which spawned several well-known products such as PostgreSQL, Sybase, and Microsoft SQL Server), and Larry Ellison's *Oracle* (1977).

Not-only-SQL data modeling

Today, there are approximately 500 known and active **database management systems (DBMS)** worldwide (as shown in *Figure 1.1*). While over one-third are relational DBMS, the past two decades have seen a rise in hundreds of non-relational (NoSQL) databases. This growth is driven by increasing data volumes, which have given rise to many big data processing frameworks that utilize both data modeling and processing techniques beyond the relational model. Additionally, evolving business demands have led to more sophisticated architectural designs, requiring more streamlined data processing.

The entry of major players into the database market has further propelled this transformation, with large technology companies spearheading the development of new database systems tailored to handle diverse and increasingly complex data structures. These companies have helped define and redefine database paradigms, providing a foundation for a variety of solutions in different industries.

As the landscape has continued to evolve, OpenAI, among other cutting-edge companies, has contributed to this revolution with diverse database systems to optimize data processing in machine learning models. In OpenAI's system architecture, a variety of databases (both commercial and open source) are used, including *PostgreSQL* (RDBMS), *Redis* (key-value), *Elasticsearch* (full-text), *MongoDB* (document), and possibly *Rockset* (a derivative of the popular *KV-library RocksDB*, ideal for real-time data analytics). This heterogeneous approach is typical in large-scale, especially highly distributed, data processing environments. Often, multiple types of databases are leveraged to meet diverse data processing needs, reflecting the difficulty—if not impossibility—of a single database type performing all functions optimally.

Complete trend, starting with January 2013

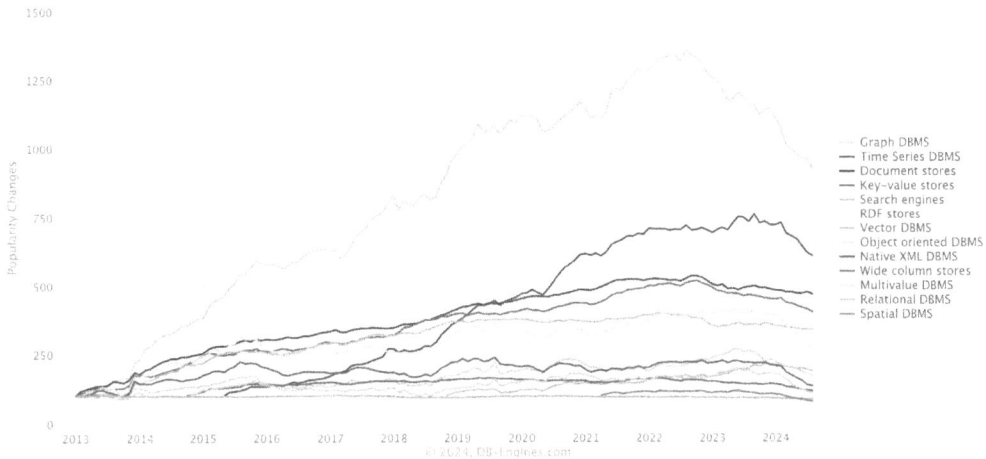

Figure 1.1: Changes in Database popularity per category (August 2024, DB-Engines)

Despite the wide range of database genres, large language models still struggle with questions requiring "deep knowledge." *Figure 1.2* illustrates how a large language model encounters challenges with queries necessitating extensive traversal.

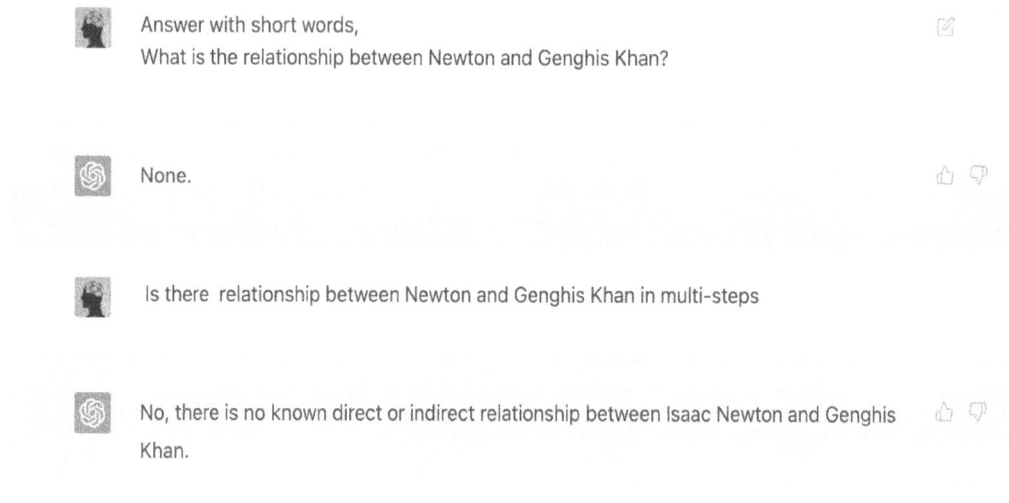

Answer with short words,
What is the relationship between Newton and Genghis Khan?

None.

Is there relationship between Newton and Genghis Khan in multi-steps

No, there is no known direct or indirect relationship between Isaac Newton and Genghis Khan.

Figure 1.2: Hallucination with LLM

The question in *Figure 1.2* involves finding causal paths (simply the shortest path) between different entities. While large language models are trained on extensive datasets, including Wikipedia, they may struggle to calculate and retrieve hidden paths between entities if they are not directly connected.

Figure 1.3 demonstrates how Wikipedia articles—represented as nodes (titles or hyperlinks) and their relationships as predicates—can be ingested into the Ultipa graph database. By performing a real-time six-hop-deep shortest path query, the results yield casual paths that are self-explanatory:

1. Genghis Khan launched the Mongol invasions of West Asia and Europe.
2. These invasions triggered the spread of the Black Death.
3. The last major outbreak of the Black Death was the Great Plague of London.
4. Isaac Newton fled the plague while attending Trinity College.

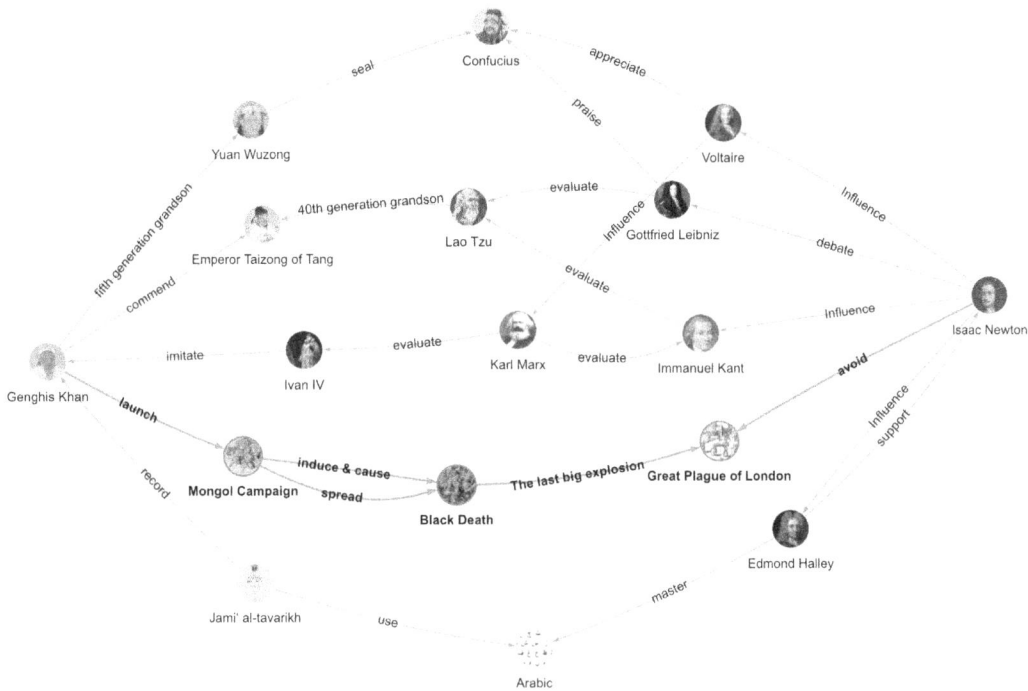

Figure 1.3: The shortest paths between entities using a graph database

The key takeaway from this section is the importance of looking beyond the surface when addressing complex issues or scenarios. The ability to connect the dots and delve deeper into the underlying details allows for identifying root causes, which in turn fosters better decision-making and a more comprehensive understanding of the world's intricate dynamics.

The rise of SQL

The introduction of the relational model revolutionized database management by offering a more structured and flexible way to organize and retrieve data. With the relational model as its foundation, SQL emerged as the standard query language, enabling users to interact with relational databases in a more efficient and intuitive manner. This section will explore how SQL's development, built upon the relational model, became central to modern database systems and continues to influence their evolution today.

The rise of the relational model

Edgar F. Codd's 1970 paper, *A Relational Model of Data for Large Shared Data Banks* (https://www.seas.upenn.edu/~zives/03f/cis550/codd.pdf) laid the foundation for the relational model. Codd proposed a table-based structure for organizing data, introducing the key concepts of relations (tables), columns (attributes), rows (tuples), primary keys, and foreign keys. When compared to the navigational model (hierarchical model), such a structure provided a more intuitive and flexible way to handle data.

> While we state that the relational model is more intuitive and flexible, it is within the context of dealing with data processing scenarios back in the 1970s-1990s. Things have gradually and constantly changed. The relational model has been facing more challenges and criticism with the rise of NoSQL and eventually the standardization of GQL. We will expand the topic on the limitations of SQL and the promises of GQL in the last section of this chapter.

The key concept of the relational model is rather simple, as simple as just five components, which are table, schema, key, relationship, and transaction. Let's break them down one by one.

Table

A table, or relation, in the relational model is a structured collection of related data organized into rows and columns. Each table is defined by its schema, which specifies the structure and constraints of the table. Here's a breakdown of its components:

- *Table Name*: Each table has a unique name that describes its purpose. For instance, a table named `Employees` would likely store employee-related information.

- *Columns (Attributes)*: Each table consists of a set of columns, also known as attributes or fields. Columns represent the specific characteristics or properties of the entities described by the table. Each column has a name and a data type, which defines the kind of data it can hold. For example, in an `Employees` table, columns might include `EmployeeID`, `FirstName`, `LastName`, `HireDate`, and `Department`. The data type for each column could be integer, varchar (variable character), date, etc.

- *Rows (Tuples)*: Rows, or tuples, represent individual records within a table. Each row contains a set of values corresponding to the columns defined in the table. For example, a row in the `Employees` table might include `101`, `John`, `Doe`, `2023-06-15`, `Marketing`. Each row is a unique instance of the data described by the table.

Schema

Another key concept tied to tables (sometimes even tied to the entire RDBMS) is the schema. The schema of a table is a blueprint that outlines the table's structure. It includes the following:

- *Column Definitions*: For each column, the schema specifies its name, data type, and any constraints. Constraints might include NOT NULL (indicating that a column cannot have null values), UNIQUE (ensuring all values in a column are distinct), or DEFAULT (providing a default value if none is specified).

- *Primary Key*: A primary key is a column or a set of columns that uniquely identifies each row in the table. It ensures that no two rows can have the same value for the primary key columns. This uniqueness constraint is crucial for maintaining data integrity and enabling efficient data retrieval. For example, EmployeeID in the Employees table could serve as the primary key.

- *Foreign Keys*: Foreign keys are columns that create relationships between tables. They refer to the primary key of another table, establishing a link between the two tables. This mechanism supports referential integrity, ensuring that relationships between data in different tables are consistent.

Here we need to talk about normalization, which is a process applied to table design to reduce redundancy and improve data integrity. It involves decomposing tables into smaller, related tables and defining relationships between them. The goal is to minimize duplicate data and ensure that each piece of information is stored in only one place.

For example, rather than storing employee department information repeatedly in the Employees table, a separate Departments table can be created, with a foreign key in the Employees table linking to it.

> The normalization concept sounds absolutely wonderful, but only on the surface. In many large data warehouses, too many tables have been formed. What was once seen as being intuitive and flexible in the relational model, can be a huge limitation and burden from a data governance perspective.

Relationships

Entity Relationship (ER) modeling is a foundational technique for designing databases using the relational model. Developed by Peter Chen in 1976, ER modeling provides a graphical framework for representing data and its relationships. It is crucial for understanding and organizing the data within a relational database. The keyword of ER modeling is graphical. The core concepts include entities, relationships, and attributes:

- *Entities*: In ER modeling, an entity represents a distinct object or concept within the database. For example, in a university database, entities might include Student, Course, and Professor. Each entity is represented as a table in the relational model.

- *Attributes*: Attributes describe the properties of entities. For instance, the Student entity might have attributes such as Student_ID, Name, Date_Of_Birth, and Major. Attributes become columns within the corresponding table.

- *Relationships*: Relationships in ER modeling illustrate how entities are associated with one another. Relationships represent the connections between entities and are essential for understanding how data is interrelated. For example, a Student might be enrolled in a Course, creating a relationship between these two entities.

The caveat about relationships is that there are many types of relationships:

- *One-to-One*: In this type of relationship, each instance of entity A is associated with exactly one instance of entity B, and vice versa. For example, each Student might have one Student_ID, and each Student_ID corresponds to exactly one student.

- *One-to-Many*: This relationship type occurs when a single instance of entity A is associated with multiple instances of entity B, but each instance of entity B is associated with only one instance of entity A. For example, a Professor might teach multiple Courses, but each Course is taught by only one Professor. If we pause here, we can immediately sense that a problem will arise when such a rigid relationship is enforced, if a course is to be taught by two or three professors (a rare scenario but it does happen), the schema and table design would need a change. And the more exceptions you can think of here, the more re-designs you would experience.

- *Many-to-Many*: This relationship occurs when multiple instances of entity A can be associated with multiple instances of entity B. For example, a Student can enroll in multiple Courses, and each Course can have multiple Students enrolled. To model many-to-many relationships, a junction table (or associative entity) is used, which holds foreign keys referencing both entities.

ER diagrams offer a clear and structured way to represent entities, their attributes, and the relationships between them:

- Entities are represented by rectangles

- Attributes are shown as ovals, each connected to its corresponding entity

- Relationships are illustrated as diamonds, linking the relevant entities

This visual framework provides a comprehensive way to design database schemas and better understand how different data elements interact within a system.

> The ER diagram is essentially the graph data model we will be discussing throughout the book. The only difference between SQL and GQL in terms of ER diagrams is that GQL and graph databases natively organize and represent entities and their relationships, while SQL and RDBMS use ER diagrams with metadata, where real data records are stored in lower-dimensional tables. It's tempting to believe that the prevalence of the relational model matches with the limited computing power at the time it was invented. Exponentially higher computing power eventually would demand something more advanced, and more intuitive and flexible as well.

Transactions

Transactions are a crucial aspect of relational databases, ensuring that operations are performed reliably and consistently. To better understand how these principles work in practice, let's explore ACID properties.

The ACID properties – **Atomicity**, **Consistency**, **Isolation**, and **Durability** – define the key attributes of a transaction. Let's explore them in detail:

- *Atomicity*: Atomicity ensures that a transaction is treated as a single, indivisible unit of work. This is crucial for maintaining data integrity, especially in scenarios where multiple operations are performed as part of a single transaction. This means that either all operations within the transaction are completed successfully, or none are applied. If any operation fails, the entire transaction is rolled back, leaving the database in its previous state. It prevents partial updates that could lead to inconsistent data states.

- *Consistency*: Consistency ensures that a transaction takes the database from one valid state to another valid state, preserving the integrity constraints defined in the schema. All business rules, data constraints, and relationships must be maintained throughout the transaction. Consistency guarantees that database rules are enforced and that the database remains in a valid state before and after the transaction.

- *Isolation*: Isolation ensures that the operations of a transaction are isolated from other concurrent transactions. Even if multiple transactions are executed simultaneously, each transaction operates as if it were the only one interacting with the database. Isolation prevents interference between transactions, avoiding issues such as dirty reads, non-repeatable reads, and phantom reads. It ensures that each transaction's operations are independent and not affected by others.

- *Durability*: Durability guarantees that once a transaction is committed, its changes are permanent and persist even in the event of a system failure or crash. The committed data is stored in non-volatile memory, ensuring its longevity. Durability ensures that completed transactions are preserved and that changes are not lost due to unforeseen failures. This property provides reliability and trustworthiness in the database system.

These attributes are best illustrated by linking them to a real-world system and application ecosystem. Considering any financial institution's transaction processing system where a transaction involves transferring funds from one account to another, the transaction must ensure that both the debit and credit operations are completed successfully (atomicity), the account balances remain consistent (consistency), other transactions do not see intermediate states (isolation), and the changes persist even if the system fails (durability). These properties are essential for the accuracy and reliability of financial transactions.

The ACID properties were introduced in 1976 by Jim Gray and laid the foundation for reliable database transaction management. These properties were gradually incorporated into the SQL standard with the SQL-86 standard and have since remained integral to relational database systems. For over fifty years, the principles of ACID have been continuously adopted and refined by most relational database vendors, ensuring robust transaction management and data integrity. When comparing relational database management systems (RDBMS) with NoSQL and graph databases, the needs and implementation priorities of ACID properties vary, influencing how these systems handle transaction management and consistency.

Modern RDBMS include robust transaction management mechanisms to handle ACID properties. These systems use techniques such as logging, locking, and recovery to ensure transactions are executed correctly and data integrity is maintained. Managing concurrent transactions is essential for ensuring isolation and consistency. Techniques such as locking (both exclusive and shared) and **multi-version concurrency control** (**MVCC**) are used to handle concurrent access to data and prevent conflicts.

Evolution of NoSQL and new query paradigms

Today, big data is ubiquitous, influencing nearly every industry across the globe. As data grows in complexity and scale, traditional relational databases show limitations in addressing these new challenges. Unlike the structured, table-based model of relational databases, the real world is rich, high-dimensional, and interconnected, requiring new approaches to data management. The evolution of big data and NoSQL technologies demonstrates how traditional models struggled to meet the needs of complex, multi-faceted datasets. In this context, graph databases have emerged as a powerful and flexible solution, capable of modeling and querying intricate relationships in ways that were previously difficult to achieve. As industries continue to generate and rely on interconnected data, graph databases are positioning themselves as a transformative force, offering significant advantages in managing and leveraging complex data relationships.

The emergence of NoSQL and big data

The advent of big data marked a significant turning point in data management and analytics. While we often date the onset of the big data era to around 2012, the groundwork for this revolution was laid much earlier. A key milestone was the release of Hadoop by Yahoo! in 2006, which was subsequently donated to the Apache Foundation. Hadoop's design was heavily inspired by Google's seminal papers on the **Google File System** (**GFS**) and MapReduce.

GFS, introduced in 2003, and MapReduce, which followed in 2004, provided a new way of handling vast amounts of data across distributed systems. These innovations stemmed from the need to process and analyze the enormous data generated by Google's search engine. At the core of Google's search engine technology was PageRank, a graph algorithm for ranking web pages based on their link structures. Named intentionally as a pun after Google co-founder Larry Page. This historical context illustrates that big data technologies have deep roots in graph theory, evolving towards increasingly sophisticated and large-scale systems.

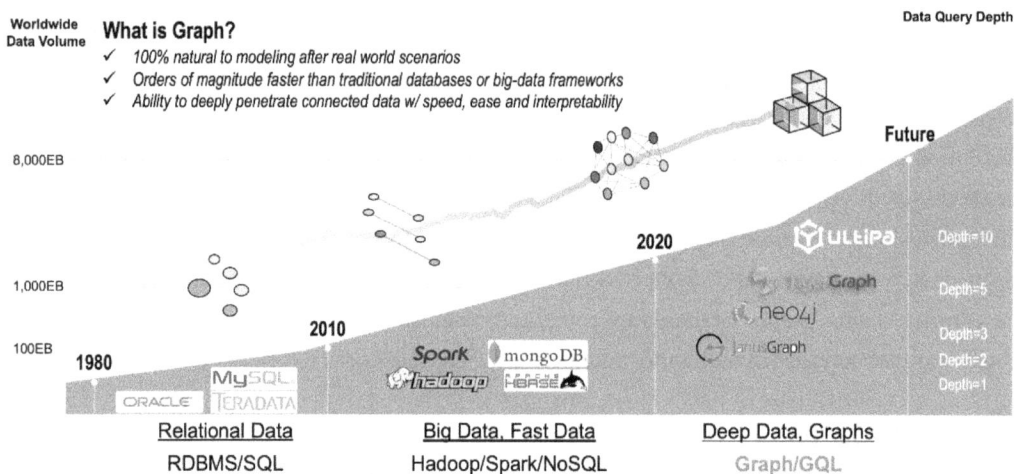

Figure 1.4: From data to big data to fast data and deep data

Examining the trajectory of data processing technologies over the past 50 years reveals a clear evolution through distinct stages:

1. ***The Era of Relational Databases (1970s-present)***: This era is defined by the dominance of relational databases, which organize data into structured tables and use SQL for data manipulation and retrieval.

2. ***The Era of Non-Relational Databases and Big Data Frameworks (2000s-present)***: The rise of NoSQL databases and big data frameworks marked a departure from traditional relational models. These technologies address the limitations of relational databases in handling unstructured data and massive data volumes.

3. ***The Post-Relational Database Era (2020s and beyond)***: Emerging technologies signal a shift towards post-relational databases, including NewSQL and **Graph Query Language** **(GQL)**. These advancements seek to overcome the constraints of previous models and offer enhanced capabilities for managing complex, interconnected data.

Each of these stages has been accompanied by the development of corresponding query languages:

1. *Relational Database—SQL*: Standardized in 1983, SQL became the cornerstone of relational databases, providing a powerful and versatile language for managing structured data.

2. *Non-Relational Database—NoSQL*: The NoSQL movement introduced alternative models for data storage and retrieval, focusing on scalability and flexibility. NoSQL databases extend beyond SQL's capabilities but lack formal standardization.

3. *Post-Relational Database—NewSQL and GQL*: NewSQL brings SQL-like functionality to scalable, distributed systems, while GQL, with the first edition released in 2024, is designed to address the needs of graph databases.

These stages reflect an evolution in data characteristics and processing capabilities:

1. *Relational Database—Data, Pre-Big Data Era*: Focused on managing structured data with well-defined schemas.

2. *Non-Relational Database—Big Data, Fast Data Era*: Emphasized handling large volumes of diverse and rapidly changing data, addressing the 4Vs—volume, variety, velocity, and veracity.

3. *Post-Relational Database—Deep Data, or Graph Data Era*: Represented a shift towards understanding and leveraging complex relationships within data, enhancing depth and analysis beyond the 4Vs.

The 4Vs – volume, variety, velocity, and veracity – capture the essence of big data:

- *Volume*: The sheer amount of data
- *Variety*: The different types and sources of data
- *Velocity*: The speed at which data is generated and processed
- *Veracity*: The reliability and accuracy of data

As data complexity grows, an additional dimension, depth, becomes crucial. This deep data perspective focuses on uncovering hidden relationships and extracting maximum value from interconnected data.

Understanding deep relationships among data is essential for various business and technological challenges:

- *Business Dimension*: Value is embedded within networks of relationships, making it critical to analyze these connections to derive actionable insights.

- *Technology Dimension*: Traditional databases struggle with network-based value extraction due to their tabular structure, which limits their ability to quickly identify deep associations between entities.

From 2004 to 2006, as Yahoo! developed Hadoop, other data processing projects emerged from different teams within the company. Yahoo!'s vast server clusters processed the massive volumes of web logs, posing significant processing challenges. Hadoop was designed to utilize low-cost, low-configuration machines in a distributed manner, but it encountered inefficiencies in terms of data processing speed and analytical depth. Despite excelling at handling large volumes and a variety of data types, these limitations led to its donation to the Apache Foundation.

The introduction of *Apache Spark* in 2014 brought a major shift. Developed by the University of California, Berkeley, Spark addressed many of Hadoop's performance issues. Its in-memory processing capabilities allowed it to process data up to 100x faster than Hadoop. With components such as GraphX, Spark enabled graph analytics, including algorithms such as PageRank and Connected Component. However, Spark's focus remained on batch processing rather than real-time, dynamic data processing, leaving gaps in real-time, deep data analysis.

The ability to process deep data involves extracting insights from multi-layered, multi-dimensional data quickly. Graph databases and GQL, the focus of this book, are designed to address these challenges. By applying graph theory principles, they enable advanced network analysis, offering unique advantages over traditional NoSQL databases and big data frameworks. Their ability to perform real-time, dynamic analysis of complex data relationships makes them well-suited to the evolving demands of data management and analysis.

This book will guide readers through the historical development, current state, and future trends of graph databases, emphasizing their relevance to market needs and technological implementation.

Graphs and graph models

Graphs offer a natural way to model entities and relationships in data, making them an essential tool in various domains. From social networks to recommendation systems, graph-based approaches provide a flexible and efficient means of representing complex structures. Let's explore the theoretical foundations of graph models and their role in modern data management.

Graph theory and graph data models

Graph database technology is fundamentally rooted in graph theory, which provides both the theoretical and practical foundations for graph computing. In this discussion, we will use the terms *graph computing* and *graph database* interchangeably, highlighting that computing plays a more pivotal role than storage in this context. This section explores the evolution of graph theory and its application to graph data modeling.

Graph theory can be traced back nearly 300 years to the groundbreaking work of the Swiss mathematician Leonhard Euler. Widely regarded as one of the greatest mathematicians, Euler laid the groundwork for this discipline with his solution to the Seven Bridges of Königsberg problem. In 1736, he abstracted the city's physical layout—which included seven bridges and two islands connected to the mainland, forming four distinct land areas—into a graph composed of nodes and edges. His work led to the development of graph theory, which focuses on the study of graphs—structures made up of *vertices* (nodes) connected by *edges* (links or relationships).

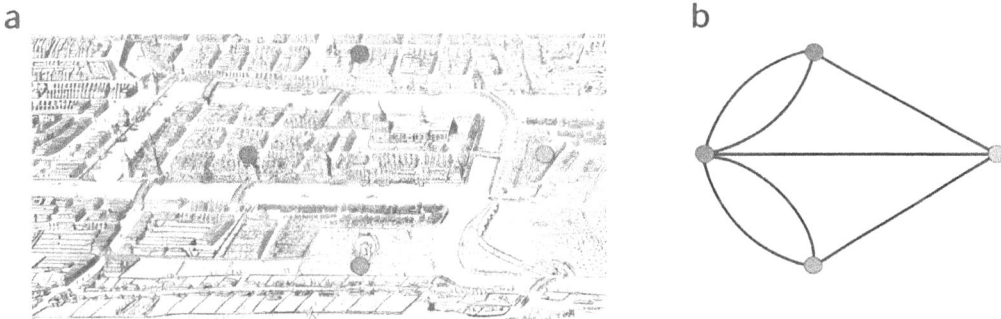

Figure 1.5: Seven Bridges of Königsberg and graph theory

Euler's exploration of the Seven Bridges problem involved determining whether it was possible to traverse each bridge exactly once in a single journey. He proved that such a path, known as a Eulerian path, was impossible in this specific configuration. Euler's criteria for a Eulerian path are still fundamental to graph theory today: a graph can have a Eulerian path if and only if it has exactly zero or two vertices with an odd degree (number of edges connected to a vertex). If all vertices have even degrees, a Eulerian circuit, a special type of path that returns to the starting point, can be found. This early work established essential graph theory concepts that continue to influence modern graph computing.

Graph theory found practical applications beyond Euler's initial problem. One notable example is the map coloring problem, which arose during the Age of Discovery and the subsequent rise of nation-states. The problem of coloring maps such that no two adjacent regions share the same color was first addressed by mathematicians in the mid-19th century. This problem led to the formulation of the Four-Color Theorem, which states that any map can be colored with no more than four colors such that no two adjacent regions share the same color. The proof of this theorem, completed with the assistance of computer algorithms in 1976, marked a significant milestone in both graph theory and computational methods.

In parallel with these developments, Johann B. Listing's introduction of topology in 1847, which included concepts such as connectivity and dimensionality, further advanced the field. Sylvester's work in 1878 formalized the concept of a graph as a collection of vertices connected by edges, introducing terminology that remains central to graph theory.

The systematic study of random graphs by mathematicians Erdős and Rényi in the 1960s laid the groundwork for understanding complex networks. Random graph theory became a fundamental tool for analyzing various types of networks, from social interactions to biological systems.

The advent of the semantic web in the early 1990s, proposed by Tim Berners-Lee, marked a significant application of graph theory to the World Wide Web. The semantic web conceptualizes web resources as nodes in a vast, interconnected graph, promoting the development of standards like the **Resource Description Framework (RDF)**. While RDF did not achieve widespread industry adoption, it paved the way for the growth of knowledge graphs and social graphs, which became integral to major tech companies such as Yahoo!, Google, and Facebook.

Graph databases are now considered a subset of NoSQL databases, providing a contrast to traditional SQL-based relational databases. While SQL databases use tabular structures to model data, graph databases leverage high-dimensional graphs to represent complex relationships more naturally. Graph databases utilize vertices and edges to encode relationships, offering a more intuitive and efficient means of handling interconnected data. This approach contrasts with the tabular, two-dimensional constraints of traditional relational databases, which often struggle with complex, high-dimensional problems.

Graph theory has various applications, including navigation, recommendation engines, and resource scheduling. Despite the theoretical alignment with graph computing, many existing solutions use relational or columnar databases to tackle graph problems. This results in inefficient solutions that fail to leverage the full potential of graph-based methodologies. As knowledge graphs gain traction, the significance of graph databases and computing continues to grow, addressing challenges that traditional databases are ill-equipped to handle.

The evolution of graph theory and its integration into graph computing reflects a broader shift toward leveraging complex, interconnected data structures. Graph databases offer promising solutions to the limitations faced by previous data management approaches, making them a crucial component of modern data infrastructure.

Property graphs and semantic knowledge graphs

The evolution of technology often follows a trajectory marked by phases of innovation, adoption, peak excitement, disillusionment, and eventual maturity. This pattern is evident in the realm of graph database (or graph computing) development, where two primary types of graph models — **Property Graphs (PGs)** and **Semantic Knowledge Graphs (SKGs)** — have emerged, each contributing to the field in distinct ways.

Property Graphs

Property graphs, also known as **Labeled Property Graphs (LPGs)**, represent one of the most influential models in graph computing. The concept of PGs revolves around nodes, edges, and properties. Nodes, also referred to as vertices or entities, and edges, the connections or relationships between nodes, can have associated attributes or properties. These attributes might include identifiers, weights, timestamps, and other metadata that provide additional context to the relationships and entities within the graph.

LPG is a term popularized by Neo4j, a graph database, where a label is considered a special kind of index that can be associated with either nodes or edges for accelerated data access. Many people use LPG and PG interchangeably.

> However, LPGs are actually a subset of property graph databases, as there are multiple ways to implement a graph database's data model. For instance, Neo4j's LPG implementation is schema-free, while GQL's PG design is schematic.

It's easy to see that, without properties (attribute fields), the expressive power of graphs would be significantly diminished. However, there is a reason for this. In the 1980s and 1990s, social behavior analytics gained traction, eventually leading to the uprising of **Social Network Services (SNSs)**. Traditionally, data analysis in SNSs focused primarily on the skeleton (or topology) of the data, and properties were not a priority. This has been the case for most of the graph-processing frameworks predating almost all PG databases.

The property graph model has seen a proliferation of implementations, including *DGraph*, *Tiger-Graph*, *Memgraph*, and *Ultipa*. These systems differ in architectural choices, service models, and APIs, reflecting the diverse needs and rapid evolution of the graph database market. The dynamic landscape of PG databases illustrates the flexibility and adaptability of this model in addressing a wide range of use cases.

Semantic Knowledge Graphs (SKGs)

In contrast to property graphs, SKGs are built upon principles derived from the **Resource Description Framework** (RDF) and related standards. SKGs focus on representing knowledge through semantic relationships, enabling more sophisticated querying and reasoning about the data.

The RDF standard, developed by the World Wide Web Consortium in 2004 (v1.0) and updated in 2014 (v1.1), provides a structured framework for describing metadata and relationships in a machine-readable format. RDF's primary query language, SPARQL, allows for querying complex data structures, but it is often criticized for its verbosity and complexity. RDF's emphasis on semantic relationships aligns with the goal of creating interoperable and extensible knowledge representations.

Despite its strong academic foundation, RDF and its associated technologies have faced challenges in gaining widespread adoption in the industry. The complexity of RDF and SPARQL has led to a preference for more user-friendly alternatives, such as JSON and simpler query languages. Exactly for this reason, property graph databases and GQL were born and are used by many graph enthusiasts and innovative enterprises who are looking to digitally transform their businesses.

While property graphs excel in data traversals with practical applications and ease of use, SKGs focus on the **Natural Language Processing** (NLP) aspect of things, offering a richer framework for semantic reasoning and interoperability. The interplay between these two models of graph stores, often in the form of using a PG database for link analysis (path-finding or deep traversals), and using an RDF store for semantic processing, reflects a broader trend toward integrating the strengths of both approaches to address diverse data challenges.

Current and future trends in graph database technology

As graph database technology continues to evolve, several key trends and advancements are shaping its development. These trends reflect the growing complexity of data environments and the increasing demand for powerful, efficient solutions.

This section explores three significant trends: **Hybrid Transactional and Analytical Processing (HTAP)**, handling sea-volume large-scale data while maintaining performance, and compliance with the emerging GQL standard.

Hybrid Transactional and Analytical Processing (HTAP)

HTAP represents a transformative approach in the graph database arena. Traditionally, databases were categorized into transactional systems such as **Online Transaction Processing** (**OLTP**) and analytical systems such as **Online Analytical Processing** (**OLAP**), each optimized for different workloads. Transactional systems focus on managing and recording day-to-day operations, while analytical systems are designed for complex queries and large-scale data analysis.

Many, if not most, graph databases and almost all graph-processing frameworks were originally designed to handle AP-centric traffic. This is also true for most NoSQL and big-data frameworks. These AP-centric graph systems tend to ingest volume data in offline mode and process the static data in online mode, meaning they are slow to ingest data in online mode. If graph database systems are to become the next mainstream database, the most critical requirement is the HTAP capabilities.

HTAP bridges this divide by enabling a single system, usually in the form of a cluster of multiple instances, to handle both transactional and analytical workloads. This integration is crucial for modern applications that require real-time analytics on live or transactional data.

In the context of graph databases, HTAP offers several advantages:

- *Performance Optimization*: Advances in HTAP technology include innovations in indexing, query optimization, and in-memory processing. These improvements help maintain high performance levels even as data volumes and query complexities increase.

- *Real-Time Insights*: HTAP enables real-time analytics on graph data, allowing organizations to gain immediate insights from ongoing transactions. This capability is particularly valuable in scenarios such as online fraud detection, recommendation engines, operation support and decision-making, and dynamic network analysis.

- *Streamlined Architecture*: By consolidating transactional and analytical processing into a single logical system, HTAP reduces the complexity of maintaining separate databases for different purposes. This integration simplifies architecture and improves data consistency across various use cases.

Recent developments in HTAP for graph databases include the adoption of in-memory processing with large-scale parallelization and distributed computing. In-memory processing allows for faster data access and query execution, while distributed computing techniques enable the scaling of HTAP systems to handle large and complex graph data.

There are different approaches to in-memory computing, primarily distinguished by their ability to update datasets in real time. One school of design may simply project data into memory space while the data stays unchanged; while another school may support real-time synchronization of in-memory data with the persistent layer, which requires more sophisticated design and engineering skills.

Handling large-scale graph data

As data volumes grow exponentially, handling sea-volume large-scale data without significant performance degradation becomes a critical challenge. Traditional graph databases often struggled with performance issues, particularly when executing deep traversal queries that required extensive computation.

Modern graph databases address these challenges through several key strategies:

1. Distributed architecture
2. Graph partitioning (sharding)
3. Hardware-aided storage and computing
4. Graph query/algorithm optimization

Let's explore them in detail.

Distributed architecture

Distributed graph databases leverage clusters of machines to distribute data and computational workloads. This architecture supports both vertical and horizontal scaling, enabling the system to handle vast amounts of data by adding higher-end hardware components or more nodes to the cluster.

Systems typically evolve from a standalone instance to master-slave or high-availability architecture, then to a distributed-consensus architecture, and eventually to horizontally scalable architecture.

For readers who are interested in scalable graph database design, it is recommended to read books such as *The Essential Criteria of Graph Databases* by Ricky Sun, published in 2024, with dedicated chapters to scalable graph database design.

Graph partitioning (sharding)

Graph partitioning techniques divide a large graph into smaller, more manageable subgraphs (shards). These partitions are contained on individual server instance nodes to be processed independently, reducing the computational load on each node. Efficient partitioning strategies minimize inter-node communication and improve overall performance.

The commonly used partitioning/sharding techniques are to cut by vertex or by edge. Note that both techniques would involve extra architectural components to be added (i.e., meta-server, name-server, shard-server, etc.) and data duplication (i.e., 2x or 3x more data points to be stored to ensure the data linkages are unbroken).

Hardware-aided storage and computing

Performance bottlenecks can be mitigated through hardware-accelerated storage and computing. In-memory databases reduce latency by storing data in RAM, SSDs offer faster data access compared to traditional hard drives, and the GPU and FPGA will help offloading the CPUs. These storage and compute solutions are increasingly integrated into graph databases to enhance performance and scalability.

Optimized graph queries and algorithms

Advancements at the hardware and software levels would require the matching graph queries and algorithms to be re-invented. Many graph algorithms were originally designed to be run in sequential mode (single-thread implementation), and have to be re-engineered to be able to harness data to vastly improve parallel computing power with modern CPUs and distributed environments, and the same holds true for many graph queries, such as path-finding, k-hoping, or just online data ingestion, which can be greatly improved with large-scale and distributed data processing. Queries and algorithms that minimize redundant computations and optimize data access patterns can significantly improve performance during deep traversals.

GQL compliance

GQL is emerging as a major standard in graph database technology, providing a unified query language for graph data. With the first edition of GQL already published, compliance with this standard is becoming a key focus for graph database vendors, as well as traditional RDBMS and NoSQL providers. Compliance helps vendors retain existing customers and attract new ones by ensuring interoperability and standardization across graph data platforms.

Key aspects of GQL compliance include the following:

- *Standardized Query Syntax*: GQL offers a standardized syntax for querying graph data, making it easier for developers to write and maintain queries across different graph database systems. This standardization promotes interoperability and reduces the learning curve associated with adopting new graph databases.

- *Advanced Query Capabilities*: GQL supports advanced querying capabilities, including pattern matching, traversal, and aggregation. By defining a comprehensive set of features, GQL will enable more sophisticated queries and analyses, enhancing the flexibility and power of graph databases.

- *Interoperability*: Compliance with GQL improves integration and interoperability between different graph databases and applications. This is particularly important for organizations that use multiple graph technologies or require data exchange between systems.

- *Industry Adoption*: As GQL gains traction, industry adoption is likely to drive further innovation and refinement. Vendors that prioritize GQL compliance will position themselves as leaders in the graph database market, attracting customers seeking standardized and future-proof solutions.

The trends in graph database technology highlight a dynamic and rapidly evolving field. HTAP is revolutionizing how graph databases handle transactional and analytical workloads, enabling real-time insights and streamlined architectures. Addressing sea-volume large-scale data handling challenges through distributed architectures, graph partitioning, and optimized algorithms ensures that graph databases can scale efficiently. Finally, GQL compliance is set to standardize and enhance graph querying, fostering greater interoperability and innovation in the industry. As these trends continue to develop, they will shape the future of (graph) database technology, driving advancements and new applications.

Why is GQL the new standard?

GQL stands as a pivotal advancement in the landscape of graph database technology. To understand why GQL represents a new standard, it is essential to explore its origins and evolution. GQL's journey mirrors broader database technologies, reflecting the ongoing quest for more intuitive, expressive, and powerful methods to query complex data structures that are often beyond the reach of tables or columns.

The genesis of GQL

The origins of GQL trace back to the early days of graph databases. In the late 20th and early 21st centuries, as the digital world grew increasingly complex, traditional relational databases began to show their limitations in handling interconnected data. While SQL-based systems excelled in managing tabular data, they struggled with the flexible and multi-dimensional relationships typical of graph-based data.

During this period, both RDF stores and graph databases gained traction. RDF stores focused on semantics and NLP, while graph databases focused on efficient data traversals. These efforts laid the groundwork for network-traversal-oriented query languages. The need for a standardized query language that could elegantly handle these graph structures became evident.

GQL emerged from the convergence of various graph query languages and best practices, aiming to unify and standardize how we interact with graph data. Its inception was driven by the need to provide a consistent, powerful query language that could serve as a universal tool for graph databases, transcending the limitations of previous, often proprietary query languages.

The GQL standardization by ISO/IEC was officially kickstarted in 2019, and the joint technical committee's project goal statement articulated why the world needs GQL:

"Using graph as a fundamental representation for data modeling is an emerging approach in data management. In this approach, the data set is modeled as a graph, representing each data entity as a vertex (also called a node) of the graph and each relationship between two entities as an edge between corresponding vertices. The graph data model has been drawing attention for its unique advantages.

Firstly, the graph model can be a natural fit for data sets that have hierarchical, complex, or even arbitrary structures. Such structures can be easily encoded into the graph model as edges. This can be more convenient than the relational model, which requires the normalization of the data set into a set of tables with fixed row types.

Secondly, the graph model enables efficient execution of expensive queries or data analytic functions that need to observe multi-hop relationships among data entities, such as reachability queries, shortest or cheapest path queries, or centrality analysis. There are two graph models in current use: the Resource Description Framework (RDF) model and the Property Graph model. The RDF model has been standardized by W3C in a number of specifications. The Property Graph model, on the other hand, has a multitude of implementations in graph databases, graph algorithms, and graph processing facilities. However, a common, standardized query language for property graphs (like SQL for relational database systems) is missing. GQL is proposed to fill this void."

Evolution pathways

The evolution of GQL is a tale of gradual refinement and adaptation. In the early days of graph databases, numerous specialized query languages emerged, each tailored to individual systems. Languages such as Cypher, OpenCypher, Gremlin, GSQL, AQL, nQL, UQL, and so on, were uniquely designed to carry out easy yet powerful recursive traversal features. But there have been cases where these languages were very challenging to learn and read, simply reflecting the language designer's preferences. In summary, they lacked the interoperability required for broader adoption. As the graph database community matured, the call for a standard language grew louder.

The development of GQL can be seen as a response to this call. The language was designed to address several key challenges: providing a unified syntax, ensuring compatibility across different graph database systems, and incorporating advanced features for querying complex graph structures. The transition from initial prototypes to a draft standard involved extensive collaboration within the graph database community, including contributions from academic researchers, industry practitioners, and standardization bodies.

The journey of GQL involved several significant milestones. The initial drafts were informed by existing graph query languages, such as Cypher used in Neo4j, Gremlin from the Apache TinkerPop project, GSQL (formerly Graph SQL) from TigerGraph, and even lots of inputs from Oracle's PL/SQL and PGQL. These languages provided valuable insights and were instrumental in shaping the foundational aspects of GQL. Moreover, as part of the ongoing development, care was taken to align GQL with the SQL/PGQ Graph Pattern Matching languages (GPM or GPML), especially with the publication of the SQL/PGQ standard in 2023. This alignment ensured consistency between the two languages, facilitating better integration across graph-based and relational systems.

As GQL continued to evolve, it incorporated feedback from a broad range of stakeholders, including those working on SQL/PGQ, and underwent rigorous testing to ensure its robustness and effectiveness.

Personal reflections on GQL's evolution

Reflecting on the evolution of GQL, Ricky Sun finds it remarkable how this language embodies the collective effort of the graph database community. It's not merely a technical achievement but a testament to the power of collaboration and innovation. GQL represents a convergence of ideas, drawing from the strengths of existing languages while introducing new concepts that address the unique challenges of graph data.

In many ways, GQL reminds me of the early days of SQL. Just as SQL revolutionized relational databases by providing a standardized way to interact with tabular data, GQL has the potential to do the same for graph databases, and maybe all other databases as well. It's exciting to witness the birth of a new standard that promises to bring clarity and coherence to the field of graph computing and beyond.

In conclusion, the evolution of GQL reflects a broader trend in technology towards standardization and interoperability. It represents a critical step forward in the quest for more effective ways to manage and query complex, interconnected data. As we move forward, GQL will undoubtedly play a central role in shaping the future of graph databases, offering a powerful and unified approach to graph querying that will benefit both practitioners and researchers alike.

Core features and capabilities

GQL addresses the limitations of previous query languages and introduces several core features designed to enhance both usability and performance. This section highlights the pivotal features that make GQL a robust and versatile tool for modern graph databases.

Flexibility and expressiveness

GQL offers a high degree of flexibility and expressiveness, allowing users to construct complex queries with relative ease. The language supports a rich set of operations for traversing and manipulating graph data, including the following:

- *Graph Data Modeling*: GQL enables users to represent complex, interconnected data in a way that reflects real-world entities and their interactions. It supports the creation and manipulation of nodes and edges, allowing users to define the structure of their graph database clearly. This includes specifying the types and attributes of nodes and edges, as well as establishing relationships and constraints. By providing a flexible and expressive framework for data modeling, GQL allows users to create schemas that capture the nuances of their data and facilitate efficient querying and analysis. This foundational capability ensures that the graph's structure aligns with the specific needs of various applications, enhancing the overall effectiveness and scalability of graph-based solutions.

- *Pattern Matching*: GQL provides powerful pattern-matching capabilities, enabling users to find specific subgraphs or structures within large datasets. This feature is essential for applications such as fraud detection, social network analysis, and recommendation systems.

- *Path Traversals*: One of the standout features of GQL is its support for deep and wide path traversals. Users can specify detailed paths through the graph, including variable-length paths and patterns that span multiple relationships, without incurring significant performance penalties. This feature sets GQL apart from SQL, which has long been criticized for lacking "recursive query" capabilities, and GQL makes that fast and easy.

- *Subgraph Extraction*: GQL allows for the extraction and creation of subgraphs based on specific criteria, facilitating the extraction of relevant portions of a graph for focused analysis or reporting.

Usability and developer experience

User experience and developer productivity are central to GQL's design. GQL's syntax is crafted to be intuitive and user-friendly, reducing the learning curve for new users and enhancing productivity for experienced developers. The language balances complexity with clarity, making it accessible for a broad range of applications.

GQL's core features and capabilities represent a significant advancement in the field of graph query languages. By addressing flexibility, interoperability, and usability, GQL sets a new standard for querying graph databases, positioning itself as a powerful tool for modern data analysis and management.

> GQL performance is implementation-specific, which means potentially the same GQL clause can experience different speeds on different vendor-created platforms. Accuracy and result validation would be another thing to carefully investigate – after all, the processing logic and results of GQL are inherently more complicated compared with the tabular SQL.

Advantages of GQL over traditional query languages

GQL represents a significant advancement in querying graph data, addressing the limitations of traditional SQL-based and non-relational query languages. This section explores the key advantages of GQL over traditional query languages, highlighting its impact on graph database management and querying.

Intuitive representation of graph data

Unlike SQL, which is built for tabular data, GQL is tailored for graph-based data structures. SQL's reliance on JOIN operations makes handling interconnected data cumbersome. In contrast, GQL's native graph orientation allows for a more intuitive representation of data relationships, using nodes and edges directly. This simplifies the querying process and makes it easier for users to understand and manipulate complex networks of data. The result is more natural and efficient queries that align closely with the underlying data model.

Simplified and expressive querying

The graph-centric syntax introduced by GQL is geared towards augmenting graph-based queries. This syntax design is more expressive when it comes to traversing relationships and patterns within the graph. Traditional query languages often require elaborate queries with nested sub-queries and multiple JOINs to achieve similar results. GQL streamlines this process by providing concise and expressive constructs for traversing nodes and edges, making it easier for users to write, understand, and maintain queries. This expressiveness not only reduces query complexity but also enhances readability and debugging.

Enhanced performance for relationship queries

GQL is designed from the bottom up to empower graph traversal. Traditional relational databases can struggle with performance when dealing with complex relationships and deep traversals. SQL queries involving multiple JOINs can become inefficient and slow, especially with large datasets. GQL, however, is optimized for handling intricate relationships and deep traversals. Its design allows for efficient pathfinding and pattern matching, which are crucial for applications such as social networks, fraud detection, and recommendation systems. The result is significantly better performance for queries involving complex relationships and connections.

Flexibility in schema design

Flexible schema design is another ostensible advantage of GQL over SQL. Traditional SQL databases often require a rigid schema that must be predefined and adhered to. Changes to the schema can be disruptive and require significant effort. In contrast, GQL supports dynamic schema design, allowing for greater flexibility in how data is represented and modified. This flexibility is particularly beneficial in graph databases where the structure of the data may evolve over time. GQL's ability to handle evolving schemas with ease means that users can adapt their data models without being constrained by rigid schema definitions.

Advanced pattern matching and analysis

Rich pattern-matching features are another area where GQL shines. GQL includes advanced pattern-matching capabilities that are inherently suited for analyzing complex graph structures. Traditional query languages, like SQL, do not natively support pattern matching in the same way and often require additional processing or external tools to achieve similar results. GQL's pattern-matching features allow users to query for specific graph patterns, sub-graphs, and relationships directly. This capability is invaluable for use cases such as network analysis, fraud detection, and social graph analysis, where understanding and identifying patterns are critical.

Streamlined integration with graph algorithms

While GQL itself focuses on querying, when a vendor implements GQL, it often ensures that GQL works seamlessly with graph algorithms, which are essential for advanced analytics and insights in graph databases. Traditional SQL queries typically operate in isolation from the algorithms used for in-depth graph analysis. GQL's design facilitates integration with graph algorithms, allowing users to execute sophisticated analytical tasks directly within the query environment. This integration enhances the ability to perform tasks such as centrality analysis, community detection, and shortest path computations without needing to switch contexts or tools.

Future-proofing and standardization

Future-proofing and standardization are other key advantages of GQL. GQL brings a level of consistency and reliability to graph querying that is often lacking in the diverse landscape of traditional query languages. The establishment of GQL as a standardized query language means that it will provide a consistent foundation for graph databases across different platforms and implementations. This standardization helps ensure interoperability and future-proofs the technology, making it easier for organizations to adopt and integrate graph databases into their existing systems.

Enhanced support for real-time applications

Many modern applications require real-time data processing and analysis. Traditional SQL databases may face limitations in handling real-time graph queries due to their tabular nature and the overhead associated with JOIN operations. GQL is designed to support real-time querying and analysis, making it well-suited for applications that demand instantaneous insights, such as live recommendation engines and real-time fraud detection systems.

Better alignment with use cases

GQL's design is inherently aligned with use cases that involve complex relationships and inter-connections. Traditional query languages often require workarounds to address these scenarios, which can lead to inefficiencies and convoluted queries. GQL's focus on graph-centric use cases ensures that it provides the right tools and features to address the unique challenges of graph data management and querying.

In summary, GQL offers a range of advantages over traditional query languages, particularly when it comes to handling graph-based data. Its intuitive graph-centric design, simplified querying, enhanced performance, and alignment with modern use cases make it a powerful tool for working with complex, interconnected data. As the field of graph databases continues to evolve, GQL's role as a standard query language will likely become even more significant, driving advancements in data management and analysis.

In the NoSQL landscape, it's interesting to note that graph databases stand out as the only database model that supports industry standards. This chapter has discussed two main declinations of the graph data model: **Property Graphs (PGs)** and **Semantic Knowledge Graphs (SKGs)**. SKGs have long had their own standards, such as W3C's RDF and SPARQL for querying. Until recently, property graphs lacked a unified standard. However, this changed with the release of GQL, providing a standard way to query property graph databases.

It's noteworthy that no other NoSQL data model, apart from graph databases, can leverage such comprehensive standards. This isn't likely a coincidence. Graph databases offer significant advantages over other NoSQL models such as key-value, document, or wide-column databases, particularly in representing and querying complex relationships.

The existence of these standards for graph databases may reflect their growing importance and the need for interoperability in increasingly complex data ecosystems. It also highlights the maturity and evolving nature of graph database technology in handling interconnected data structures.

Summary

In this chapter, we explored how database query languages have evolved, moving from relational and NoSQL models to the emergence of the graph model. We looked at the challenges traditional databases face when handling complex relationships and how graph databases provide a more intuitive way to manage interconnected data. By tracing the history of data management—from early record-keeping methods to the rise of SQL—we set the stage for understanding why GQL has become necessary and how it's shaping the future of data querying.

Next, we'll dive into the fundamentals of GQL and graph theory. We'll cover essential graph terminology, explore the structure of the GQL catalog system, and see how different value types are handled in GQL. The chapter also includes executable GQL code, giving you a chance to try things out in your own environment or with GQL Playground by Ultipa Graph.

2

Key Concepts of GQL

Understanding the structure of a new query language is crucial for anyone looking to harness the full potential of graph databases. GQL's unique approach to querying allows for more intuitive and powerful data retrieval, making it an essential tool for developers and data scientists alike. By grasping the fundamentals of GQL, you'll be able to write more efficient and effective queries.

This chapter introduces the key concepts of GQL and graph theory. The foundational knowledge covered here will enhance your understanding of the remaining sections of the book. You will explore general graph terminology, understand the hierarchical design of the GQL catalog system, and learn how to handle various value types using GQL. The chapter includes executable GQL code that you can run either in your own GQL environment or using the GQL Playground environment provided by Ultipa Graph.

This chapter covers the key concepts of GQL. If you're already familiar with these concepts, please feel free to move on to the next chapter. However, if you need a refresher, make sure you review this chapter for a brief overview of the basic data types and objects in GQL before proceeding. These concepts will be used in subsequent chapters, so don't worry if you don't understand some parts right away.

This chapter will cover the following topics:

- Graph terms and definitions
- GQL catalog system
- GQL values
- GQL patterns
- Brief introductions to GQL sessions, transactions, and procedures

Since many graph definitions have alternative names or methods, this book will assume specific definitions to ensure consistency and clarity throughout the text.

Graph terms and definitions

Graphs come in various types, each with distinct characteristics. GQL primarily focuses on **property graphs**. Modern graph databases adhere to the property graph model and support both directed and undirected graphs.

Graph element

The GQL standard defines a set of fundamental graph elements, each assigned a standard name and optional aliases that can be selected by implementation providers. For consistency and clarity, this book will use a single confirmed name for each element:

- *Node, also known as a vertex*: In GQL, a node represents an individual entity in the graph, for example, a person, place, or product. Each node can have zero or more labels that classify its role in the data model and can hold properties as key-value pairs to store metadata or descriptive attributes.

- *Edge, also known as a relationship*: An edge represents a connection or relationship between two nodes, defining how those entities are related. In GQL, edges can also have zero or more labels and properties.

> In this book, we will use *node* as the default term to represent nodes or vertices, and *edge* as the default term to represent edges or relationships.

To visualize graph elements, nodes can be thought of as points, and edges as the connections linking these points in a graph, much like the components of a network. *Figure 2.1* illustrates these definitions in the context of a property graph.

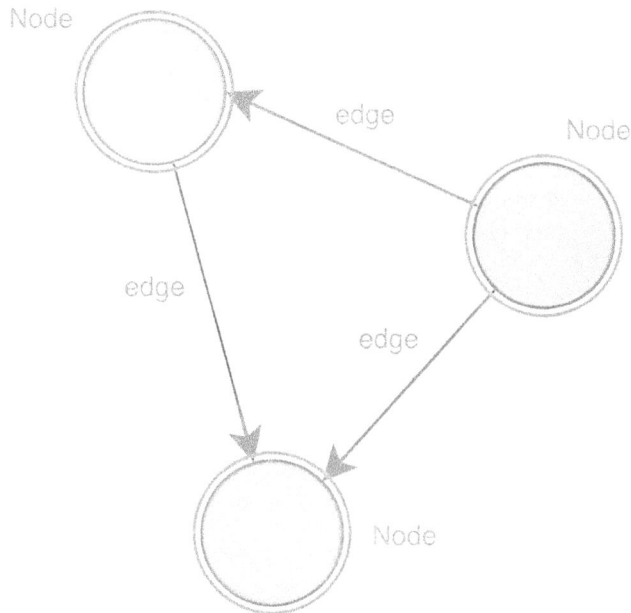

Figure 2.1: Nodes and edges within a graph

Directed and undirected edge

The type of edge—whether directed or undirected—directly shapes how relationships between nodes are represented and queried. Understanding these edge types is crucial for working with different graph structures, as they influence data modeling:

- *Directed edge*: A directed edge defines a one-way relationship between two nodes. One node is the **start node** (or source node) and the other is the **end node** (or destination node). The direction implies the flow of a one-way relationship between the two nodes.

- *Undirected edge*: An undirected edge does not have a specified direction, connecting two nodes. Unlike directed edges, undirected edges do not have a start node or end node.

In both cases, the nodes connected by a directed or undirected edge are considered **endpoints** of that edge.

> The terms *start node* and *end node* will be used in this book to represent the endpoints of directed edges.

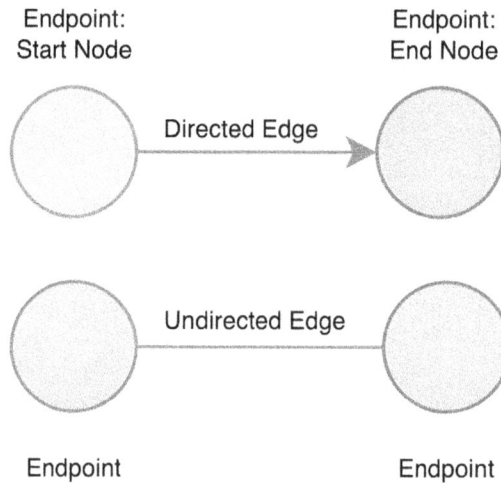

Figure 2.2: Endpoint, start node, and end node

Label

In the GQL standard, labels serve as identifiers, which define the type or category of a node, or an edge, within a graph for a quick understanding of the graph's model. These help organize the graph data model, making it easier to interpret and query.

For example, the :User label could be assigned to nodes representing users, while the :Follows label could be assigned to edges that represent social relationships between users. The typical graph structure could be visualized as follows:

Figure 2.3: User follows user

Property

Properties are key-value pairs, associated with both nodes and edges, where the key is the property name and the value represents the property value. Properties enable nodes and edges to hold structured, queryable data. For example, a :User node might have an age:18 property. A node or edge can contain zero or many properties, and values can vary in type depending on the data model.

Property graph

The property graph model organizes data as a set of nodes and edges, where each node or edge can have multiple properties with either static or dynamic value types. Property graphs can support directed or undirected edges and can take the form of a simple graph, multigraph, or even an empty graph.

Throughout this book, the term *graph* will specifically refer to a property graph.

Simple and multigraph

In GQL-based systems, understanding the distinction between a simple graph and a multigraph is important to design and query graph models.

A simple graph allows only one edge between any pair of nodes. This model is well suited for scenarios where a single, clearly defined relationship exists between two entities.

On the other hand, a multigraph permits multiple edges between the same pair of nodes, even if edges share the same label. This enables richer and more complex relationship modeling.

Some graph database systems may offer variations of simple graphs, such as those supporting multiple edge types between two nodes (but still, under the same type, only one edge is allowed).

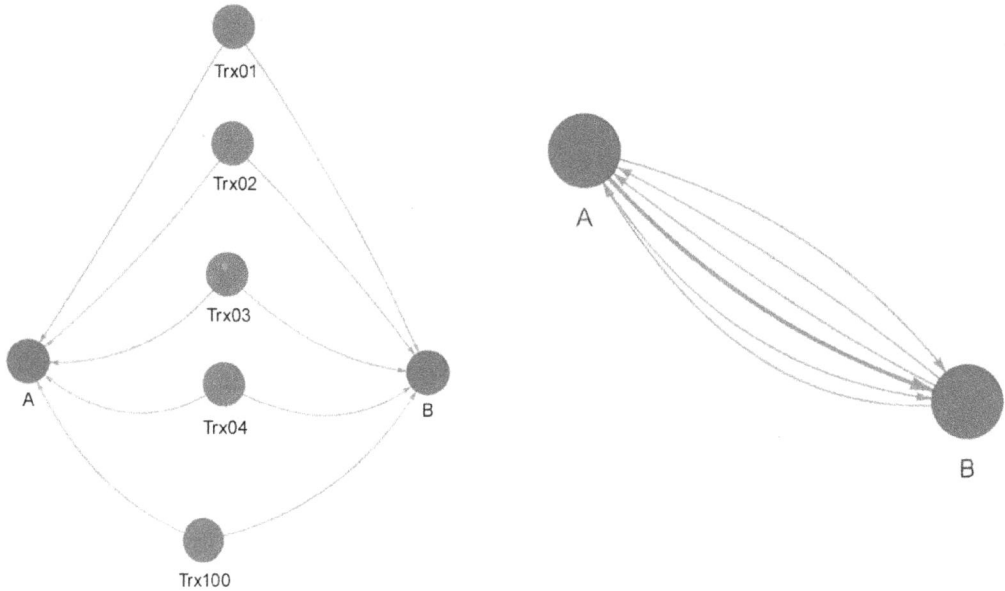

Figure 2.4: Simple graph versus multigraph

Graph traversal and computational operations in a multigraph data structure are inherently more complex than in a simple graph. This complexity arises because all operations must account for the presence of multiple edges between any two nodes.

In this book, all examples and queries will be run in a multigraph environment, where multiple edges may connect two nodes.

Directed, undirected, and mixed graph

The terms directed, undirected, and mixed define how the edges behave with respect to the directionality of edges in a graph:

- ***Directed graph***: All edges have a defined direction, meaning each edge links a *source node* and a *destination node*.

- ***Undirected graph***: Edges have no direction. Each edge simply connects two nodes without indicating a source or destination.

- ***Mixed graph***: A combination of directed and undirected edges, coexisting within the same graph.

This distinction can be easily understood through the illustration in *Figure 2.5*.

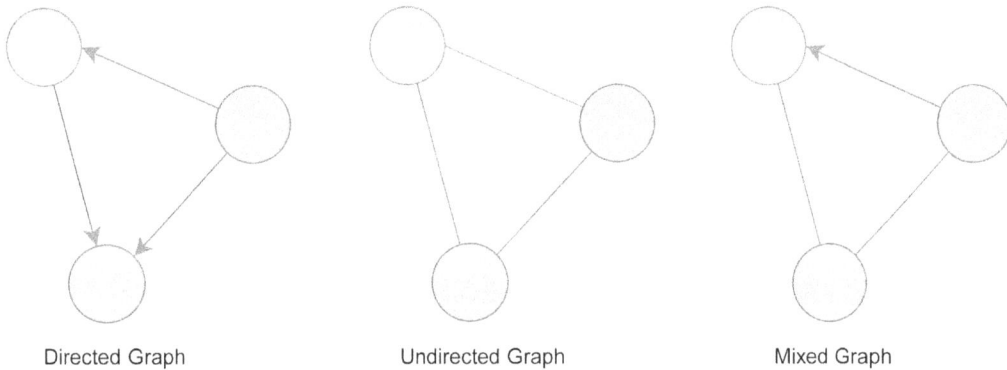

Directed Graph   Undirected Graph   Mixed Graph

Figure 2.5: Directed graph, undirected graph, and mixed graph

> GQL's ability to filter based on edge direction makes directed graphs highly adaptable for most graph requirements. Consequently, all examples and queries in this book will be executed on a directed graph.

Empty graph

An empty graph is a valid graph instance in GQL, defined as a graph that contains zero nodes and zero edges.

Path

In GQL, a *path* is a sequence that alternates between nodes and edges. By definition, a path always starts and ends with a node, resulting in an odd-numbered sequence of elements. GQL supports path retrieval as part of pattern-matching queries.

Depending on the use case and query, a path can follow or restrict repeated nodes and edges. There are several types of paths in graph theory:

- **Euler path**: A path that visits each edge exactly once, ensuring that all edges are distinct
- **Hamiltonian path**: A path that visits each node exactly once, ensuring that all nodes are distinct

Beyond these, the evolving GQL specifications introduce additional path modes, including WALK, TRAIL, ACYCLIC, and SIMPLE, along with various match modes. These advanced concepts will be explored in more detail in later chapters of this book.

> In this book, we will use the Euler path as the default path mode for querying paths.

In the next section, you will explore other elements of GQL.

GQL catalog system

So far, you've explored elements that exist *within* the graph. In this section, you will delve into additional elements *outside* the graph using GQL.

The GQL standard also introduces the catalog system, which organizes GQL objects into a structured hierarchy. Catalogs classify objects as either primary or secondary. Understanding this system is crucial for managing and navigating GQL components effectively.

GQL objects

The following list describes the primary and secondary GQL objects (see *Figure 2.6* for a diagram of GQL objects):

- **Primary GQL objects**: These objects may hold other GQL objects. They include the following:
    - **GQL directory**: Can be the root catalog and contains other GQL directories or GQL schemas

- *GQL schema*: Can be the root GQL catalog and contains graph, graph type, binding table, and named procedure
- *Graph and graph type*: Represent specific graph instances and their types
- *Binding table*: Associates variables with values for use in queries or procedures
- *Named procedure*: Predefined procedures that can be executed within the query

- *Secondary GQL objects*: These define the types used to enforce structure in a graph:

    - *Node type*: Specifies the structure and allowed properties for nodes in a graph
    - *Edge type*: Specifies the structure, source, target roles, and allowed properties for edges in a graph

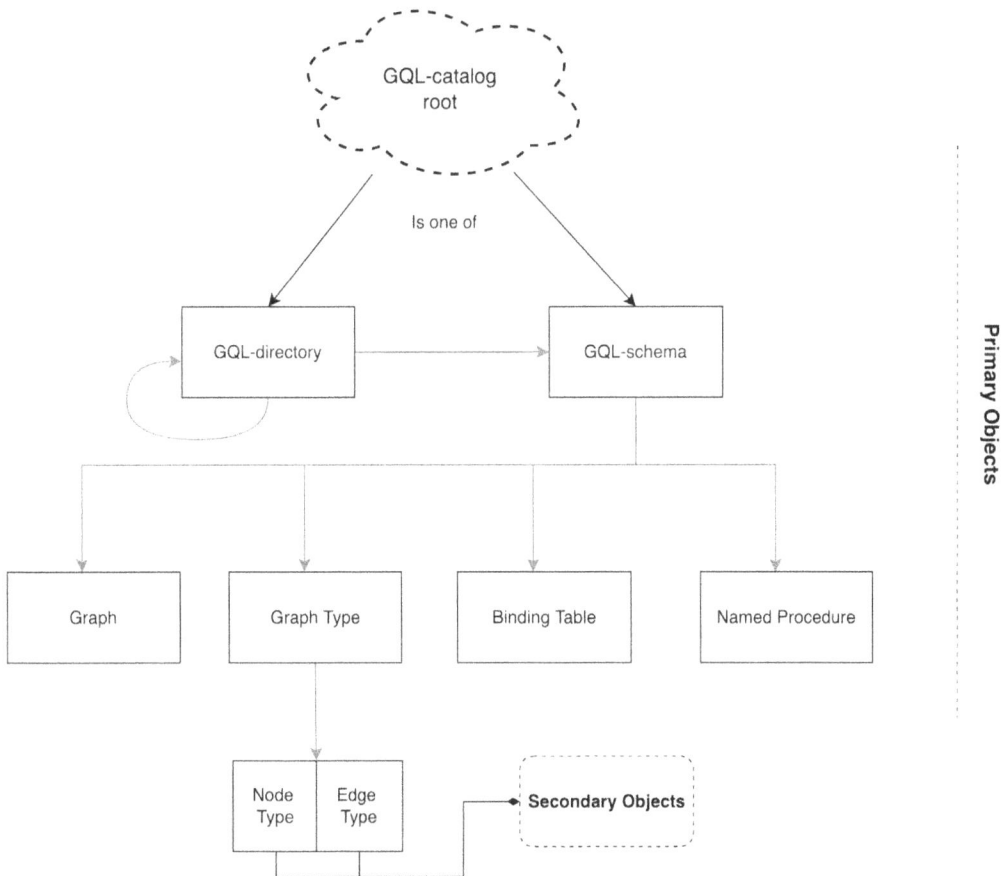

Figure 2.6: Components of GQL catalog

The GQL implementer may optionally support the GQL directory and GQL schema. If the provider doesn't support creating multiple GQL directory or GQL schema objects, it means GQL will always use the default GQL directory and GQL schema.

> In this book, all examples assume the use of a default schema as the root GQL catalog.

Binding tables

In GQL, a binding table (illustrated in *Figure 2.7*) is a primary object that comprises a collection of zero or more (possibly duplicate) records of the same record type. These tables are typically used to carry data during the execution of GQL and serve several key functions:

- **Iteration construct**: Binding tables are the primary mechanism for iterating over data during the execution of procedures. They help manage and process multiple records efficiently.

- **Intermediate results**: They serve as containers for intermediate results generated by GQL statements. For example, binding tables can hold the results of graph pattern matches.

- **Execution results**: Binding tables are used to return results to the client as part of the final execution outcome. They facilitate the delivery of query results or procedural outputs.

For example, the following GQL snippet demonstrates how binding tables are used to drive pattern matching and return query results. The MATCH statement iterates over the binding table records and retrieves nodes a and b to another binding table. Finally, the RETURN statement returns nodes to a new binding table as the outcome.

```
GQL:
FOR friendName IN ["Joey", "Yuna", "Wendy"]
MATCH (a {name: friendName })-[]-(b)
RETURN a, b
```

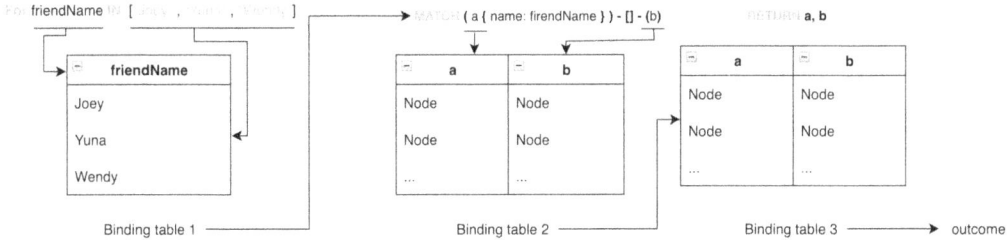

Figure 2.7: Binding tables

GQL values

In GQL, *values* are distinct from *objects* and represent atomic units of data that can be assigned, passed, or compared within queries and procedures. Values serve as parameters, property assignments, return results, and internal variables—much like primitive data types in programming languages.

Here's a closer look at the different types of GQL values and their roles.

NULL and material values

A null value in GQL, represented by the NULL keyword, signifies an unknown or empty property. In GQL, NULL is not equal to any other value, including another NULL. Comparisons involving NULL always yield false unless the operation is explicitly designed to handle null logic.

Any non-NULL value is called a material value, meaning it contains an explicit, meaningful piece of data. Material values can include strings, numbers, Booleans, or other concrete data types depending on the context.

> In this book, when a value is described as NOT NULL, it refers to a material value.

Reference value

A reference value represents a globally resolved reference to a GQL object, such as a graph, node, or edge. These objects can be either primary or secondary. If the referenced object is deleted or invalidated, the reference value also becomes invalid.

Comparable value

In GQL, comparable values are those that can participate in ordering, equality, and inequality comparisons. The definition of what constitutes a comparable value may vary among different GQL implementations. The standard distinguishes between the following:

- *Essentially comparable values*: These values can be compared directly within their category, for example, two numerical values, such as an integer and a float, strings such as ABC and XYZ, or Booleans (TRUE or FALSE).

  GQL-compliant systems must guarantee comparison behavior for comparable values within a category.

- *Universally comparable values*: These are the values from different categories that can be compared by implicitly converting their data types, for instance, comparing a numerical value 12 with a string value 12:

  - If the values are universally comparable values and the comparison operator is = (equal), the result would be false. For instance, the number 12 is not equal to '12'.

  - Otherwise, the result is determined by the implementation. For example, the number 13 could be greater than the string '12' if the GQL implementation supports implicitly converting the string '12' to the number 12 during comparison.

We will explore more details of comparable values next.

GQL value types

GQL value types include both dynamic and static types. Static types are further divided into predefined and constructed types. You will explore these types through executable GQL examples.

Dynamic types

A dynamic type is a flexible type that can encompass two or more static types. The actual type of a dynamic value is determined during the execution of GQL statements.

Examples of dynamic types include the following:

- *ANY*: Represents any valid GQL value type. Variables assigned ANY can hold any data type at different points during execution.

- *INT | Float*: Indicates that the value may be an integer or a floating-point number.

- *Type 1 | Type 2 | Type3 ...*: A union of specific types. The variable or property can hold any one of the listed types at runtime.

Here's an example in GQL:

```
GQL:
LET a = 1
LET a = "Hello GQL"
RETURN a
```

In this example, the a variable is initially assigned an integer value, then reassigned a string value. The type of a is initialized as ANY and changes from integer to string during execution. This illustrates that the dynamic type of a variable is determined at runtime.

Static types

A static type is a fixed type that does not change during runtime and is typically explicitly defined. Static types help to optimize performance, as the type is known during compiling and all the operations can be processed without any type testing.

Static types are categorized into *predefined types* and *constructed types*.

Predefined types

Predefined values in GQL refer to various atomic types, encompassing a wide range of fundamental data types essential for graph operations.

GQL categorizes the predefined types into the following groups:

- *Boolean types*: BOOL or BOOLEAN
- *String types*: STRING, CHAR, or VARCHAR
- *Binary types*: BYTES or BINARY
- *Numeric types*:
    - *Exact numeric types*: INT, UNIT, or DECIMAL
    - *Float numeric types*: FLOAT or DOUBLE
- *Temporal types*: DATETIME, TIME, DATE, DURATION, etc.
- *Reference value types*: Specialized types for references to elements such as nodes, edges, paths, etc.
- *Immaterial types*: NULL, representing the absence of a material value

In this book, type tables will organize GQL data types by categories: Boolean, character string, byte string, numeric, temporal, reference, and immaterial.

If a data type includes angle brackets (<>) in its notation, such as CHAR(<size>), it means the type expects a parameter.

If a type supports multiple syntaxes, they will be separated by a vertical bar (|). For instance, the CHAR type can be defined as CHAR | CHAR(size) and can be either unconstrained or parameterized.

Boolean

A Boolean type represents one of three logical states: true, false, or unknown. The unknown state is represented by the null value.

For example, to define a Boolean value in GQL, we would do the following:

```
GQL:
LET VALUE a BOOL = TRUE RETURN a
```

This query defines and returns the value of a as TRUE.

GQL supports various keywords and syntaxes to operate on values and return results. This query uses the LET VALUE keyword to define the a variable, and BOOL to set its type to Boolean. The = operator assigns the value TRUE to the a variable. Finally, the RETURN keyword is used to return the result a to the client.

Alternatively, you can use the BOOLEAN keyword instead of BOOL for the same operation.

Another example to generate a Boolean value by comparison is as follows:

```
GQL:
RETURN 2 > 1 AS a
```

This query returns the a variable as the comparison result of 2 > 1, because 2 is greater than 1, so a should be TRUE. The AS keyword creates an alias for the results of 2 > 1 to be returned.

Character string type

A character string is a possibly empty sequence of characters drawn from the Universal Coded Character Set repertoire specified by The Unicode® Standard.

Character String Types		
Type	**Description**	**Constructor**
CHAR	CHAR is a fixed-length character string. The length is always fixed no matter how many characters will be stored inside. If `<size>` is omitted, the default size is 1.	CHAR | CHAR(`<size>`)
VARCHAR	VARCHAR is a flexible character string with a `<max>` length. The default `<max>` length should be at least 2^{14}-1. The length of VARCHAR is the number of characters stored inside.	VARCHAR | VARCHAR(`<max>`)
STRING	STRING is the same as VARCHAR, but it can be defined with a `<min>` and `<max>` length. The `<min>` length should be 0 or a positive integer. If `<min>` is equal to `<max>`, the STRING value is a fixed-length string. The size of STRING is the number of characters stored inside. The `<max>` length should be at least 2^{14}-1 as well.	STRING | STRING(`<max>`) | STRING(`<min>`,`<max>`)

Table 2.1: Character string types and their descriptions

For example, to define a CHAR value, do the following:

```
GQL:
LET VALUE s CHAR(10) = "hello" RETURN s, CHAR_LENGTH(s)
```

This query defines a CHAR variable, s, and assigns a string, "hello", to it. The CHAR_LENGTH(s) function returns the length of the s variable. Since the data type is CHAR(10), which is a fixed-length character string, the actual stored value is hello (i.e., hello followed by five spaces) and the result of CHAR_LENGTH(s) is 10.

For example, to define a STRING value, you would use the following:

```
GQL:
LET VALUE s STRING = "hello" RETURN s, CHAR_LENGTH(s)
```

This query defines and returns the string s and its length CHAR_LENGTH(s) is 5, which is the actual length of the stored string.

Byte string

A byte string represents a sequence of bytes (octets). Like character strings, byte strings can have varying or fixed lengths based on the type.

Byte String Types		
Type	Description	Constructor
BYTES	BYTES is a sequence of octets with optional <min> and <max> length limitations. The length of BYTES is the actual bytes stored inside. The default <max> should be at least 2^{16}-2=65,534 bytes. If the <min> is equal to <max>, the BYTES is a fixed-length byte string.	BYTES | BYTES (<max>) | BYTES (<min>,<max>)
BINARY	BINARY is a fixed-length sequence of octets. No matter how many bytes are stored inside, the length of BINARY is always fixed. If the size is not specified, the default size is 1 byte.	BINARY |BINARY(<size>)
VARBINARY	VARBINARY is a variable number of bytes. It is similar to BYTES but only <max> can be set. VARBINARY can support a large number of bytes to store unstructured data such as images.	VARBINARY | VARBINARY(<max>)

For example, to define a BYTES value, do the following:

```
GQL:
LET VALUE icon BYTES(1024) = 0x3C42819981423C00 RETURN icon
```

The query returns a binary icon. The maximum size of the icon is 1 KB.

Numeric type

GQL supports two classes of numeric data: exact numeric data and approximate numeric data.

Exact numeric data stores values with a high degree of precision that must be exactly equal to the actual value. It is either signed or unsigned. Signed numeric data is either positive, zero, or negative. Unsigned numeric data is always non-negative.

Approximate numeric types store values with a precision that may be close, but not always exactly equal, to the actual value. These types are always signed.

Exact numeric type		
Type	Description	Constructor
INT	INT is a signed number with a range. The range is from (-2^{x-1}) to $(2^{x-1} - 1)$, where x is <size>. INT8 is from -128 to 127. INT32 is from -2,147,483,648 to 2,147,483,647.	INT|INT8 | INT16 | INT32 INT64 | INT128 | INT256 | INT(<size>)
SMALLINT	-32,768 to 32,767	SMALLINT
BIGINT	-9,223,372,036,854,775,808 to 9,223,372,036,854,775,807	BIGINT
UINT	UINT is an unsigned number with a range. The range is from 0 to 2^x, where x is <size>. UINT8 is from 0 to 256. UINT32 is from 0 to 4,294,967,295.	UINT8 | UINT16 | UINT32 UINT64 | UINT128 | UINT256| UINT(<size>)

Exact numeric type		
Type	**Description**	**Constructor**
USMALLINT	0 to 65,535	SMALLUINT
UBIGINT	0 to 18,446,744,073,709,551,615	BIGUINT
INTEGER	INT and UINT are all the alternatives of INTEGER. For example, UINT8 is an alternative to UNSIGNED. INTEGER8 INT32 is an alternative to SIGNED INTEGER32, and SIGNED can be omitted.	INTEGER8 | INTEGER16 | INTEGER32 | INTEGER64 | INTEGER128| INTEGER256 | INTEGER(<size>) | SMALL INTEGER | BIG INTEGER
DECIMAL	DECIMAL is an exact number with limited digits. For example, DECIMAL(5,2) means the number can store five digits in total and two digits after the decimal point.	DECIMAL(<precision>,<scale>)
Approximate numeric type		
Type	**Description**	**Constructor**
FLOAT	Floating-point number with precision and scale specified. For example, FLOAT32 and FLOAT(23,7) take precision 23 with scale 7, which can be displayed as 123456789012345.1234567. The default precision and scale for different float sizes follows the rules from IEEE standard 754:2019.	FLOAT|FLOAT8 | FLOAT16 | FLOAT32 | FLOAT64 | FLOAT128 | FLOAT256 | FLOAT(<precision>,<scale>)
REAL	Same as FLOAT32.	REAL

Exact numeric type		
Type	Description	Constructor
DOUBLE	Same as FLOAT64.	DOUBLE | DOUBLE PRECISION

Two numeric numbers are essentially comparable values:

```
GQL:
LET VALUE age1 INT = 18, VALUE age2 FLOAT = 18.0
RETURN age1 = age2
```

In this example, age1 (of type INT8) and age2 (of type FLOAT32) are essentially comparable. The comparison age1=age2 evaluates to TRUE because both values are *comparable* and numerically equal. Here's what you can run:

```
GQL:
LET VALUE pNumber DECIMAL(5,2) = 18.001 RETURN pNumber
```

In this case, pNumber is defined as DECIMAL(5,2), meaning it allows up to two decimal places. However, 18.001 has three decimal places, which exceeds the allowed scale. Consequently, an error is raised because the provided value does not fit within the specified precision and scale constraints.

> A GQL implementation is not required to support all of the numeric data types. How-ever, a claim of conformance must specify a complete set of value types that are supported as the types of property values. At a minimum, this set should include the following:
>
> - The Boolean type, specified by BOOLEAN or BOOL.
> - The signed regular integer type, specified by SIGNED INTEGER, INTEGER, or INT.
>
> The approximate numeric type, specified by FLOAT. The size of numeric types is implementation-defined.

Temporal type

GQL supports two classes of temporal data: ***temporal instant data*** and ***temporal duration data***. The string formats for date, datetime, and duration adhere to the ISO 8601 standard, as detailed here: https://en.wikipedia.org/wiki/ISO_8601.

Temporal instant data represents specific points in time, used to capture exact moments, such as event dates, logging times, or creation dates. Temporal instant data can use the ISO 8601 format, which is structured in three parts:

- *Date part*:

    - **Rules:** [YYYY] represents the four-digit year, [MM] represents the two-digit month, and [DD] represents the two-digit day

    - **Example:** 2019-03-14 matches the date format of [YYYY-MM-DD]

- *Time part*:

    - **Rules:** [hh] represents hours (00 to 24), [mm] represents minutes (00 to 59), and [ss] represents seconds (00 to 59)

    - **Example:** 12:00:59 matches the time format of hh:mm:ss

- *Time zone part*:

    - **Rules:** Z or a time offset from UTC, e.g., ±[hh]:[mm], ±[hh][mm], or ±[hh].

    - **Example:** +0100 matches ±[hh][mm].

    - The time zone part can be represented as Z (which stands for UTC) or as an offset from UTC. For example, +0100 indicates a time zone that is one hour ahead of UTC.

With the rules of date, time, and time zone, 2019-03-14T12:00:59Z matches the format YYYY-MM-DDThh:mm:ss:Z. The T character represents "time" in the time string, which can be replaced or removed if the context is clear.

The temporal instant type can be declared by a record value as well, with the key fields named year, month, and day.

Temporal instant type		
Type	**Description**	**Constructor**
ZONED DATETIME	ZONED DATETIME captures the date, the time, and the time zone: ZONE_DATETIME("2019-03-14T12:00:59Z")	CURRENT_TIMESTAMP | ZONED_DATETIME(<time string>) | ZONED_DATETIME(<time record>)

Temporal instant type		
Type	Description	Constructor
LOCAL DATETIME	LOCAL DATETIME captures the date and the time without the time zone: LOCAL_DATETIME("2019-03-14T12:00:59")	LOCAL_TIMESTAMP | LOCAL_DATETIME(<time string>) | LOCAL_DATETIME(<time record>)
DATE	DATE captures the date only: DATE ("2019-03-14")	CURRENT_DATE | DATE(<date string>) | DATE(<date record>)
ZONED TIME	ZONED TIME captures the zoned time without the date: ZONED_TIME ("12:00:59Z")	CURRENT_TIME | ZONED_TIME(<time string>) | ZONED_TIME(<time record>)
LOCAL TIME	Same as ZONED TIME but without the time zone: ZONED_TIME ("12:00:59")	LOCAL_TIME(<time string>) | LOCAL_TIME(<time record>)

For example, to define a zoned datetime, do the following:

```GQL
GQL:
LET myDate = ZONED_DATETIME("2019-03-17T12:00:59+01:00")
RETURN myDate
```

This query declares and returns the myDate zoned datetime.

The sample code defines a variable named myDate and assigns a ZONED DATETIME type value to it. The 2019-03-17T12:00:59+01:00 time string follows the ISO 8601 format YYYY-MM-DDThh:mm:ss±hh:mm, which contains the following time details:

- **Date:** March 17, 2019
- **Time:** 12:00:59
- **Time zone:** UTC+01:00

Alternatively, to define the same datetime value with a record, do the following:

```
GQL:
LET myDate = ZONED_DATETIME({
    year:2019,
    month:3,
    day:17,
    hour: 12,
    minute: 0,
    second: 59,
    timezone: '+01:00'
})
RETURN myDate
```

This query returns the same value.

Temporal duration data represents the period between two temporal instant data points, capturing a span of time. Durations are typically used for shifting a time point or calculating the difference between two exact time points, for instance, a counting-down system or reminder system. Duration can be as granular as years to nanoseconds.

Temporal duration data can be represented using two types of units: YEAR TO MONTH and DAY TO SECOND. These units offer different levels of precision for duration data. YEAR TO MONTH stores durations in terms of years and months, while DAY TO SECOND stores durations in terms of days, hours, minutes, and seconds.

The duration string format also follows the string template of the ISO 8601 standard, which is P[year]Y[month]MT[day]DT[hour]H[hour]S[second].

For example, P5Y6MT6H10S represents the following duration:

- P: Period
- 5Y : 5 years
- 6M: 6 months
- 6H: 6 hours
- 10S: 10 seconds

Temporal duration type		
Type	**Description**	**Constructor**
DURATION	DURATION captures a time difference, which could be a positive, zero, or negative value: DURATION("P5Y6MT6H10S")	DURATION(<duration string>) | DURATION(<duration record>) | ABS(<duration expression>)

Here's a syntax we can use:

```
GQL:
LET period = DURATION("P1D") RETURN period
```

This sample code defines a DURATION type value named period and returns it. The value of period is a one-day duration. Here's the syntax:

```
GQL:
LET date1 = DATE("2015-06-01"), date2 = DATE("2015-06-02")
RETURN DURATION_BETWEEN(date1,date2)
```

This GQL defines two date values, where date1 minus date2 is used to calculate the period from date2 to date1. The result is minus one day, equivalent to -DURATION("P1D").

NULL or immaterial

NULL is a special value that is sometimes included in other value types.

A NOT NULL constraint can typically be set in a property type specification. The nullable feature is supported by GQL implementers. A NOT NULL value is a material value.

If NULL is assigned as a value of BOOLEAN, the value will be UNKNOWN. The meaning of NULL is equivalent to UNKNOWN. Note that comparing two NULL values returns FALSE, which is the same as comparing two UNKNOWN values. Sometimes, NULL values are considered the same value in GROUP BY clauses. We will discuss this in detail in *Chapter 4, GQL Basics*.

The following GQL example demonstrates how NULL interacts with various operations:

```
GQL:
RETURN "a" + NULL AS r1, 1 - NULL AS r2, NULL + NULL AS r3
```

The GQL return statement includes three result item expressions: `"a" + NULL`,

`1 - NULL`, and `NULL + NULL`. All the results are `NULL`.

In most expressions, if either the left or right value is `NULL`, the result is `NULL`. The following example shows this behaviour:

```
GQL:
RETURN NULL = NULL AS r1, NULL IS NULL AS r2, NULL IS NOT NULL AS r3
```

The GQL return statement includes three return item expressions: `NULL = NULL`, `NULL IS NULL`, and `NULL IS NOT NULL`. The expression results are `FALSE`, `TRUE`, and `FALSE`, respectively.

> NULL is not equal to another NULL value. The only way to check for a NULL value is by using the `[IS]` or `[IS NOT]` predicate operator.

There are more functions for the `NULL` value. We will explore them in *Chapter 6, Working with GQL Functions*.

Reference type

Earlier in this chapter, we learned about reference values when discussing the GQL values concept. A reference type value could refer to GQL object data such as a node, edge, graph, or binding table. These references act as pointers to graph elements, rather than storing the element content directly. Here's an example code:

```
GQL:
MATCH p = (a)-[e]-(n) RETURN n, e, p LIMIT 1
```

The GQL returns values using three references:

- `p` is a `PATH` reference – referring to the traversed paths
- `n` is a `NODE` reference – referring to the matched end nodes
- `e` is an `EDGE` reference – referring to the edges from a to n

Constructed types

Constructed types, sometimes called composite types in other programming languages, are data types created by combining other data types according to a specific structure. In GQL, examples of constructed types include the path value type, the list value type, and the record type.

Path value type

A path is a sequence of nodes and edges that represent the path with an ordered offset. It may contain one or more nodes and zero or more edges. The path length is determined by the number of edges.

Take the following example:

```
GQL:
MATCH p = () - [] - () RETURN p, PATH_LENGTH(p) LIMIT 1
```

The GQL returns a path, p: PATH(NODE-EDGE-NODE), and the path length using PATH_LENGTH(p). The length is 1 because there is one edge in the path.

Another example demonstrates a path that consists of a single node and no edges:

```
GQL:
MATCH p = () RETURN p, PATH_LENGTH(p) LIMIT 1
```

The GQL returns a path, PATH(NODE), and the length is 0 because there are no edges in the path.

> If the number of nodes in a path is 0, the path can be considered as NULL, which is an empty path.

List value type

A list value is a collection of ordered items. Each item has its own offset, starting from 0. Items in a list can have one or more different value types, including NULL values. Some GQL executors may not support multiple types in a single list.

> In this book, multiple types and NULL are allowed in the same list.

For example, to declare a list, do the following:

```
Let myList = ["a", 2, NULL]
```

The myList list contains three items. The offsets are as follows: a is at offset 0, 2 is at offset 1, and NULL is at offset 2. The list is composed of these values with three predefined types.

Two lists can be concatenated using the concatenation operator:

```
GQL:
RETURN ["a", "b"] || ["c"]
```

> Besides lists, other types, such as strings and paths, are also capable of concatenation. You will see more examples in *Chapter 6, Working with GQL Functions*.

Record value type

In GQL, a *record* is a collection of fields, each consisting of a field name and an associated value. GQL records can be either *open* (flexible) or *closed* (fixed) types:

- *Open record*: Allows fields to be assigned values dynamically without being restricted to predefined types
- *Closed record*: Restricts fields to predefined types, meaning only values that match the declared field types can be assigned

Here's an example:

```
GQL:
Let myRecord = {name: "Pearl", age: 18} RETURN myRecord
```

In this example, the myRecord record has two fields: the name field, with a string value of Pearl, and age, with an integer value of 18. The myRecord is an open record.

To declare a record with fixed fields and types, do the following:

```
GQL:
LET VALUE myRecord {name STRING, age INT8} = {name: "Pearl", age: 18}
RETURN myRecord
```

The query declares a closed record and returns it.

GQL providers may not support all data types and might offer partial support based on system characteristics. For example, a GQL provider might support the string type but not CHAR or VARCHAR, which can still meet most real-world requirements. You will explore more details in *Chapter 10, Conformance to the GQL Standard*.

The following diagram shows all major classes of data types as defined in the GQL and ISO standards.

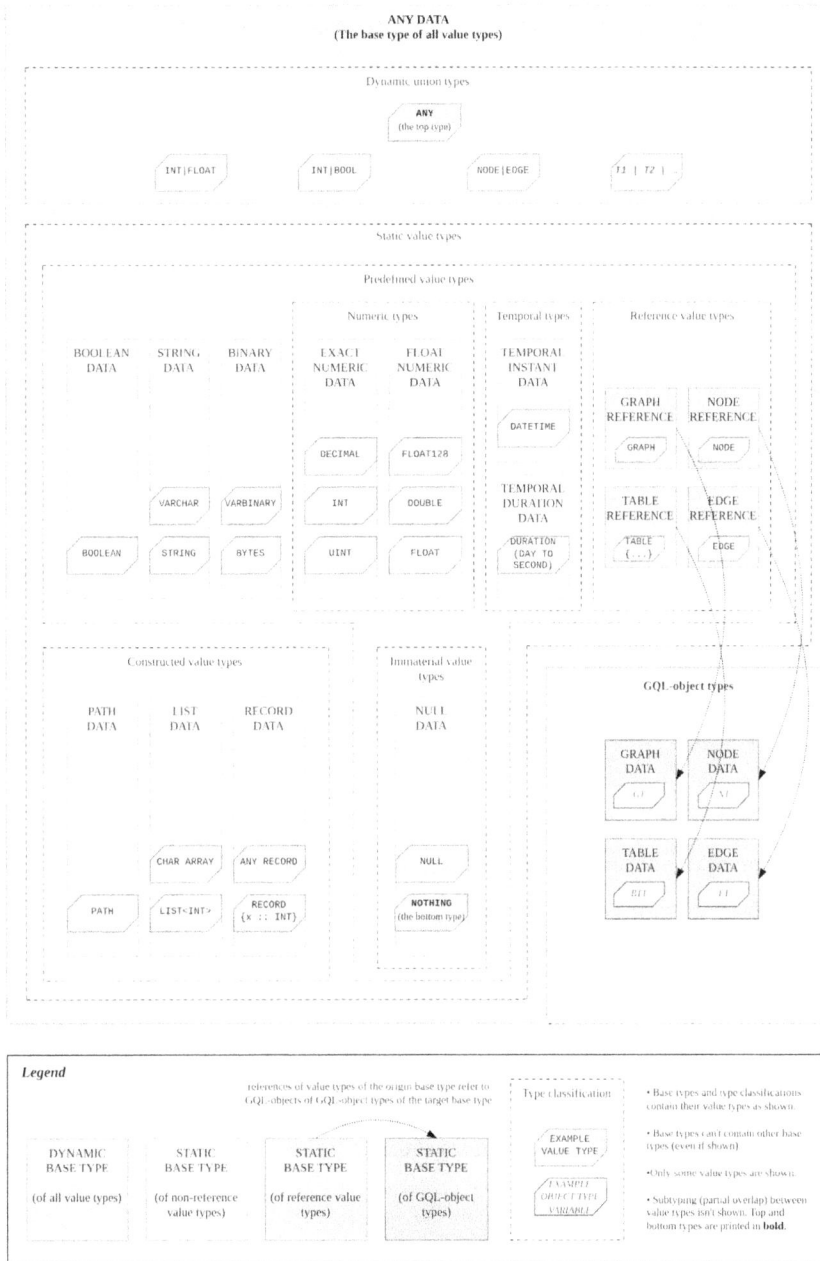

Figure 2.8: Major classes of data type

Graph patterns

The **graph pattern** describes a particular structure of nodes and edges, and their labels and properties. The graph pattern is mainly used for retrieving nodes, edges, paths, and subgraphs within a graph that conforms to it.

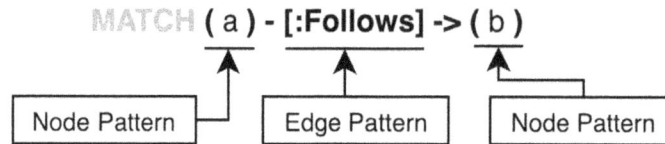

Figure 2.9: A MATCH statement with patterns

This example shows a path pattern composed of two node patterns and one edge pattern: (a) and (b) are node patterns to match the nodes and -[:Follows]-> is an edge pattern to match the edges in the paths.

The details of patterns will be discussed in later chapters of this book.

Element patterns

Element patterns are the basic components of a graph pattern and consist of node patterns and edge patterns:

- A node pattern specifies a node to be matched in the graph and is syntactically represented by a pair of parentheses
- An edge pattern specifies an edge to be matched and can be expressed either as a full edge pattern or as an abbreviated form, depending on the inclusion of variable names, labels, or direction

Path patterns

A path pattern is built recursively from element patterns using operations such as concatenation, grouping, and quantification. GQL supports prefixes for path patterns. Path mode prefixes such as TRAIL, ACYCLIC, SIMPLE, and WALK control how paths are traversed. Path search prefixes such as ALL, ANY K, and ANY SHORTEST select a finite set of matches from each partition.

Graph patterns

A graph pattern contains a list of path patterns. GQL supports two match modes for a graph pattern: DIFFERENT EDGES, which restricts a matched edge from being bound to more than one edge variable, and REPEATABLE ELEMENTS, which imposes no such restriction.

Other topics

This chapter provided a brief introduction to GQL programs, sessions, transactions, and procedures. These concepts may initially seem complex, but they will be explained in greater detail in later chapters. For now, it's helpful to understand that a GQL program consists of procedures or direct statements executed within a GQL session. A GQL session encompasses context elements such as authorization identifiers, time zones, the current graph, transactions, and other parameters relevant to the GQL request:

- *GQL program*: A GQL program is a collection of commands and procedures written in GQL, designed to execute specific operations within a GQL environment.

- *GQL session*: A GQL session is a sequence of GQL requests issued by a GQL agent on behalf of a single user via a GQL client within the same GQL environment.

- *GQL transaction*: A GQL transaction is a series of actions defined by GQL syntax that must be either fully completed or fully failed. A single GQL session can manage multiple transactions.

- *GQL procedure*: A GQL procedure is a block of GQL code that performs specific operations during execution. Some GQL implementers may offer built-in named procedures.

- *GQL statement*: A GQL statement is one of the following:

    - Catalog modifying statement
    - Data modifying statement
    - Query statement – this includes focus statements and ambient statements

An ambient linear query uses the current session graph. You will learn more details about sessions in *Chapter 8, Configuring Sessions*.

A focused linear query contains a USE GRAPH clause. This overrides the current session graph for the life of the statement.

An example of a focused linear query statement:

```
USE GRAPH MyGraph
MATCH (n)-[]-(m) RETURN n, m
```

The diagram in *Figure 2.10* illustrates how different GQL environment components relate to each other.

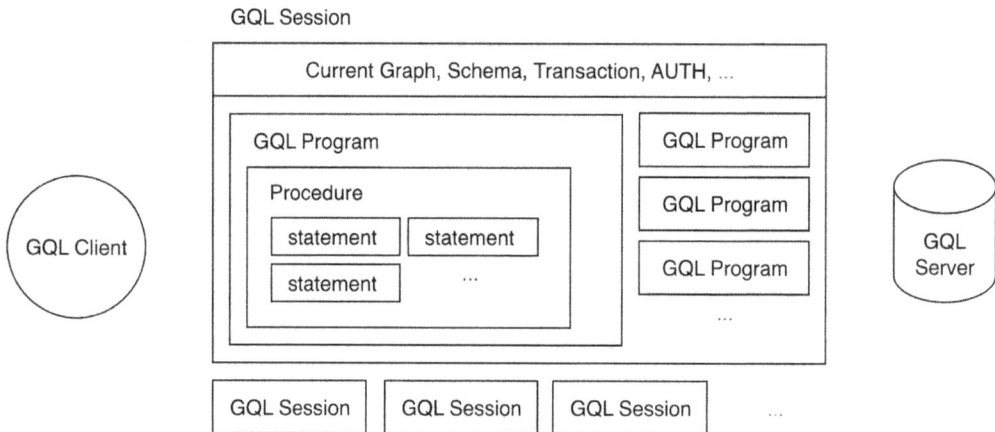

Figure 2.10: GQL environment illustrated

GQL status code

The GQL status code describes the status of a GQL request. The status is normally included in the response data. The GQL status code follows the ISO standard: `https://standards.iso.org/iso-iec/39075/ed-1/en/ISO_IEC_39075(en)-conditions.xml`.

You can also find the definition of "status code" in *Chapter 14, Glossary and Resources*.

Summary

In this chapter, you have gained a foundational understanding of GQL and graph theory, which is crucial for effectively understanding the next chapters. You explored essential graph terminology, the hierarchical design of the GQL catalog system, and how to handle various value types using GQL. Additionally, you learned about GQL patterns and received brief introductions to GQL sessions, transactions, and procedures.

In the next chapter, you will learn how to quickly get started with GQL, executing queries on GQL Playground to create and drop graphs, insert and delete data, and query graph data.

Get This Book's PDF Version and Exclusive Extras

Scan the QR code (or go to packtpub.com/unlock). Search for this book by name, confirm the edition, and then follow the steps on the page.

Note: *Keep your invoice handy. Purchases made directly from Packt don't require an invoice.*

3

Getting Started with GQL

In the previous chapter, you explored the fundamental concepts of graphs. Building on that conceptual foundation, this chapter will take you on a journey to acquiring practical experience in interacting with graph data using GQL. You will learn how to formulate and execute GQL queries against a graph database, which is essential for querying, manipulating, and analyzing graph-structured data.

To execute GQL queries, you will need access to a graph database that supports GQL syntax and behavior. This book uses Ultipa Graph, a high-performance property graph database, to provide a consistent and hands-on learning experience. Ultipa Graph includes GQL Playground – a dedicated web-based development and testing environment.

Using GQL Playground, you'll take your first steps in writing queries, inserting and retrieving data, performing data manipulations, and visualizing query results.

By the end of this chapter, you will have completed your first set of GQL exercises, giving you the foundational understanding necessary to follow the advanced topics covered in subsequent chapters.

This chapter covers the following topics:

- How to access and use GQL Playground
- Analyzing and building a graph according to the requirements
- Writing GQL queries to insert, delete, and update the graph data
- Cleaning the graph data

Introduction to Ultipa Graph

Ultipa Graph was founded by Ricky Sun in 2019. Prior to its founding, Ricky and his team encountered critical limitations with existing graph products, particularly in areas such as scalability, flexibility, and deep traversal performance. Ultipa Graph was developed to address these needs with an emphasis on high performance and architectural innovation.

Ultipa has revolutionized the graph database landscape. Leveraging high-density parallel graph computing infrastructure and concurrent memory data structures, Ultipa has built a cutting-edge graph database system. This system parallelizes all operations, queries, calculations, and graph algorithms, ensuring unparalleled performance.

Beyond performance, Ultipa offers a suite of environmental software for high-visualization manipulations, drivers for various programming languages, and public cloud services for enhanced flexibility. Ultipa has empowered numerous top banks and large institutions worldwide, driving innovation and delivering significant value to their customers.

To support learning and knowledge sharing in graph technologies, Ultipa provides two free services:

- **GQL Playground**, which allows users to execute GQL queries
- A **free version of the Ultipa Graph database** on Ultipa Cloud, supporting both GQL and **Ultipa Query Language** (**UQL**), Ultipa's native query language.

> Ultipa Cloud is Ultipa's **database-as-a-service** (**DBaaS**) offering, which simplifies the process of deploying Ultipa Graph databases and provides access to companion services such as Ultipa Manager, a powerful graph **database management system** (**DBMS**). To start using Ultipa Cloud, visit `https://cloud.ultipa.com/`.

Next, let's explore GQL Playground, which will be used throughout this book as the primary interface for executing GQL queries and interacting with Ultipa Graph databases.

Guide to GQL Playground

GQL Playground is a comprehensive, all-in-one platform designed for executing GQL queries, validating GQL syntax, and visualizing graph data. It serves as both an educational and practical tool, allowing users to easily learn and refine their GQL skills.

Whether you are a beginner looking to understand the basics or a seasoned professional aiming to test queries, GQL Playground offers a user-friendly interface and robust features to support your journey.

Setting up your Ultipa account

Before assessing GQL Playground, you must create an Ultipa account. To register, do the following:

1. Open `https://www.ultipa.com/login` in your web browser.

2. Click **Sign In**, then click **Sign up now** to create an Ultipa account using your email address and password.

Alternatively, you may register or log in using Google **Single Sign-On** (**SSO**) for streamlined access.

If you already have an Ultipa account, simply enter your credentials on the login page to proceed.

Accessing GQL Playground

Once logged in, navigate to GQL Playground at `https://www.ultipa.com/gql-playground`. The Playground interface appears as illustrated in *Figure 3.1*.

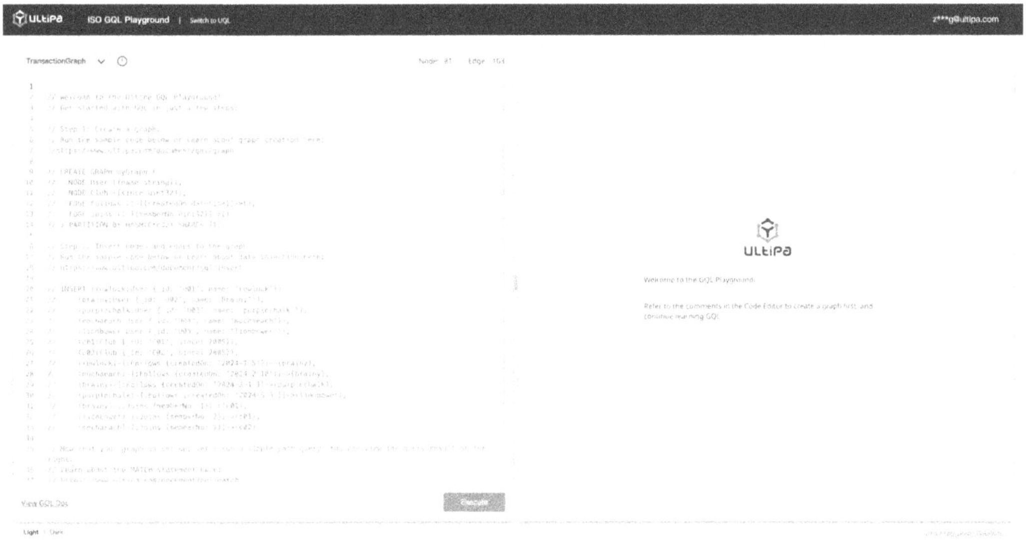

Figure 3.1: GQL Playground supported by Ultipa

There are two panels in the playground:

- **GQL IDE**: This panel provides syntax highlighting for editing GQL queries, delivering the convenience and functionality of modern IDEs – such as tools like Visual Code Studio. Once you have created a graph, you can switch graphs using the drop-down menu in the top-left corner.

- **Results visualizer**: Located on the right side of the screen, this panel presents query results in various formats, including graph view, table view, and path lists. In the graph view, you can drag nodes to explore details about nodes and edges, as well as adjust the graph's layout for better visualization.

> Graphs created in GQL Playground are temporary and will be automatically deleted after a set period of time. It is not recommended to store critical or long-term data within Playground. For advanced features and persistent data storage, consider deploying databases using Ultipa Cloud: (`https://cloud.ultipa.com`).

Now that you've familiarized yourself with GQL Playground, let's start using it through hands-on exercises to begin writing and executing your first GQL queries.

Hands-on GQL

The best way to learn a new query language is by using it hands-on. In this section, you'll apply GQL by creating and dropping graphs, inserting and deleting data, and executing queries to retrieve information. GQL Playground offers a controlled and interactive environment for performing these tasks, enabling both experimentation and practical learning.

Scenario script

Here is a simple story to start our graph journey. We will convert this story into a graph using GQL Playground.

In the heart of Paris, where the city lights twinkle like stars, lived Boyard, a 24-year-old banker at X-Bank. His best friend, Gison, a 23-year-old tech wizard at Y-Tech, was always up for an adventure. One crisp evening, Boyard decided to introduce his charming colleague, Areith, to the vibrant nightlife of Paris. Areith, a stunning 23-year-old with a captivating smile, had just moved to the city and was eager to explore. They will go to Z-Club where Boyard and Gison often went.

Creating the graph and building the graph model

Before creating the graph model, we will abstract entities and relationships from the story and draw the graph on a whiteboard, as shown in *Figure 3.2*:

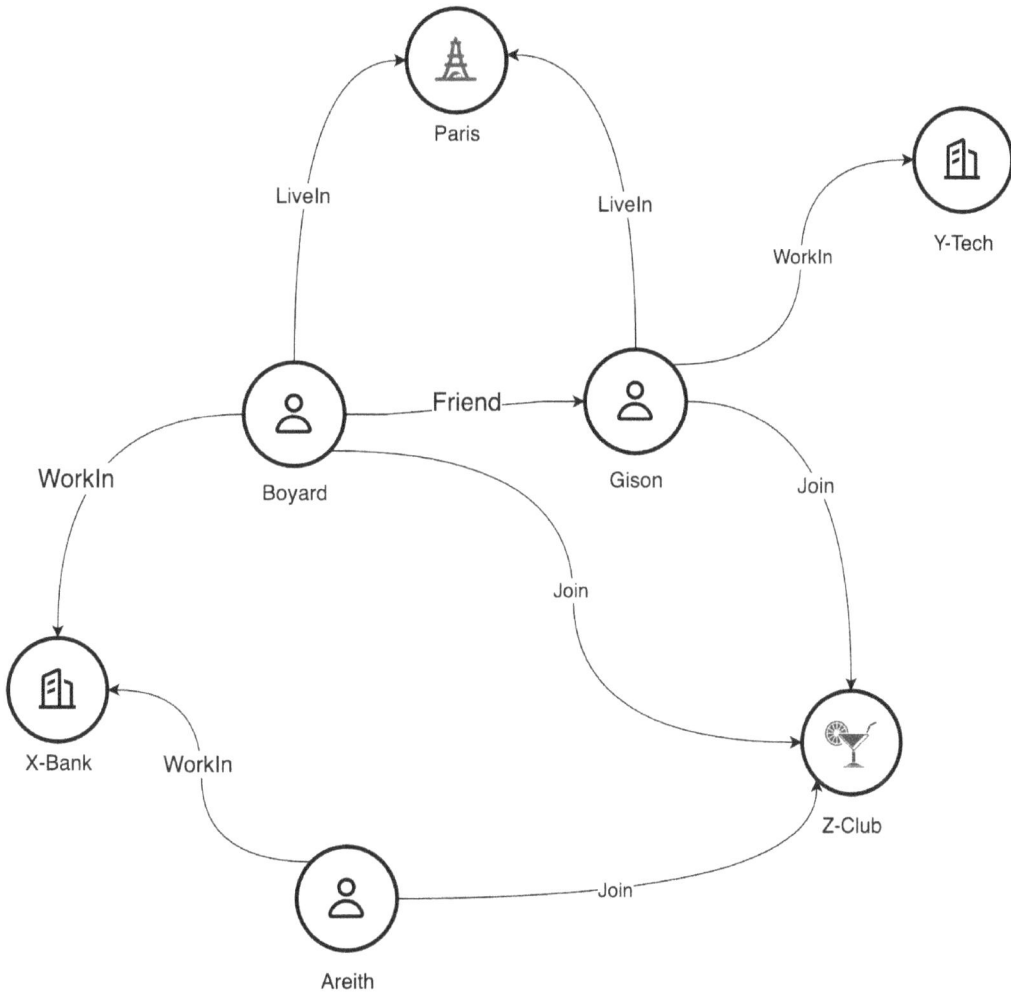

Figure 3.2: Entities and relationships extracted from the story

It's a simple process. Once all entities are connected through actions, events, and other relation-ships, the graph takes shape naturally.

> *"Graphs are a projection of the real world."*
>
> *— Jason ZHANG, Director of R&D at Ultipa*

You can analyze and extract nodes and edge types. This scenario yields the following:

- *Node types*: Person, Company, Club, and City
- *Edge types*: Friend, WorkIn, Join, and LiveIn

By aggregating all the nodes and edges into these types, you can derive a graph model as shown in *Figure 3.3*:

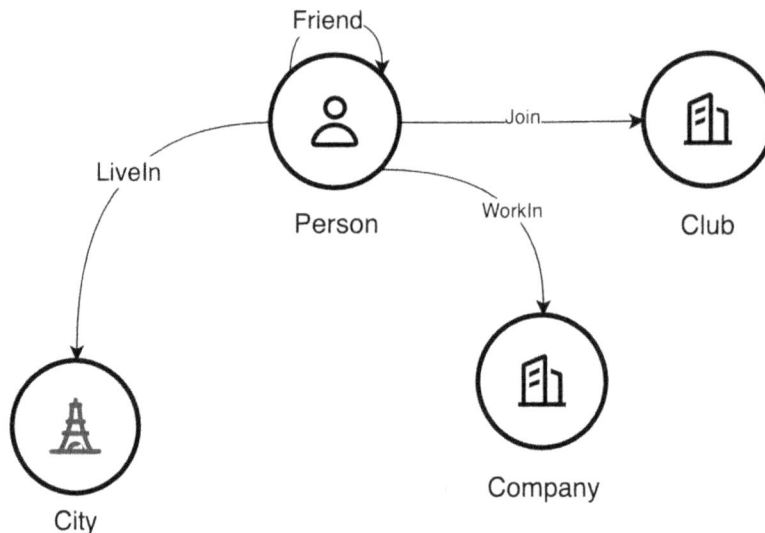

Figure 3.3: The graph model derived from Figure 3.2

The graph model is crucial because it defines the structure of the graph, including the types of nodes and edges that will be created along with the graph.

You can now create this graph using GQL in Playground by executing the following query:

```
GQL:
CREATE GRAPH StoryGraph {
    NODE Person ({name string, gender string}),
```

```
    NODE Club ({name string, score float}),
    NODE Company ({name string}),
    NODE City ({name string}),
    EDGE Friend ()-[{}]->(),
    EDGE Join ()-[{memberNo int32}]->(),
    EDGE WorkIn ()-[{startOn date}]->(),
    EDGE LiveIn ()-[{startOn date}]->()
}
```

The new graph, StoryGraph, involves the following node and edge types, as well as labels and properties:

- The Person node type, with two properties, name (string) and gender (string)
- The Club node type, with the name (string) and score (float) properties
- The Company node type, with the name (string) property
- The City node type, with the name (string) property
- The Friend edge type with no properties
- The Join edge type, with the memberNo (int32) property
- The WorkIn edge type, with the StartOn (date)
- The LiveIn edge type, with the StartOn (date)

> In GQL Playground, when you create a node or edge type with an explicit type name but without specifying a label set, the label set defaults to the type name. For example, NODE Person ({}) is equivalent to NODE Person (:Person {}). You will learn about this in more detail in the next chapter.
>
> In Ultipa Graph, each node has the _id (string type) and _uuid (uint64 type) system properties. Each edge has the _uuid (uint64 type) system property, and _from (string type) and _to (string type), which correspond to the source and destination node IDs.

Inserting nodes and edges

After creating the graph model, you can use the INSERT statement to insert graph data (nodes and edges) into the StoryGraph graph:

```
GQL:
INSERT
    (boyard:Person {_id: "P1", name: "Boyard", gender: "male"}),
```

```
(gison:Person {_id: "P2", name: "Gison", gender: "male"}),
(areith:Person {_id: "P3", name: "Areith"}),
(zclub:Club {_id: "C1", name: "Z-Club", score:  7.2}),
(xbank:Company {_id: "CO1", name: "X-Bank"}),
(ytech:Company {_id: "CO2", name: "Y-Tech"}),
(paris:City {_id: "CT1", name: "Paris"}),
(boyard)-[:Join {memberNo: 1}]->(zclub),
(gison)-[:Join {memberNo: 9}]->(zclub),
(boyard)-[:WorkIn {startOn: "2023-5-3"}]->(xbank),
(areith)-[:WorkIn {startOn: "2024-12-22"}]->(xbank),
(gison)-[:WorkIn {startOn: "2022-11-12"}]->(ytech),
(gison)-[:Friend]->(boyard),
(gison)-[:LiveIn]->(paris),
(boyard)-[:LiveIn]->(paris)
```

This query inserts seven nodes, labeled :Person, :Club, :Company, and :City, along with eight edges, labeled :Join, :WorkIn, :LiveIn, and :Friend. Some of their properties are specified with values during insertion. These nodes and edges are connected, as illustrated in *Figure 3.2*. With properties, the current graph tells the story with more details.

If an associated property does not have a specified value, such as the gender property of the areith node, its value will be set to null.

> In GQL Playground, the _uuid property is automatically generated by the system and cannot be manually assigned.

Querying the graph

In the previous section, your graph, StoryGraph, was established and the data was inserted. Next, you can interact with the graph to retrieve the anticipated data. For this, you can use the RETURN statement to return the desired result.

For example, to retrieve all one-step paths from the graph, use the following:

```
GQL:
MATCH p=()->() RETURN p
```

This query retrieves all direct relationships between nodes.

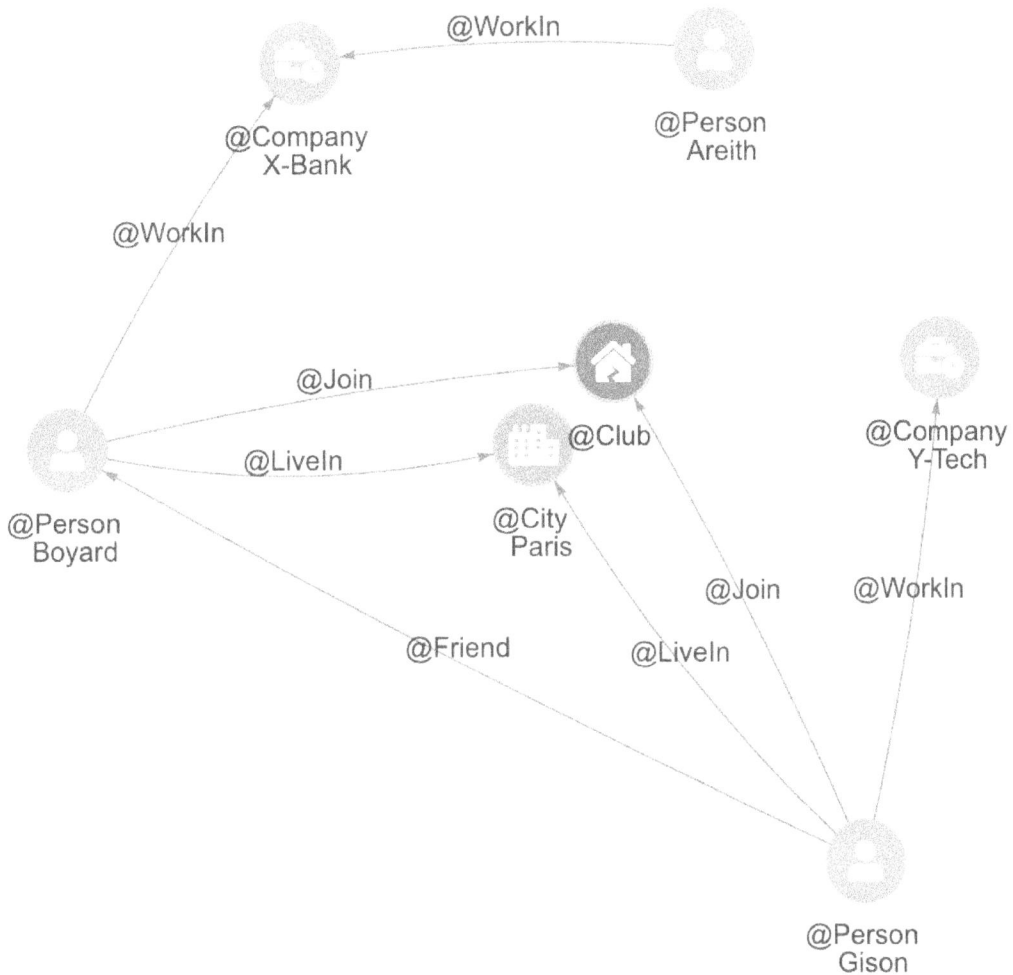

Figure 3.4: The query showing all direct relationships

You can also use the RETURN statement to return a string value directly:

```
GQL:
RETURN "Hello GQL"
```

Alternatively, you can return the result of a value expression:

```
GQL:
RETURN 1 + 1
```

Reading data

The MATCH statement is used to retrieve data from the database using various graph patterns. The data you can read from a graph includes nodes, edges, and paths.

Nodes

In GQL, nodes are represented by a pair of parentheses, (). In the following table are some examples of node patterns:

Node Pattern	Description
()	Matches any anonymous node.
(:Person)	Matches any anonymous node labeled :Person.
(n:Person)	Matches any node labeled :Person and binds it to the n variable.
({name: "Kavi Moore"})	Matches any anonymous node where the name property is Kavi Moore.
(n:Club WHERE n.score > 7)	Matches any node labeled :Club where its score value exceeds 7, bound to the n variable.

Table 3.1: Node pattern examples

For example, to retrieve all nodes, use the following:

```
GQL:
MATCH (nodes) RETURN nodes
```

This query retrieves all nodes from the graph.

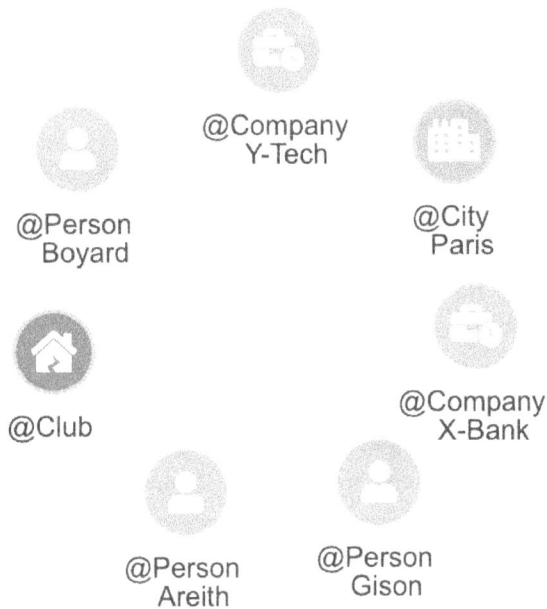

Figure 3.5: The graph with the retrieved nodes

To retrieve nodes with a node label, filter by using the following code:

```
GQL:
MATCH (p:Person) RETURN p
```

This query retrieves all nodes labeled :Person.

Figure 3.6: All nodes labeled :Person

To retrieve nodes with a node label and property filter, use the following:

```
GQL:
MATCH (p:Person {name: "Boyard"}) RETURN p
```

Alternatively, use the following:

```
GQL:
MATCH (p:Person WHERE p.name = "Boyard") RETURN p
```

These two queries return the same node, named Boyard.

Next, let's explore how to retrieve edges.

Edges

In GQL, edges are represented by square brackets, [ ], along with the indication of edge direction (->, <-, -). The following are some examples of edge patterns:

Edge Pattern	Description
-[]-	Matches any anonymous edge in any direction.
-[e:Join]->	Matches any edge labeled :Join pointing right, bound to the e variable.
<-[e:Join {memberNo: 1}]-	Matches any edge labeled :Join pointing left, where its memberNo value is 1, bound to the e variable.
-[e WHERE startOn < DATE("2022-1-1")]-	Matches any edge in any direction, where its startOn value is earlier than 2011-1-1, bound to the e variable.

Table 3.2: Edge pattern examples

For example, to return all edges, use the following:

```
GQL:
MATCH -[edges]-> RETURN edges
```

This query returns all edges as a list.

@Friend

_uuid	_from	_to	_from_uuid	_to_uuid
6	P2	P1	3098478742654156802	10448353334522806273

@Join

_uuid	_from	_to	_from_uuid	_to_uuid	memberNo
2	P2	C1	3098478742654156802	216176080648667140	9

@Workin

_uuid	_from	_to	_from_uuid	_to_uuid	startOn
5	P2	CO2	3098478742654156802	13907120047366602758	2022-11-12T00:00:00

@LiveIn

_uuid	_from	_to	_from_uuid	_to_uuid	startOn
7	P2	CT1	3098478742654156802	16212964156091924487	null

@Join

_uuid	_from	_to	_from_uuid	_to_uuid	memberNo
1	P1	C1	10448353334522806273	216176080648667140	1

@Workin

_uuid	_from	_to	_from_uuid	_to_uuid	startOn
3	P1	CO1	10448353334522806273	8863088464711647237	2023-05-03T00:00:00

@LiveIn

_uuid	_from	_to	_from_uuid	_to_uuid	startOn
8	P1	CT1	10448353334522806273	16212964156091924487	null

Figure 3.7: Graph database edge relationships with metadata and connections.

To return edges with a specific label, use the following query:

```
GQL:
MATCH -[e:Friend]-> RETURN e
```

This query returns all :Friend edges in the graph:

@Friend

_uuid	_from	_to	_from_uuid	_to_uuid
6	P2	P1	3098478742654156802	10448353334522806273

Figure 3.8: :Friend Edge Representation in GQL Result Table

Next, let's explore how to retrieve paths.

Paths

Finding nodes and edges in a graph is very similar to retrieving rows from tables in a relational database. However, a graph is designed to solve more complex issues, such as deep data searches.

A path always starts and ends with a node and alternates between nodes and edges. Therefore, you can concatenate node patterns and edge patterns recursively to build a path pattern.

For example, if you want to find the employees of X-Bank, you can use GQL as follows:

```
GQL:
MATCH (:Company {name: "X-Bank"})<-[:WorkIn]-(employees:Person)
RETURN employees
```

This query returns Areith and Boyard. The path pattern starts from the :Company node with the name X-Bank, goes through an incoming :WorkIn edge, and reaches a :Person node. The last :Person node is bound to the employees variable in order to be returned.

@Person
Areith

@Person
Boyard

Figure 3.9: Employees of X-Bank returned via :WorkIn edge traversal.

Alright, here is another question: *How does Areith know Gison?*

While this is straightforward to answer in the natural world, it becomes a complex matter when dealing with large datasets, especially those stored in tables. Graphs, being projections of the real world, can address this kind of question using a natural method: finding the path between Areith and Gison. We identified the employees of X-Bank by performing a path finding that entails one edge in each path. To analyze unknown relationships between nodes, we typically use multi-hop path finding.

To find the paths from Areith to Gison within 1 to 3 hops, do the following:

```
GQL:
MATCH (areith:Person WHERE areith.name = "Areith"),
      (gison:Person WHERE gison.name = "Gison"),
      p =(areith)-[]-{1,3}(gison)
RETURN p
```

The following is the one path returned by the preceding GQL query. In GQL Playground, you will see detailed information about each node and edge involved in the path. Here we write this path in a simple form, with only the name property of the nodes and the direction of the edges, as illustrated in *Figure 3.10*:

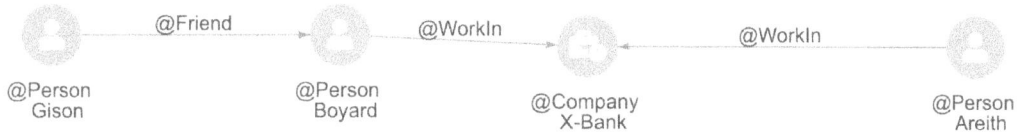

Figure 3.10: Path from Gison to Areith via X-Bank using Friend and WorkIn edges.

With the results, we can assume that Areith met Gison through her colleague Boyard. The graph visualization itself provides a self-explanatory capability.

Updating nodes and edges

To update the property values of existing nodes and edges, you can retrieve the target nodes or edges from the database using the MATCH statement and set values by using the SET statement.

Considering the previous example, after Areith met Gison and Boyard in Z-Club, Areith gives a high score to the Z-Club, which improves its score. Now, we can use the MATCH and SET statements to retrieve the Z-Club node and set its score to 7.4:

```
GQL:
MATCH (zclub:Club {name: "Z-Club"})
SET zclub.score = 7.4
```

Another way to update the score of the club that Areith visited to 7.4 is as follows:

```
GQL:
MATCH (:Person {name: "Areith"})-[:Join]->(c:Club)
SET c.score = 7.4
```

Now, Areith is also a friend of Gison, so we can add a :Friend edge between them:

```
GQL:
MATCH (areith:Person {name: "Areith"}),
      (gison:Person {name: "Gison"})
INSERT (areith)-[:Friend]->(gison)
```

Then, to retrieve the relationship between Areith and Gison, we can do the following:

```
GQL:
MATCH (areith:Person {name: "Areith"}),
      (gison:Person {name: "Gison"}),
      p=(areith)-[]-{,3}(gison)
RETURN p
```

This query retrieves all the possible paths from Areith to Gison within three steps.

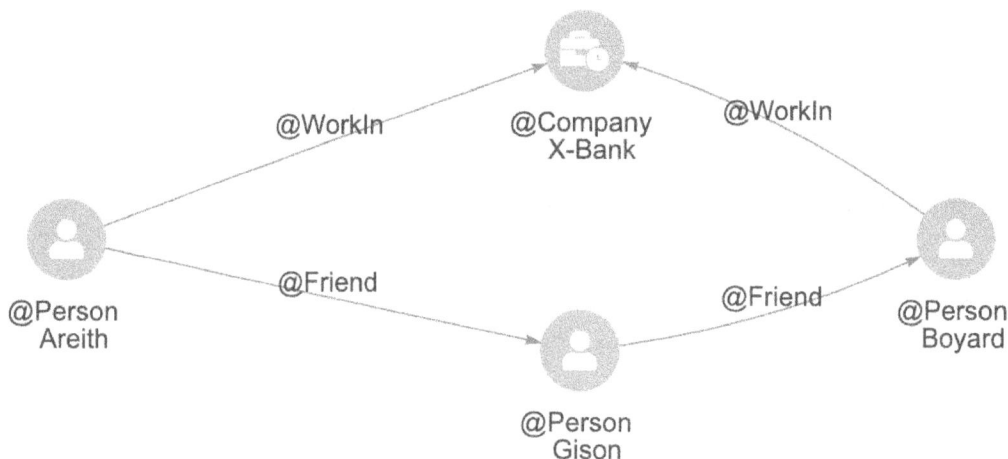

Figure 3.11: Multiple paths connecting Areith and Gison via Friend and WorkIn edges.

Given that graphs created in Ultipa Graph are all directed graphs, you must set a direction for each edge when inserting it even though the relationship is not explicitly directional. However, you can ignore directions when querying the graph.

For instance:

```
MATCH p = (areith)-[:Friend]-(gison) RETURN p
```

This query will retrieve both paths: `(areith)-[:Friend]->(gison)`, and `(gison)<-[:Friend]-(areith)`.

Now that we've utilized data modification statements to insert and modify nodes and edges, let's attempt to delete graph data.

Deleting nodes and edges

You can delete existing nodes and edges from the graph. The DELETE statement is used for this purpose. The nodes or edges to be deleted must first be retrieved from the database using the MATCH statement.

The story continues: Boyard wants to give himself a long-term break, so he decides to leave X-Bank. So, we can delete the relationship between Boyard and X-Bank:

```
GQL:
MATCH (:Person {name: "Boyard"})-[e:WorkIn]-
      (:Company {name:"X-Bank"})
DELETE e
```

Because of Boyard's decision, the boss of Z-Club wants to give himself a long-time break too, so he decides to close the club:

```
GQL:
MATCH (c:Club {name: "Z-Club"}) DELETE c
```

An error will occur during the execution of this deletion query because there are still other connections to the Z-Club node. In GQL, by default, it is prohibited to delete a node that has edges connected to it.

To force the deletion of nodes along with the deletion of edges connected to those nodes, you can use the DETACH DELETE statement:

```
GQL:
MATCH (c:Club {name: "Z-Club"})
DETACH DELETE c
```

This query deletes the Z-Club node and all the edges connected to it.

Dropping graph

You can drop a graph using the DROP GRAPH statement:

```
GQL:
DROP GRAPH StoryGraph
```

By dropping the graph, you have successfully concluded this comprehensive journey to getting started with GQL, including graph creation, data querying, graph modification, and data deletion.

Summary

In this chapter, we made our initial attempts at using GQL by learning how to create and manage graph data using intuitive pattern-based queries. We explored GQL Playground and constructed our own graph model called `StoryGraph`, which introduced us to the process of defining nodes and edges. Through examples, we practiced retrieving data using the `MATCH` statement, learning how to identify specific nodes, edges, and paths based on labels, properties, and relationships.

We also learned how to handle updates in the graph by modifying node and edge properties with the `SET` statement, demonstrated through scenarios such as updating the score of clubs or adding new friendships between people. Additionally, we practiced managing data life cycle operations by using the `DELETE` and `DETACH DELETE` statements to safely remove edges and nodes, while understanding the constraints around connected nodes. Finally, we saw how to conclude graph operations entirely by dropping the graph structure with the `DROP GRAPH` statement.

By following these examples, you've built a foundation in querying, modifying, and managing graph data in GQL. This sets the stage for the next chapter, where you'll explore GQL's statements and clauses in more detail, and apply your knowledge through hands-on, executable tutorials designed for deeper learning. Let's move forward and continue the journey.

Good luck!

4

GQL Basics

In the previous chapter, you got a quick start with GQL by creating graphs and manipulating data, providing a brief overview of how to operate graph data. Now, it's time to dive deeper! In this chapter, you'll explore the fundamentals of GQL, uncovering the power of GQL statements and learning how to match data and return results tailored to your needs. Get ready to unlock the full potential of GQL and transform the way you interact with graph data!

This chapter will cover the following topics:

- GQL statements
- Modifying GQL catalogs
- Retrieving graph data
- Modifying graph data
- Composite query statements
- Other clauses

Technical requirements

All the queries are located in the repository at https://github.com/PacktPublishing/Getting-Started-with-the-Graph-Query-Language-GQL/tree/main/Ch04.

GQL statements

In GQL, a statement defines one or more operations that are executed as part of a procedure. Each operation updates the current context and produces a result. GQL uses leading keywords to identify different parts of a statement, without any delimiters between operations. GQL statements can be categorized into **Data Definition Language** (DDL), **Data Query Language** (DQL), **Data Manipulation Language** (DML), and **Data Control Language** (DCL).

This chapter will cover all the statements. Here's a brief introduction to each:

- *DDL*: DDL allows managing schemas and graphs:

    - Creating or deleting GQL schemas or directories.

    - Managing graphs and graph types.

- *DQL*: DQL statements retrieve data using pattern matching and filtering. GQL provides a powerful set of querying constructs:

    - MATCH is used for graph pattern matching.

    - FILTER restricts matches based on conditions.

    - LET introduces intermediate variables.

    - FOR allows iteration over results.

    - RETURN specifies what data to project as output.

- *DML*: DML statements modify the content of a graph by inserting, updating, or deleting graph data:

    - Inserting nodes and edges:

        - INSERT: Adds new nodes and edges to a graph by specifying graph patterns that define the structure and properties of the new elements. It can also insert a path or subgraphs.

    - Updating nodes and edges:

        - SET: Updates properties and labels of existing nodes and edges, including label sets and property values.

        - REMOVE: Removes properties or labels of existing nodes and edges.

- Deleting nodes and edges:

    - DELETE: Removes nodes and edges from a graph. The optional DETECH/ NODETACH keyword can be added before the DELETE statement to define whether the statement will delete the related edges when deleting nodes.

- *DCL*: GQL does not currently define standard DCL statements. However, certain database implementations may support the following:

    - Grant and revoke privileges on graphs and systems for users and roles.

    - Managing users and roles.

Linear query statements

In GQL, a **linear query statement** refers to a query where each operation is executed in a sequence, without any branching or conditional logic. The result is delivered in a straightforward, linear progression.

Here's an example of a linear query:

```
GQL:
MATCH (l:Lang)-[:FOUNDED_BY]->(c:Company)
FILTER l.name = "GQL"
RETURN c
```

This query works as follows:

1. MATCH identifies all paths where a language node (Lang) is connected to a company node (Company) with a FOUNDED_BY relationship.

2. The FILTER statement ensures the language name is GQL.

3. The RETURN statement outputs the results.

Each step feeds into the next and the query is executed in a linear fashion: the results flow from the MATCH statement to the FILTER statement, then to the RETURN statement, and finally are output to the client.

In *Chapter 2, Key Concepts of GQL*, you were introduced to statement types, such as **Catalog Modifying Statements** and **Data Modifying Statements**. In this chapter, you'll learn about these in the *Modifying catalogs* and *Modifying graph data* sections. Additionally, you'll explore how to query data using various GQL query statements in the *Retrieving graph data* section.

Let's begin with modifying GQL catalogs.

Modifying catalogs

Now that you're familiar with GQL statements, it's time to explore how GQL catalogs are managed. This includes working with schemas, graphs, and graph types—key components of the GQL catalog structure.

GQL provides CREATE statements for defining new GQL schemas and graphs and corresponding DROP statements for removing them. As mentioned in *Chapter 2*, *Key Concepts of GQL*, both schemas and graphs are regarded as GQL objects within its hierarchical catalog design system.

In this section, you'll focus on how to create and drop GQL schemas.

CREATE and DROP GQL schema

A GQL schema serves as a logical workspace that contains graphs, graph types, binding tables, and named procedures. It helps users manage their graph data in independent domains.

Creating a GQL schema

A GQL schema can be created at the root of a GQL catalog or within a GQL directory.

To create a GQL schema, use the following syntax:

```
CREATE SCHEMA [ IF NOT EXISTS ] <schema path>
```

For example, to create a schema within the root path, you could use the following:

```
GQL:
CREATE SCHEMA /root/my_schema
```

This query creates a new GQL schema, my_schema, under the /root directory.

> Schema and directory management are not supported in GQL Playground. To execute this query, use Ultipa Powerhouse on Ultipa Cloud.
>
> Some graph database systems may support GQL predefined schema references such as HOME_SCHEMA and CURRENT_SCHEMA. In this book, we use HOME_SCHEMA as the default schema to store all the graphs. By default, CURRENT_SCHEMA refers to the same schema.

Dropping a GQL schema

To remove a schema, use the DROP SCHEMA statement:

```
GQL:
DROP SCHEMA /root/my_schema
```

This query drops the my_schema GQL schema.

CREATE and DROP graph

Creating and dropping graphs are foundational operations for building a graph database. In GQL, these are performed using the CREATE GRAPH and DROP GRAPH statements.

Creating a graph

Creating a graph is one of the first essential steps when using GQL to address real-world problems. This involves modeling data as a graph structure, enabling both efficient storage and powerful computation over connected data.

When designing a graph model, users should focus on three key considerations:

1. Define the problem to be solved, including the desired outcomes and the algorithms that might be employed.
2. Determine the types of nodes and edges, along with their properties and the types of those properties.
3. Connect the nodes using the appropriate edge types to effectively solve the problem.

Creating a graph serves a dual purpose: it tackles the challenge of data storage along with facilitating the computation of desired results using the graph model. These two goals should guide the graph's design.

The CREATE GRAPH statement in GQL is used to create property graphs. It supports operations such as IF NOT EXISTS to avoid duplication or CREATE OR REPLACE GRAPH to overwrite an existing graph.

Here is the syntax for creating a graph:

```
CREATE { [ PROPERTY ] GRAPH [ IF NOT EXISTS ] | OR REPLACE [ PROPERTY ]
GRAPH }
<catalog graph parent and name> { <open graph type> | <of graph type> } [
<graph source> ]
```

This allows flexibility in how graphs are created:

- As an open-type graph, which does not have a fixed graph structure
- From existing graph-type definitions
- By duplicating an existing graph with its structure and data

For example, to create a graph representing a network of database query languages, founders, and locations, use the following GQL:

```
GQL:
CREATE GRAPH QLGraph {
    NODE Lang ({name string, year int32}),
    NODE Company ({name string}),
    NODE Person ({name string}),
    NODE Category ({name string}),
    EDGE FOUNDED_BY ()-[{}]->(),
    EDGE WORKED_FOR ()-[{}]->(),
    EDGE LOCATED_IN ()-[{startYear int32}]->(),
    EDGE LIVES_IN ()-[{}]->(),
    EDGE BELONGS_TO ()-[{}]->()
}
```

If a graph with the same name already exists, a standard `CREATE GRAPH` statement will result in an error. To avoid this, GQL provides the `IF NOT EXISTS` option:

```
GQL:
CREATE PROPERTY GRAPH IF NOT EXISTS QLGraph {
    <property type definitions>
}
```

To remove an existing graph and recreate it with the same name, use `OR REPLACE`:

```
GQL:
CREATE OR REPLACE GRAPH QLGraph {
    <property type definitions>
}
```

Note that the `PROPERTY` keyword is optional in the `CREATE GRAPH` statement:

```
GQL:
CREATE GRAPH QLGraph {
```

```
        <property type definitions>
}
```

Creating a new graph with an existing graph or graph type

GQL allows you to create new graphs based on existing graphs or graph types, making it easier to reuse structures and maintain consistency across different graphs.

Reusing an existing graph

You can create a new graph based on an existing one. This is useful when you want to keep the same structure but not necessarily copy the data.

- Using LIKE: This creates a new graph with the same node and edge types as an existing graph but without any data. It's useful when you only need the structure.

    ```
    GQL:
    CREATE GRAPH NewQLGraph LIKE QLGraph
    ```

- Using AS COPY OF: This creates a new graph with both the same structure and data as the original graph. It's ideal when you want to clone the entire graph, including its data.

    ```
    GQL:
    CREATE GRAPH NewQLGraph AS COPY OF QLGraph
    ```

Reusing an existing graph type

Instead of using an existing graph, you can use a graph type. A graph type defines the structure (node and edge types and properties) without any data. Using a graph type ensures consistency and reusability across different graphs.

- The :: operator specifies that you're using a graph type to create the new graph.

    ```
    GQL:
    CREATE GRAPH NewQLGraph :: QLGraphType
    ```

- Alternatively, the TYPED keyword can be used instead of ::, which results in the same behavior.

    ```
    GQL:
    CREATE GRAPH NewQLGraph TYPED QLGraphType
    ```

    This query performs the same action as the query above.

On the other hand, you can also omit both operators:

```
GQL:
CREATE GRAPH NewQLGraph QLGraphType
```

These methods allow you to create a new graph with a predefined structure without including any data.

Dropping a graph

In GQL, you can remove an existing graph using the `DROP GRAPH` statement. This is useful when a graph is no longer needed or needs to be recreated from scratch.

To drop a graph named `NewQLGraph`, use the following query:

```
GQL:
DROP GRAPH NewQLGraph
```

However, if the graph does not exist, executing this statement will result in an error. To avoid such errors, you can include the `IF EXISTS` clause, which ensures that the statement executes only if the graph is present:

```
GQL:
DROP GRAPH IF EXISTS NewQLGraph
```

This query checks for the graph's existence before attempting to drop it, ensuring a safer execution path, especially in automated scripts or pipelines.

In the next section, you'll learn how to manage graph types, which define the structural blueprint of a graph.

The CREATE and DROP graph types

GQL supports both `CREATE` and `DROP` graph types. These graph types can serve as fundamental structures for generating new graphs.

Creating a graph type

A graph type in GQL defines the structure of a graph—specifying the types of nodes, edges, and their properties—without containing any data. It is reusable when creating new graphs.

Here's the syntax to create or replace a graph type:

```
CREATE { [ PROPERTY ] GRAPH TYPE [ IF NOT EXISTS ] | OR REPLACE [ PROPERTY
] GRAPH TYPE }
<catalog graph type parent and name> <graph type source>
```

The syntax is similar to the graph creation syntax, with the addition of the TYPE keyword following the GRAPH keyword.

To create a graph type, use the following GQL:

```
GQL:
CREATE GRAPH TYPE QLGraphType {
    NODE Lang ({name string, year int32}),
    NODE Company ({name string}),
    NODE Person ({name string}),
    NODE Category ({name string}),
    EDGE FOUNDED_BY ()-[]->(),
    EDGE WORKED_FOR ()-[]->(),
    EDGE LOCATED_IN ()-[{startYear int32}]->(),
    EDGE LIVES_IN ()-[]->(),
    EDGE BELONGS_TO ()-[]->()
}
```

To avoid errors when the graph type already exists, include IF NOT EXISTS:

```
GQL:
CREATE GRAPH TYPE IF NOT EXISTS QLGraphType {
    <property type definitions>
}
```

This query only creates the QLGraphType graph type if it does not exist.

Another way to force the creation of the graph type is by using the OR REPLACE keywords:

```
GQL:
CREATE OR REPLACE GRAPH TYPE QLGraphType {
    <property type definitions>
}
```

This query creates a graph type, QLGraphType, and deletes any existing graph type with the same name.

Creating a new graph type with an existing graph or graph type

You can create a new graph type from an existing graph or graph type by using the LIKE clause:

```
GQL:
CREATE GRAPH TYPE QLGraphModel LIKE QLGraph
```

This query creates a new graph type, QLGraphModel, by copying the graph structure from a graph named QLGraph.

To create a graph type by copying another graph type with the COPY OF clause, use the following query:

```
GQL:
CREATE GRAPH TYPE QLGraphModel2 COPY OF QLGraphModel
```

This query copies the node and edge type definitions from QLGraphModel.

Dropping a graph type

Using the DROP statement can drop a graph type:

```
GQL:
DROP GRAPH TYPE QLGraphModel2
```

This query drops the graph type QLGraphModel2.

To avoid an error occurring when the graph type does not exist, add an IF EXISTS clause before the graph type name:

```
GQL:
DROP GRAPH TYPE IF EXISTS QLGraphModel2
```

This query prevents an error occurring when QLGraphModel2 does not exist.

Retrieving graph data

Having explored how to manage graphs and graph types, this section will teach you how to retrieve data from a graph using GQL. The MATCH statement is central to querying the graph, enabling you to search for nodes, edges, paths, or subgraphs based on specific patterns.

The MATCH statement will be explored in two parts in this book. This section will cover the fundamental aspects of the MATCH statement, while an advanced discussion will be presented in *Chapter 07, Delve into Advanced Clauses*. This approach allows for a gradual and comprehensive understanding of the MATCH statement's capabilities within GQL.

The syntax of the MATCH statement is as follows:

```
[OPTIONAL] MATCH <match mode> <path pattern list>
```

- [OPTIONAL]: This keyword enables the MATCH statement to assign null values to results (binding variables) if no match is found, allowing the query to continue executing without interruption.

- <match mode>: GQL supports two match modes:

    - DIFFERENT EDGES: Prevents the same edge from appearing more than once in a record.

    - REPEATABLE ELEMENTS: Permits the repetition of elements, including nodes or edges, in a record.

    - If no match mode is specified, a default mode can be set by the GQL implementor.

- <path pattern list>: It consists of one or multiple path patterns. The multiple path patterns can be disconnected or connected by using common node or edge variables. Path patterns in GQL also include a variety of path modes, which will be explored in detail in later chapters.

MATCH is introduced here with fundamentals. Advanced usage (e.g., OPTIONAL, recursion, path modes, etc.) will be explored in *Chapter 07, Delve into Advanced Clauses*.

In GQL Playground, MATCH DIFFERENT EDGES is used as the default mode. For simplicity, the DIFFERENT EDGES keywords will be omitted in the example queries.

Matching with node patterns

Node patterns are fundamental components of path patterns and are used for retrieving nodes. Within a node pattern, you can declare a variable to bind the matching nodes and set labels and search conditions. A node pattern starts and ends with (and).

Here's the node pattern syntax:

```
([<variable>][<is label>][<search conditions>])
```

Here are the definitions within the node pattern syntax:

- `<variable>`: This binds a variable to the nodes that matched in the graph.
- `<is label>`: This specifies which labels the pattern matches. If `<is label>` is omitted, it will match any label.

    - `IS A or :A` matches nodes labeled A.
    - `IS A|B or :A|B` matches nodes labeled A or B.
    - `IS A&B or :A&B` matches nodes labeled A and B.
    - `IS !A or :!A` matches nodes that are not labeled A.

- `<search conditions>`: It has two possible forms, the `WHERE` clause or the property specification. If it's omitted, the search condition will always be true.

> The `<variable>` name should start with an `Underscore(_)` or a Unicode `ID_Start` character, followed by Unicode `ID_Continue` characters. If you are interested in the details of the `UnicodeID` characters, visit https://www.unicode.org/reports/tr31/.

Label and search condition definitions are flexible—GQL supports both `IS` and `:` for labels, and both the `WHERE` clause and property specification for filtering.

Here are some examples to `MATCH` with node patterns:

Node Pattern	Description
`()`	Any anonymous node.
`(:Person)` `(is Person)`	Any anonymous node labeled `Person`.
`(n IS Person|Company)`	Any node labeled `Person` or `Company`, bound to the variable n.
`({name: "GQL"})` `(WHERE name = "GQL")`	Any anonymous node where its name is GQL.
`(n is Lang WHERE name = "GQL")`	Any node labeled `Lang` where its name is GQL.

Table 4.1: Node pattern examples

Let's take an example to match all nodes in a graph:

```
GQL:
MATCH (n) RETURN n
```

This query returns all nodes from the current graph.

> To execute the examples, you need to initialize the graph data using the query located in the Ch04/initial_data.gql file.

To match nodes with a specific label, you can use the following:

```
MATCH (n IS Lang) RETURN n
```

Alternatively, you can use :Lang:

```
MATCH (n:Lang) RETURN n
```

Both queries return all nodes labeled Lang.

You can add more conditions by using a WHERE clause within a node pattern:

```
MATCH (n IS Lang WHERE n.name = "GQL") RETURN n
```

This query returns all nodes with the Lang label where the name is GQL.

Alternatively, you can use the following query to retrieve the same data:

```
MATCH (n:Lang {name: "GQL"}) RETURN n
```

If you want all nodes except Lang nodes, use the following query:

```
MATCH (n IS !Lang) RETURN n
```

If you want to retrieve all nodes with a Person or Company label, use the following:

```
MATCH (n IS Person|Company) RETURN n
```

Matching with edge patterns

Edge patterns are another fundamental component of path patterns. Within an edge pattern, you can declare a variable to bind to the matching edges, set labels, and define search conditions. An edge pattern starts and ends with [and].

Here's the edge pattern syntax:

```
<direction-symbols><left bracket>
[<element filter>]
<right bracket><direction-symbols>
```

These are the definitions within the edge pattern syntax:

- `<direction-symbols>`: Represents the direction of the edges. The direction can be left, right, undirected, or any. *Table 4.2* contains the list of different directions.

- `[<element filler>]`: It includes `[<variable>][<is label>][<search conditions>]`, which are similar to the node pattern.

Edge Pattern	Direction
`-[]-`	Any
`-[]->`	Right
`<-[]-`	Left
`~[]~`	Undirected
`~[]~>`	Undirected or right
`<~[]~`	Undirected or left
`<-[]->`	Left or right

Table 4.2: Edge pattern directions

Edge Pattern	Description
`-[]-`	Any anonymous edge in any direction.
`-[e:LOCATED_IN]->` `-[e IS LOCATED_IN]->`	Any edge labeled `LOCATED_IN` pointing right, bound to the variable e.

Table 4.3: Edge pattern examples

To match all edges with any direction, use the following:

```
GQL:
MATCH -[edges]- RETURN edges
```

In a directed graph, this query returns all edges twice because an edge from a to b can be represented as a->b and b<-a when the direction is not restricted.

You can avoid returning duplicate edges by specifying a direction:

```
GQL:
MATCH -[edges]-> RETURN edges
```

This query returns each edge only once.

Edges can be filtered by labels and properties. For example, to match all LOCATED_IN edges, use the following:

```
GQL:
MATCH -[edges IS LOCATED_IN]-> RETURN edges
```

This query returns all edges with the LOCATED_IN label.

```
GQL:
MATCH -[edge IS LOCATED_IN WHERE edge.startYear > 2000]->
RETURN edge
```

This query returns the edges with the LOCATED_IN label where the startTime property is larger than 2000.

Matching with path patterns

Once you're familiar with node and edge patterns, you can combine them with path patterns or graph patterns, which represent a sequence of connected nodes and edges. In this section, we focus on the TRAIL path mode, which allows repeated nodes but not repeated edges. As discussed when discussing the GQL concepts, path modes include ACYCLE, TRAIL, WALK, and SIMPLE.

In GQL, a path pattern can include optional variable declarations, path prefixes, and a sequence of node and edge patterns. The general syntax looks like this:

```
[<path variable declaration>][<path pattern prefix>]<path pattern
expression>
```

Let's break this down:

- <path variable declaration>: This declares the variable that is bound to the paths.
- <path pattern prefix>: There are two types of prefixes. The first pertains to the path mode prefix, which can be ACYCLE, TRAIL, WALK, or SIMPLE. If omitted, TRAIL will be used as the default in GQL Playground. The second is the path search prefix, which can be ANY, ALL, or SHORTEST. We will discuss more about the path prefixes in *Chapter 7, Delve into Advanced Clauses*.
- <path pattern expression>: This is a concatenation of node and edge patterns. It must begin and end with node patterns, with node and edge patterns alternating in the sequence.

To match and return paths from any node to any node with any direction, do the following:

```
GQL:
MATCH p=()-[]-() RETURN p
```

This query returns paths by the variable p. Each path contains two nodes and one edge. Since the edge pattern matches undirected edges, the path connects the start and end nodes in any direction.

Edge pattern abbreviation

In path patterns, the edge patterns can be abbreviated using the following mappings:

Full Edge Pattern	Abbreviated Edge Pattern
-[]-	-
-[]->	->
<-[]-	<-
<~[]~	<~
~[]~>	~>

Table 4.4: Edge pattern abbreviations

To match all paths between any two nodes, regardless of direction, you can use an abbreviated GQL pattern:

```
GQL:
MATCH p=()-() RETURN p
```

In GQL, the MATCH path statement enables users to define variables for both path patterns and element patterns (node or edge patterns) simultaneously.

For example, consider the task of matching a path from a Lang named "GQL" to a Person and retrieving both the path and the person nodes.

The GQL query would be as follows:

```
GQL:
MATCH p=(l IS Lang WHERE l.name = "GQL")-(founder IS Person)
RETURN p, founder
```

Finding paths across multiple hops is a fundamental feature of graph databases. For instance, to identify languages that have the same category as GQL, the query can be structured as follows:

```
GQL:
MATCH (l IS Lang WHERE l.name = "GQL")-(IS Category)-(otherLangs IS Lang)
RETURN otherLangs AS languages
```

Connected and disconnected path matching

In GQL, path matching can either be connected or disconnected, depending on how the path patterns are defined and whether they share common variables. If the path patterns share common declared or binding element variables, the matching is considered *connected*. Otherwise, it is *disconnected*.

Matching with connected path patterns

Path patterns can be connected by common variables and produce connected paths or subgraphs.

To search databases supporting GQL using connected path matching, the query might be the following:

```
GQL:
MATCH (l IS Lang WHERE l.name = "GQL"),
      (l)-(c:Category)
RETURN c AS category
```

The (l IS Lang WHERE l.name = "GQL") and (l)-(c:Category) path patterns are linked through the variable l.

Another example involves finding query languages in the same category as GQL and UQL. The query might look like this:

```
GQL:
MATCH (gql IS Lang WHERE gql.name = "GQL"),
      (uql IS Lang WHERE uql.name = "UQL"),
      (gql)-(c IS Category)-(uql),
      (c)-(otherLanguages IS Lang)
RETURN otherLanguages
```

In the default match mode, as outlined in this book, DIFFERENT EDGES are employed in the MATCH statement. This approach ensures that the companies identified do not include Facebook and Microsoft, since the edges linking these individuals to the country have been traversed before executing the path pattern.

Matching with disconnected path patterns

Disconnected path patterns occur when there are no shared variables between them. In this case, the results are generated by computing the **Cartesian product** of the result sets from the individual patterns, meaning all combinations of nodes from each pattern are included in the final result.

Let's take the example of searching for both Person and Location in a graph using disconnected path patterns in a single MATCH statement:

```
GQL:
MATCH (person IS Person), (location IS Location)
RETURN person, location
```

In this query, the (person IS Person) and (location IS Location) patterns are disconnected. Consequently, the results will perform a Cartesian product between Person and Location. The number of returned records is equal to the product of the number of person nodes and the number of location nodes.

Matching with quantified path patterns

Quantified path matching in GQL allows you to specify how many times a path pattern or edge pattern should be repeated. This is particularly useful for matching paths with a specific number of hops, or when you need to repeat edge patterns or path fragments within a query.

Repeated edge patterns

An edge pattern is the minimal repeatable unit within a path pattern. GQL permits defining a range from 0 to a positive integer to specify how many times an edge should repeat.

For example, to find paths from a node named GQL to any other node, with either 1 hop or 2 hops, you can structure the query like this:

```
GQL:
MATCH p=(n WHERE n.name = "GQL")-[]-()
RETURN p
```

```
UNION
MATCH p=(n WHERE n.name = "GQL")-[]-()-[]-()
RETURN p
```

This query retrieves paths from GQL to other nodes within 1 or 2 hops. However, writing 30 different queries for 30 hops doesn't make sense!

Quantified path matching simplifies this by specifying the range of edge repetitions:

```
GQL:
MATCH p=(n WHERE n.name = "GQL")-[]-{1,2}()
RETURN p
```

In this query, the -[]-{1,2} fragment repeats the -[]- edge pattern from 1 to 2 times, where {1,2} serves as the quantifier of the edge pattern.

GQL defines several quantifiers:

Quantifier	Example	Description
Fixed quantifier	{2}	Denotes an exact repeat number, represented as an unsigned integer, equivalent to {2,2}.
General quantifier	{1,30} {1,} {,30}	Specifies a range with lower and upper bounds as unsigned integers. Bounds can be omitted, implying no lower or upper limit, and at least one bound is required.
*	*	Indicates a range from 0, equivalent to {0,}.
+	+	Indicates a range from 1, equivalent to {1,}.

Table 4.5: Quantifiers

Repeated path patterns

In a graph where nodes and edges are of the same type, simply repeating an edge pattern might seem sufficient. However, the complexity of real-world scenarios often requires repeating a path fragment to accurately model these situations.

For instance, consider the task of finding a path from a node named Meta to another node named Apache Software Foundation. A query with repeated path fragments might look like this:

```
GQL:
MATCH (meta {name: "Meta"}),
      (apache {name: "Apache Software Foundation"})
MATCH p=(meta)-[]-(()-[]-()){2}-[]-(apache)
RETURN p
```

In the provided GQL query, meta and apache act as the start and end nodes connected to a quantified path pattern: (()-[]-()){2}. The quantifier {2} specifies that this fragment should be repeated two times. We can expand the quantified path pattern as follows:

```
(meta)-[]-()-[]-()()-[]-()-[]-(apache)
```

There are two node patterns that are concatenated consecutively, ()(), between the repetition, and they will be merged into one node pattern, (). Therefore, the path pattern is equivalent to this:

```
(meta)-[]-()-[]-()-[]-()-[]-(apache)
```

Let's analyze what will happen with this GQL query:

```
GQL:
MATCH (meta {name: "Meta"}),
      (apache {name: "Apache Software Foundation"})
MATCH p=(meta)-(()-[]-(IS !Company)){1,2}-(apache)
RETURN p
```

The path pattern is equivalent to this:

```
(meta)-()-[]-(IS !Company)-(apache)
```

Or, this:

```
(meta)-()-[]-(IS !Company)()-[]-(IS !Company)-(apache)
```

In the second case, the two node patterns that are put together, (IS !Company)(), are treated as a single node pattern, (IS !Company), with their search conditions merged.

Therefore, the path pattern is equivalent to this:

```
(meta)-()-[]-(IS !Company)-(apache)
```

Or, this:

```
(meta)-[]-()-[]-(IS !Company)-[]-(IS !Company)-[]-(apache)
```

Simplified path patterns and full path patterns

GQL supports both simplified and full path patterns. The simplified path pattern is a more concise expression of edge labels, often used in regular expressions. On the other hand, the full path pattern includes both node and edge patterns, along with parenthesized path patterns.

For those interested in exploring simplified path patterns, which can be expressed as regular expressions of edge labels, please refer to ISO/IEC 39075:2024 at `https://www.iso.org/standard/76120.html`, specifically the `<simplified path pattern expression>` section.

Returning results

In the previous section, you explored how to use the `MATCH` statement to retrieve graph data. Those queries also include the `RETURN` statement, which outputs the results. In this section, you will delve into the `RETURN` statement to explore its details.

Here's the syntax of the `RETURN` statement:

```
RETURN [DISTINCT | ALL] {* | <return item list>} [Group By clause]
```

Or, this:

```
RETURN NO BINDINGS
```

These are the definitions within the `RETURN` syntax:

- `[DISTINCT | ALL]`: Specifies whether to deduplicate results. If omitted, `RETURN ALL` will be the default setting.
- `*`: Returns all variables from previous statements.
- `<return item list>`: Returns explicitly defined items. Each item can be a value expression or a variable, and new alias names can be defined using the `AS` keyword.
- `GROUP BY`: Groups results based on specified values within the results.
- `RETURN NO BINDINGS` or `FINISH`: Executes the query without returning any results. Useful for executing queries to retrieve system statistics without returning data.

In previous sections, you used `RETURN` statements to yield results such as nodes, edges, and paths.

To retrieve all variables from the MATCH path statements, consider the following GQL example:

```
GQL:
MATCH p=(lang IS Lang)-(category IS Category) RETURN *
```

In this example, RETURN * equates to RETURN p, lang, category.

To retrieve the Lang nodes and return all unique year values, use the following:

```
GQL:
MATCH (lang IS Lang) RETURN DISTINCT lang.year
```

In this GQL statement, the RETURN clause outputs the deduplicated values from the year property of the nodes referenced by the lang variable.

```
GQL:
MATCH (c IS Category)-[]-(l IS Lang)
RETURN count(l), c.name AS categoryName
GROUP BY categoryName
```

Using this GQL, you can count the languages of each category. The query uses AS to rename c.name to categoryName, which is then used in the GROUP BY clause. Note that in the first version of GQL, the GROUP BY clause can only use variable references; a syntax error will occur if written as GROUP BY c.name.

Filtering records

The FILTER statement is used to select records that meet the specified search conditions from the current incoming working table, that is, the intermediate result set produced by previous statements.

Here's the filter statement syntax:

```
FILTER [WHERE] <search condition>
```

For example, to filter all Lang nodes with year greater than 2000, use the following:

```
GQL:
MATCH (l IS Lang) FILTER WHERE l.year > 2000 RETURN l
```

Or, simply this:

```
GQL:
MATCH (l IS Lang ) FILTER l.year > 2000 RETURN l
```

This query retrieves the same results as the following GQL:

```
GQL:
MATCH (l IS Lang WHERE l.year > 2000 ) RETURN l
```

Or, the following:

```
GQL:
MATCH (l IS Lang) WHERE l.year > 2000 RETURN l
```

The distinction between a FILTER query and a MATCH WHERE query lies in whether the WHERE clause is part of the graph pattern matching. This can lead to varying behavior in graph database executors, such as filtering data during graph traversal in a MATCH statement or filtering data from all results of MATCH statements without a search condition. For this query, using MATCH WHERE could potentially offer better performance compared to using MATCH FILTER. However, it's GQL implementation dependent.

Differences between FILTER and WHERE

The FILTER statement and the WHERE clause in the MATCH statement both apply conditions to queries, but they differ in their timing and evaluation process. The WHERE clause is part of the MATCH statement and is evaluated during the graph pattern-matching process. Conversely, the FILTER statement is applied after the preceding statements have been executed, refining the results further by applying additional conditions.

> In some graph database systems, using WHERE with MATCH instead of FILTER can optimize query execution more effectively.

Sorting and paging results

GQL defines the ORDER BY, SKIP, and LIMIT clauses to sort results, skip a specified number of rows, and limit the number of records returned. These clauses facilitate the implementation of paginated results.

Sorting (ORDER BY)

The ORDER BY clause is used to sort query results based on one or more value expressions.

The syntax of ORDER BY is as follows:

```
ORDER BY <sort specification>
```

`<sort specification>`:

```
{ASC | DESC} <value expression> [NULLS {FIRST | LAST}]
```

Here are the definitions within the sorting syntax:

- ASC | DESC: This sorts results in ascending or descending order, respectively. The keywords ASCENDING and DESCENDING are also valid alternatives.
- `<value expression>`: This can be any valid value expression, such as lang.year, lang.name, or lang.year - 10.
- NULLS FIRST or LAST: This determines the position of NULL values in the ordered list. NULLS FIRST places NULL before non-NULL values, whereas NULLS LAST places them after.

> Graph databases often have default behaviors when sorting options are omitted. In GQL, by default, it sorts ASC with NULLS FIRST and DESC with NULLS LAST.

To return all query languages sorted by year in ascending order and put NULLs first, use the following:

```
GQL:
MATCH (g IS Lang) RETURN g ORDER BY g.year ASC
```

This is functionally the same as this simpler form:

```
GQL:
MATCH (g IS Lang) RETURN g ORDER BY g.year
```

To place NULL values at the end of the sorted results, use the following:

```
GQL:
MATCH (g IS Lang) RETURN g ORDER BY g.year ASC NULLS LAST
```

Limiting records

GQL uses the LIMIT clause to restrict the number of records from the working table.

Here's the syntax you can use:

```
LIMIT <unsigned integer>
```

LIMIT can be applied after any statement such as MATCH, FILTER, RETURN, and so on.

For example, to return only one query language node from all query language nodes, you'd use this:

```
GQL:
MATCH (n:Lang) RETURN n LIMIT 1
```

LIMIT can also be placed after MATCH statements, achieving the same result:

```
GQL:
MATCH (n:Lang) LIMIT 1 RETURN n
```

LIMIT can be applied multiple times within a GQL query for different purposes:

```
GQL:
MATCH (n:Lang) LIMIT 5
MATCH (n)-(c IS Category) LIMIT 2
RETURN c LIMIT 1
```

Skipping records

GQL uses SKIP and OFFSET (interchangeable keywords) to skip a number of records from a working table.

Here's the syntax to skip records:

```
{SKIP|OFFSET} <unsigned integer>
```

SKIP can be applied after any statement such as MATCH, FILTER, RETURN, and so on.

To skip the first query language node retrieved from the MATCH statement, use the following:

```
GQL:
MATCH (n:Lang) SKIP 1 RETURN n
```

You can also place SKIP at the end of the query and receive the same result:

```
GQL:
MATCH (n:Lang) RETURN n SKIP 1
```

`SKIP` can be applied multiple times in a query as well:

```
GQL:
MATCH (n IS Lang) SKIP 1
MATCH (n)-(c IS Category) SKIP 2 RETURN c
```

Each `SKIP` applies to its respective statement, letting you fine-tune how many records are by-passed at each stage.

Paging records

With `SKIP` and `LIMIT` clauses, you can now retrieve results page by page.

Here's the syntax for paging records:

```
SKIP <page_size> * <page_num - 1> LIMIT <page_size>
```

This code snippet allows you to calculate which records to skip and how many to retrieve, based on the desired page number and size.

For example, to retrieve the second page of the query language nodes list, and limit it to 5 records for each page, you'd use the following:

```
GQL:
MATCH (n IS Lang) RETURN n SKIP 5 LIMIT 5
```

`SKIP 5` is calculated from `5 * (2 - 1) = 5`, which matched the formula `<page_size> * <page_num - 1>`.

Grouping and aggregating results

GQL supports using the `GROUP BY` clause at the end of the `RETURN` statement to group the final result set based on specific values. Grouping records is usually used with aggregating functions to summarize or analyze sets of records.

Here's the syntax you can use:

```
GROUP BY {<group element list> | ()}
```

Grouping records

To group records in GQL, you must reference binding variables declared in earlier clauses such as `MATCH`, `LET`, or `RETURN`. These group elements define how the results are partitioned before applying aggregation functions.

For example, to group query language nodes by their categories and return the count of language nodes in each group, use the following:

```
GQL:
MATCH (g IS Lang)-(c IS Category)
RETURN count(g), c.name as cateName
GROUP BY cateName
```

What will happen if you replace count(g) with g?

```
GQL:
MATCH (g IS Lang)-(c IS Category)
RETURN g, c.name as cateName
GROUP BY cateName
```

This adjustment will result in selecting only the first query language node from each group.

Aggregating records

If a query includes an aggregation function and omits GROUP BY or uses ( ) as the group element, all records will be aggregated into a single group:

```
GQL:
MATCH (g IS Lang)-(c IS Category)
RETURN count(g), c GROUP BY ()
```

You could also use this:

```
GQL:
MATCH (g IS Lang)-(c IS Category)
RETURN count(g), c
```

Both queries will return the same result, aggregating all records into one group.

> In the first version of GQL, `<group element>` can only be a binding variable reference and cannot use an expression. So, in the previous example, a LET to declare a new variable reference to the property value is required.

Modifying graph data

GQL defines linear data-modifying statements to support inserting, updating, and deleting data. These statements allow users to efficiently manage and manipulate their datasets, ensuring that data can be dynamically adjusted to reflect changes.

Inserting graph data

GQL employs the INSERT statement to create nodes, edges, or paths within the current graph. As we have learned about using graph patterns, these patterns can also be utilized for data insertion.

To insert graph data, use the following syntax:

```
INSERT <graph pattern list>
```

A graph pattern list can include nodes, edges, or paths. Let's take a closer look at how to insert nodes, edges, and paths.

Inserting nodes

When inserting nodes, you define the node's label and properties. Each node is represented in a graph pattern that specifies its label and then its properties.

For example, to insert two nodes into the QLGraph, use the following query:

```
GQL:
INSERT (:Lang {name: "UQL"}), (:Company {name: "Ultipa"})
```

This query inserts two nodes: one with the Lang label and a name property set to UQL, and another with the Company label and a name property set to Ultipa.

Inserting edges

Edges represent relationships between nodes. To insert an edge, you must define both the start and end nodes, as well as the edge type between them.

For example, to insert an edge from UQL to the corresponding category, use the following query:

```
GQL:
MATCH (g:Lang {name: "UQL"}), (c:Category {name: "Graph"})
INSERT (g)-[:BELONGS_TO]->(c)
```

This query inserts an edge labeled **BELONGS_TO** that connects the nodes g and c.

Inserting paths

Now that you've learned how to insert nodes and edges by matching start and end nodes, GQL allows the simultaneous insertion of nodes and edges in a path-inserting statement.

For example, to insert a path from the query language node (UQL) and connect it to the company node (Ultipa) via a FOUNDED_BY edge, use the following:

```
GQL:
INSERT (:Lang {name: "UQL"})-[:FOUNDED_BY]->(:Company {name: "Ultipa"})
```

Alternatively, the path pattern can be separated into two node patterns and one path pattern for clearer readability:

```
GQL:
INSERT (uql:Lang {name: "UQL"}),
       (ultipa:Company {name: "Ultipa"}),
       (uql)-[:FOUNDED_BY]->(ultipa)
```

The declared binding variables can be returned. Therefore, the query can return the newly inserted graph data:

```
GQL:
INSERT (uql:Lang {name: "UQL"}),
       (ultipa:Company {name: "Ultipa"}),
       (uql)-[e:FOUNDED_BY]->(ultipa)
RETURN uql, ultipa, e
```

This query inserts the nodes and edges and returns them.

Updating data

To update nodes or edges in GQL, the SET statement is used to modify the properties or labels of graph elements. This statement allows you to update values based on variable references and expressions.

The basic syntax for the SET statement is as follows:

```
SET <set item list>
```

Here are the definitions within the updating syntax:

- `<set item list>`: There are three types of set items:

    - Updating a property value to a variable reference:

        `<property of variable reference> = <value expression>`

    - Updating all property values to a variable reference:

        `<variable reference> = <property value specification>`

    - Updating the label of a variable reference:

        `<variable reference> IS <label name>`

These updates can be applied to both nodes and edges, depending on the element you are modifying.

For example, to update a specific property value for a node, you can use the SET statement. For instance, to set the year property of the UQL node to 2019, the query would look like this:

```
GQL:
MATCH (uql IS Lang WHERE uql.name = "UQL")
SET uql.year = 2019
```

To change all property values in one SET statement, use the following query:

```
GQL:
MATCH (uql IS Lang WHERE uql.name = "UQL")
SET uql = { name: "Ultipa Query Language", year: 2019 }
```

Note that if the uql node has other properties other than name and year, their values will be removed and replaced with NULL.

Or, to set all properties separately, use the following query:

```
GQL:
MATCH (uql IS Lang WHERE uql.name = "Ultipa Query Language")
SET uql.name = "UQL", uql.year = 2019
```

The updated graph element can be returned as well – use the following query:

```
GQL:
MATCH (uql IS Lang WHERE uql.name = "UQL")
SET uql.name = "Ultipa Query Language",
    uql.year = 2019
RETURN uql
```

To set the label of the node, use the following query:

```
GQL:
MATCH (uql WHERE uql.name = "Ultipa Query Language")
SET uql IS Lang
```

This query sets the Lang label to the uql node. You can use SET uql :Lang alternatively.

Let's change the name back to UQL:

```
GQL:
MATCH (uql WHERE uql.name = "Ultipa Query Language")
SET uql.name = "UQL"
```

Deleting data

To delete nodes or edges in GQL, the DELETE statement is used. This statement allows you to remove graph elements, including nodes and edges.

The syntax for the DELETE statement is as follows:

```
[DETACH | NODETACH] DELETE <delete item list>
```

Here are the definitions within the Delete syntax:

- DETACH: Removes the node along with all its connected edges.
- NODETACH: Deletes the node only if no edge connects to it; an error occurs if edges are present. If neither DETACH nor NODETACH is specified, NODETACH is the default.
- <delete item list>: References to node and edge graph elements.

To delete a node named SQL, use the following:

```
GQL:
MATCH (g IS Lang WHERE g.name = "SQL")
DELETE g
```

This query causes an error when the SQL node has connected edges in the graph. To prevent this error, you can remove all related edges before removing the node:

```
GQL:
MATCH (g IS Lang WHERE g.name = "SQL")-[e]-()
DELETE e
DELETE g
```

Alternatively, using NODETACH DELETE has the same behavior:

```
GQL:
MATCH (g IS Lang WHERE g.name = "SQL")
DETACH DELETE g
```

Removing properties and labels

Besides deleting nodes and edges, GQL also offers the REMOVE statement to remove properties and labels from nodes and edges.

Here's the syntax for removing properties and labels:

```
REMOVE {<variable property reference> | { <variable reference> <is label>
}}
```

Here are the definitions within the syntax:

- <variable property reference>: Refers to the property of a variable, such as n.name, which is the name property of the n variable.
- <variable ref> <is label>: Represents the label of a variable, such as n IS Lang, which indicates the Lang label of the n variable.
- All variables used for removing properties or labels should be node or edge variables.

For example, to remove a property value, use the following:

```
GQL:
MATCH (g WHERE g.name = "GQL") REMOVE g.year
```

This query removes the value of the year property from the node.

For example, to remove a label, use the following:

```
GQL:
MATCH (g WHERE g.name = "GQL") REMOVE g IS Lang
```

This query removes the Lang label from the node.

> GQL Playground does not allow you to remove or modify the label of nodes and edges.
>
> Different graph database providers may support various graph types, such as open and closed graphs. As a result, removing a label or property can trigger different operations – for example, a property might be completely removed, or it might be set to null.

Composite query statements

A composite query statement combines a list of linear query statements with query conjunctions. The query conjunctions could be UNION, EXCEPT, INTERSECT, or OTHERWISE.

Here's the syntax of the composite query:

```
<query> <conjunction> <query>
```

Here are the definitions within the syntax:

- <query>: Represents any linear query statement or another composite query.

- <conjunction>: Represents conjunction keywords such as UNION, EXCEPT, INTERSECT, and OTHERWISE. You will explore this later in this section.

- The two <query> instances of the composite query must return variables with the same variable names.

Next, you will explore the usage of the UNION conjunction.

Retrieving union records

The GQL UNION conjunction merges results from two queries sharing the same returning variable name. UNION supports both UNION ALL and UNION [DISTINCT], allowing for the retention of all results or the deduplicated results.

Following is an example of combining two linear query statements with a UNION conjunction to yield a unified result:

```
GQL:
MATCH (n:Lang) LIMIT 3 RETURN n
UNION
MATCH (n:Lang) LIMIT 4 RETURN n
```

This query returns two groups of nodes as a single set, removing repeated results. As a result, the maximum number of nodes in the output should be 4. This is equivalent to UNION DISTINCT, where DISTINCT is implicitly applied.

By changing UNION to UNION ALL, duplicated records will be retained in the result:

```
GQL:
MATCH (n:Lang) LIMIT 3 RETURN n
UNION ALL
MATCH (n:Lang) LIMIT 4 RETURN n
```

This query returns 7 nodes.

Excluding records from another query

GQL allows for the exclusion of results from one query based on the results of another:

```
GQL:
MATCH (n:Lang)-(c:Category) RETURN c LIMIT 10
EXCEPT
MATCH (n:Lang)-(c:Category) RETURN c LIMIT 1
```

This query returns records from the first query, excluding those also obtained from the second query. This is equivalent to EXCEPT DISTINCT, where DISTINCT is implicitly applied.

Changing EXCEPT to EXCEPT ALL will return a result set including rows from the first query that do not appear in the second query, without removing duplicates:

```
GQL:
MATCH (n:Lang)-(c:Category) RETURN c LIMIT 10
EXCEPT ALL
MATCH (n:Lang)-(c:Category) RETURN c LIMIT 1
```

Retrieving intersected records

GQL supports returning the intersection of the result sets from different queries:

```
MATCH (n:Lang)-(c:Category) RETURN c LIMIT 10
INTERSECT
MATCH (n:Lang)-(c:Category) RETURN c LIMIT 2
```

This query retrieves records that exist in both the first and the second queries while removing duplicates.

This operation is analogous to INTERSECT DISTINCT, where DISTINCT is implicitly applied. If you opt for INTERSECT ALL, the intersected records will be returned without duplicate removal:

```
MATCH (n:Lang)-(c:Category) RETURN c LIMIT 10
INTERSECT ALL
MATCH (n:Lang)-(c:Category) RETURN c LIMIT 2
```

Other clauses

GQL also offers other clauses such as YIELD, AT SCHEMA, and USE GRAPH.

The YIELD clause

The YIELD clause is instrumental for selecting and renaming variables from the current working table. It specifies which variables are available for subsequent statements. The YIELD clause can be utilized with either CALL named procedure statements or MATCH statements.

To select only the g variable from the working table containing p and g, use the following:

```
GQL:
MATCH p=(g:Lang) YIELD g RETURN g
```

You can select results from a named procedure as follows (this query needs the support of HDC services – you will explore how to use HDC services in *Chapter 7*):

```
GQL:
CALL hdc.algo.degree("gql_g1",{
    params: {}
}) YIELD results
RETURN results
```

This query calls a procedure provided by GQL Playground. The procedure is a graph algorithm that calculates degree centrality for nodes in the "gql_g1" graph using default parameters. The result of the procedure is defined as the results variable, which is a binding table with two columns: the node UUID and degree centrality.

The AT SCHEMA clause

GQL allows you to declare the current working schema scope with the AT SCHEMA clause:

```
GQL:
AT /root/<schema_name> ...
```

This query sets a new current schema.

The USE graph clause

GQL also allows you to declare the current working graph scope. Any query with the USE GRAPH clause is considered a focused linear statement.

Here's the syntax of the USE GRAPH clause:

```
USE <graph_name>
```

Here is an example of retrieving nodes from a target graph:

```
GQL:
USE StoryGraph
MATCH (n) RETURN n
```

This query returns all nodes from the *StoryGraph* graph. This query is a focused linear statement.

Users can set the current working graph using the USE clause or session settings. In GQL Playground, you can select the graph from the top-left drop-down graph list, which sets the current graph for the session.

Using the USE clause can overwrite the graph settings in session configurations.

You will explore more about session operations in *Chapter 8, Configuring Sessions*.

> In GQL Playground, a default GQL schema serves as the root catalog and the current schema.

Summary

In this chapter, you have gained a comprehensive understanding of the basic usage of GQL. You have learned how to manipulate GQL catalogs, including schemas, graphs, and graph types, as well as how to insert and retrieve graph data using the MATCH statement. Additionally, you have mastered sorting records, paging results, and modifying graph nodes and edges according to your needs.

In the next chapter, you will explore a variety of expressions and operators. These tools will enable you to efficiently manipulate data, set precise conditions, and perform calculations. You will also learn how to use comparison and logical operators to enhance your queries.

Get This Book's PDF Version and Exclusive Extras

Scan the QR code (or go to packtpub.com/unlock). Search for this book by name, confirm the edition, and then follow the steps on the page.

Note: Keep your invoice handy. Purchases made directly from Packt don't require an invoice.

5

Exploring Expressions and Operators

Expressions and operators are the foundation of value manipulation in GQL. They enable you to filter nodes and relationships, compute metrics over graph structures, construct dynamic labels, and transform properties on the fly. In every MATCH, WHERE, RETURN, or SET clause, value expressions and operators turn raw graph data into the precise results your applications and reports require. Understanding their behavior, precedence, and interaction is essential for writing clear, efficient queries. Note that assignment occurs in SET clauses rather than inline within filtering expressions.

This chapter will cover the following topics:

- Understanding GQL operators

  - Comparison operators
  - Mathematical operators
  - Boolean operators
  - Assignment and concatenation operators

- Using value expressions

  - Boolean value expressions
  - Common value expressions
  - Other expressions

Technical requirements

Before stepping into this chapter, you should have acquired skills in the basic usage of GQL and learned how to create graphs and execute queries with it. All queries are located in the repository at `https://github.com/PacktPublishing/Getting-Started-with-the-Graph-Query-Language-GQL/tree/main/Ch05`.

Understanding GQL operators

GQL provides a variety of operators to manipulate values within expressions. These operators enable users to construct search conditions, assign values to variables, compare values to produce predicate results, combine multiple values into one, perform mathematical operations, and utilize built-in functions, among other tasks.

In this section, we will explore the following operators:

- Comparison operators
- Mathematical operators
- Boolean operators
- Assignment operators

Comparison operators

In *Chapter 2, Key Concepts of GQL*, we learned about essentially comparable values and universally comparable values. Here's a quick recap: Essentially comparable values can be directly compared, such as two numbers or two identical values. In contrast, universally comparable values typically require a data type conversion implemented by the GQL provider, such as comparing a datetime property with a time string. In this section, we will learn how to use comparison operators to compare values.

GQL specifies comparison predicate operations, which we have already touched upon in the sections about the `FILTER` statement and `MATCH WHERE` statement. These queries utilize comparison operations to search graph data according to our desired criteria.

The list of comparison operators is as follows:

Symbol	Description	Example
=	equals	v1 = v2
>=	greater than or equal to	v1 >= v2
>	greater than	v1 > v2
<=	less than or equal to	v1 <= v2
<	less than	v1 < v2
<>	not equal	v1 <> v2

Table 5.1: Comparison operators

In *Table 5.1*, the >=, >, <=, and < operators can be used for numeric, string, time, boolean, and null values.

Comparison operators can be used in the following parts of queries:

- In WHERE clauses, to specify search conditions within MATCH statements
- In FILTER statements, to define filter conditions for working tables
- In boolean value expressions, to yield a truth value

Let's explore examples of essentially comparable values first.

General comparisons

You can compare two static values of the same data types or two numeric values:

Example	Result	Description
"a" = "a" 1 >= 1 1 < 2 2 <> 1	TRUE	Comparing two static values returns TRUE as they fit the comparison rules.
"a" = "b" 2 <= 1 1 > 1.1 1 <> 1	FALSE	Comparing two static values returns FALSE as they don't fit the comparison rules.

Table 5.2: Examples of comparing values of the same type or numeric values

You can test any of these examples by executing a simple GQL query with the RETURN statement:

```
GQL:
RETURN 1 <> 1
```

GQL Playground supports ! = as an alternative operator of <>.

Comparing list values

GQL allows for the comparison of lists. If two lists contain the same elements in the exact same order, they are considered equal.

Example	Result	Description

`[1,2,3] = [1,2,3]`
 	
`[] = []`
	TRUE	Two lists have the same values in the exact same order.

`[1,2,3] = [1,3,1]`
 	
`[1,2] = [1,2,3]`
	FALSE	Two lists have different values or the same values in different orders, returning FALSE.

Table 5.3: Examples of comparing lists

Comparing record values

Record values can be compared. If two records have the same fields with the same values, they are considered equal.

Example	Result	Description
`{a:1} = {a:1}`	TRUE	Two records have the same field names and the same values, even if they are in a different order.

`{a:1} = {a:1, b: 2}`
 	
`{a:1} = {a:2}`
	FALSE	Two records have different fields or values.

Table 5.4: Examples of comparing records

Comparing paths

Graph data is comparable using GQL, including paths, nodes, and edges. The node and edge values follow the same rules as comparing records, while paths follow the rules of list comparison, as a path can be viewed as a list of nodes and edges.

Example	Result	Description
MATCH (a), (c) LIMIT 1 MATCH ()-[b]->() LIMIT 1 LET p1=PATH[a,b,c], p2=PATH[a,b,c] RETURN p1=p2	TRUE	Comparing two paths declared by two LET statements.
MATCH p1=(:Lang {name:"GQL"})-(:Category {name: "Graph"}) MATCH p2=(:Lang {name:"GQL"})-(:Category {name: "Graph"}) RETURN p1=p2	TRUE	Comparing two paths retrieved from two path-matching statements.

Table 5.5: Examples of comparing paths

Comparing string values

GQL allows three ways to determine the comparison result of two strings:

- UCS_BASIC: Determined entirely by the Unicode scalar values of the characters in the character strings being sorted. You can find more details here: https://en.wikipedia.org/wiki/Unicode.

- UNICODE: Determined by the Unicode collation algorithm. You can find more details here: https://www.unicode.org/reports/tr10.

- Customized rules to compare strings.

> UCS_BASIC is the default method to compare strings in GQL Playground.

Example	Result	Description
"b" > "a"	TRUE	The scalar value of b is 98, while a is 97.
"ba" > "b"	TRUE	The first chars of the two strings are equal, the second char of the right string is empty, and a is greater than empty.
"c" > "ba"	TRUE	The scalar value of c is greater than that of b.

Table 5.6: Examples of comparing strings

To run the examples, we can use the RETURN statement:

```
GQL:
RETURN "b" > "a"
```

Comparing byte string values

A byte string is a possibly empty sequence of bytes (octets). Like character strings, byte strings can be compared using operators such as < and >. Byte strings are typically represented in the X'<hexadecimal digits sequence>' format—for example, the GQL string is represented as X'47514C'.

Example	Result	Description
X'0102' > X'0101' X'0102' > X'01'	TRUE	The first byte is the same, X'01', but the second byte, X'02', is greater than X'01' or empty.
X'02' > X'0102'	TRUE	The first byte X'02' is greater than X'01'.

Table 5.7: Examples of comparing byte strings

> In GQL, two byte strings can be considered equivalent if all elements of the shorter string match those of the longer string at the same positions, with the longer string padded with X'00' at the end. For example, X'0102' is equivalent to X'01020000'. Depending on the implementation, GQL also allows X'0102' less than X'01020000'. In GQL Playground, it used the second rule, which is X'0102' < X'01020000'.

Comparing temporal values

Temporal values can be treated as numeric values since time is quantified using units such as seconds, hours, days, and years. Therefore, comparing temporal values is akin to comparing numeric values.

To compare two temporal values, the GQL query engine calculates the duration, which is the difference between the two temporal points. If the duration is 0, the values are equal; if the duration is negative, the left value is less than the right; otherwise, the left value is greater than the right.

Examples	Results	Descriptions

`LET d1 = DATE("2019-03-14"),`
 	
`    d2 = DATE("2019-03-15")`
 	
`RETURN d2 > d1`
	TRUE	d2 is greater than d1 as the duration between d1 and d2 is one day, which is a positive value.

Table 5.8: Examples of comparing temporal values

Up until now, we have learned about how to compare static values and constructed values; they are essentially comparable. Next, let's talk about universally comparable values.

Comparing values with different types

GQL defines universally comparable values, enabling comparisons across different value types. For the equals(=) operator, the comparison of any two universally comparable values returns FALSE.

GQL providers can design the rules for other comparison operators when comparing varied types. The rules and examples in this section reflect the behaviors of GQL Playground.

> When comparing universally comparable values, GQL permits implementers to define specific behaviors. *The examples in this book align with GQL Playground's implementation.*

Comparing string and numeric values

GQL Playground converts a string value to a numeric value if one operand is a number and the other is a string. Here's how to perform this conversion:

1. Identify numeric characters (0-9 and the decimal point).
2. Extract the substring from the beginning of the string up to the first non-numeric character (excluded).
3. Convert the string to a numeric value of the same type as the other numeric operand.
4. If the other numeric operand is a positive integer, convert the string to a UINT64 number.
5. If the other numeric operand is a negative integer (e.g., -1), convert the string to an INT64 number.

6. If the other numeric operand is a floating-point number (e.g., 1.0), convert the string to a DOUBLE number.

    a. When converting the string to UINT64 or INT64, discard any decimal part found in the string.

Example	Result	Description
`10 > "9"`	TRUE	Converts string `"9"` to numeric value 9.
`"11.2a" > 10`	TRUE	Converts string `"11.2a"` to 11
`"11.2a" > 11.1`	TRUE	Converts string `"11.2a"` to 11.2.
`"11.9" > 11`	FALSE	Converts `"11.9"` to 11 (discards decimal part) for UINT64 comparison.
`"a11" > 1`	FALSE	Converts `"a11"` to 0 as it lacks numeric characters at the beginning.

Table 5.9: Examples of comparing string and numeric values

Universally comparable values may exhibit different behaviors in various GQL environments. The behaviors in *Table 5.9* are specific to GQL Playground. Since Ultipa Graph is developed in C++, the conversion methods and rules adhere to certain aspects of the C++ programming language.

Comparing string and temporal values

Similar to string-numeric comparisons, strings can be converted to temporal values in GQL Playground. Note that comparison behavior depends on the GQL implementation. For a string to be compared with temporal values, it must do the following:

*   Adhere to a date, datetime, or duration format per the ISO 8601 standards: `https://en.wikipedia.org/wiki/ISO_8601`

*   Be converted to date, datetime, or duration based on the type of the other temporal value

Example	Result	Description

`let d1 = DATE("2024-10-31")`
 	
`RETURN d1 < "2024-11-01"`
	TRUE	A date format string will be converted to the DATE type for comparison.

Table 5.10: Examples of comparing string and temporal values

Comparing a boolean and values of other types

To compare a boolean with other data types such as string or numeric values, consider the following examples:

Example	Result	Description

`RETURN TRUE = 1`
 	
`RETURN TRUE > 0`
 	
`RETURN FALSE = 0`
	TRUE	TRUE is interpreted as 1 and FALSE as 0.

`RETURN TRUE = "true"`	FALSE	The boolean TRUE is not equivalent to the "true" string.
`RETURN TRUE = ("true" = "true")`	TRUE	`("true" = "true")` returns TRUE and `TRUE = TRUE` returns TRUE.

Table 5.11: Comparing boolean and other values

Mathematical operators

GQL provides mathematical operators that facilitate expressions executing mathematical calculations. The list of mathematical operators is as follows:

Symbol	Description	Example
+	Addition	`v1 + v2`
-	Subtraction	`v1 - v2`
*	Multiplication	`v1 * v2`
/	Division	`v1 / v2`

Table 5.12: Mathematical operators

Mathematical operators can be applied to any two numeric values or numeric value expressions.

Boolean operators

Boolean operators are used for two boolean values or value expressions, returning a truth result upon execution.

Symbol	Description	Example
NOT	NOT TRUE returns FALSE. NOT FALSE returns TRUE.	NOT TRUE
AND	Returns true if both values are true.	v1 AND v2
OR	Returns true if at least one value is true.	v1 OR v2
XOR	True if only one is true, not both. v1 XOR v2 is equivalent to (v1 OR v2) AND NOT (v1 AND v2).	v1 XOR v2
IS	Returns true if two booleans are equal.	v1 IS TRUE

Table 5.13: Boolean operators

Below are the truth tables for various comparison operators, where NULL is used to represent the truth value UNKNOWN.

> In *Chapter 2, Key Concepts of GQL*, it is mentioned that the truth value of UNKNOWN is represented by NULL, and they can be used interchangeably.

Here are the results with two truth values using the AND operator:

AND	TRUE	FALSE	NULL
TRUE	TRUE	FALSE	NULL
FALSE	FALSE	FALSE	FALSE
NULL	NULL	FALSE	NULL

Table 5.14: Truth table of AND

Here are the results with two truth values using the OR operator:

OR	TRUE	FALSE	NULL
TRUE	TRUE	TRUE	TRUE
FALSE	TRUE	FALSE	NULL
NULL	TRUE	NULL	NULL

Table 5.15: Truth table of OR

Here are the results with two truth values using the XOR operator:

XOR	TRUE	FALSE	NULL
TRUE	FALSE	TRUE	NULL
FALSE	TRUE	FALSE	NULL
NULL	NULL	NULL	NULL

Table 5.16: Truth table of XOR

Here are the results with two truth values using the IS operator:

IS	TRUE	FALSE	NULL
TRUE	TRUE	FALSE	FALSE
FALSE	FALSE	TRUE	FALSE
NULL	FALSE	FALSE	TRUE

Table 5.17: Truth table of IS

Assignment and other operators

GQL offers other operators such as assignment and concatenation operators.

Assignment operator

The assignment operator is utilized for assigning values within statements such as LET and SET.

Here's an example:

```
GQL:
LET a = 1 RETURN a
```

The = operator serves as an assignment operator. For examples of value constructions, refer to *Chapter 2, Key Concepts of GQL*.

The assignment operator can also be used to define path variables for path patterns in the MATCH statement:

```
GQL:
MATCH p = ()-() RETURN p
```

The symbol of the assignment operator is the same as the equal comparison operator. Its semantics depend on the context.

Assignment can also be used in the SET statement:

```
GQL:
MATCH (n:Lang WHERE n.name = "GQL") SET n.year = 2024
```

In this query, there are two = symbols. The first is a comparison operator to match the value of the name node property, and the second is an assignment operator to set the value for the year property.

> If an = symbol is used to declare variables or set values (in the path pattern, a SET statement, or a LET statement), it functions as an assignment operator. Otherwise, it is a comparison operator.

Concatenation operator

The concatenation operator can be used for concatenating values such as strings or lists.

To concatenate two strings, use the following query:

```
GQL:
RETURN "a" || "b"
```

The query returns the string ab.

> GQL Playground also supports + as an alternative concatenation symbol to ||. Therefore, "a" + "b" is equivalent to "a"||"b".

In this section, you explored GQL operators for comparison, mathematics, boolean assignments, and concatenations. Additionally, GQL offers operators for predicates.

Other predicate operators

GQL offers predicate operators (or predicates) for evaluating value type, checking data existence, and determining whether a node is the source or destination of an edge and whether an edge is directed.

Predicating value type

GQL offers IS TYPED and IS NOT TYPED predicates to check whether the value type is as expected.

For example, to check if the value type is a string, use the following:

```
GQL:
LET v = "hello"
RETURN v IS TYPED STRING
```

This query returns true as the result, as the value 'v' is a string type.

The value type predicate operators are useful for checking the current value type and performing further operations, such as revising the data type and cleaning graph data. This helps avoid errors when encountering unexpected values.

Predicating source and destination nodes

You explored the MATCH statement and learned how to use it to retrieve edges, each containing source and destination nodes. Besides filtering nodes at the node pattern level, you can also use the source and destination node predication operators for filtering.

For example, to filter edges with specific source or destination nodes, use the following:

```
GQL:
MATCH (n {name: "SQL"})
MATCH p = ()-[e]->()
FILTER n IS SOURCE OF e OR n IS DESTINATION OF e
RETURN p
```

This query returns edges where either the source or destination node is P1.

Predicating labels

GQL offers the IS LABELED and IS NOT LABELED predicates to check whether a node or edge contains specific labels.

For example, to check whether a node has a label, use the following:

```
GQL:
MATCH (n) WHERE n IS LABELED Lang
RETURN n
```

This query returns all nodes with the label Lang.

> In GQL Playground, If the node type is Lang, it will also be returned.
>
> GQL playground offers extended operators such as CONTAINS, IN, BETWEEN, and so on. You can visit https://www.ultipa.com/docs/gql/operators for more details.

Up to this point, you have explored GQL data values, various value types, GQL operators, and additional predicate operations. In the next section, you will learn how to generate different values using value expressions.

Using value expressions

A value expression specifies values in GQL. The GQL standard divides value expressions into boolean and common value expressions. Common value expressions include numeric, string, datetime, duration, list, record, path, and reference value expressions. Value expressions produce a value and can be used in most GQL statements and clauses.

Boolean value expressions

A Boolean value expression produces a truth value as a result. In the previous section, we covered comparison and boolean operators, commonly included in Boolean value expressions.

Here's an example of a Boolean value expression:

```
GQL:
LET a = TRUE, b = FALSE RETURN a OR b
```

In this query, a OR b is a boolean expression that produces a truth value result. This expression uses Boolean operators.

Here's another example:

```
GQL:
LET a = 1 RETURN a > 0
```

Here a > 0 is an expression using comparison operators. Its result is a truth value, so this expression is a boolean value expression.

Nested value expressions

In daily usage, multiple value expressions often appear in a nested style.

Here's an example:

```
GQL:
LET a = 1, b = 10
RETURN ((a > 0 AND b > 5) OR b > 20) IS TRUE
```

In this example, parentheses define expression priority, executed in the following steps:

1. Execute `a > 0` , `b > 5` to get `((TRUE AND TRUE) OR b > 20) IS TRUE`.

2. Execute `(TRUE AND TRUE)` to get `(TRUE OR b > 20) IS TRUE`.

3. Execute `(TRUE OR b > 20)` to get `TRUE IS TRUE`.

4. The final result is `TRUE`.

Common value expressions

In GQL, common value expressions relate to strings, numbers, temporal values, lists, records, graph data, and data references.

> This chapter introduces expressions with some functions. The next chapter will cover all functions in GQL for each value type.

String expressions

To specify a string value, use tring constructors, string functions, or expressions that yield a string. In *Chapter 2, Key Concepts of GQL*, we learned how to declare a string or a byte string. Here, we will explore using concatenation operators and string functions.

Here is an example of concatenating two strings:

```
GQL:
RETURN "a" || "b"
```

In this query, `"a" || "b"` is a string expression that specifies a concatenated string "ab".

Here is an example of using a string function:

```
GQL:
RETURN UPPER("a")
```

The query returns the string A.

Numeric expressions

To specify a numeric value, use numeric constructors, mathematical operators, and numeric functions.

Here's an example of a mathematical operation:

```
GQL:
RETURN (1 + 1) * 2
```

The query returns 4 from the expression (1 + 1) * 2.

Here's an example of using a numeric function:

```
GQL:
RETURN ABS(1-10)
```

This will return 9 as the positive form of -9. The numeric value expression ABS(1-10) combines a numeric function and a sub-expression, which involves a math operation using a numeric operator.

Temporal expressions

Temporal expressions are used for specifying temporal values and are divided into datetime expressions and duration expressions.

Datetime expressions

To define a datetime, use constructors, datetime functions, and mathematical operations. For more on date time construction, refer to *Chapter 2, Key Concepts of GQL*. You can add or subtract duration values with datetime expressions.

Here's an example:

```
GQL:
LET d = DATE("2024-10-29")
RETURN d + DURATION("P1D")
```

This query returns the date 2024-10-30, effectively adding one day to the date variable d.

Duration expressions

To define duration, use constructors, functions, and mathematical operations. As per ISO 8601 standards, durations are specified in YEAR to MONTH or DAY to SECOND units. Operations can include addition, subtraction, multiplication, and division.

Here's an example:

```
GQL:
LET d = DURATION("P1Y10M")
RETURN d - DURATION("P1Y")
```

This query yields a duration of 10 months.

Attempting operations on incompatible units, such as DURATION("P1Y") - DURATION("PT1D"), will result in an exception.

To derive a duration value from comparing two datetime values, use the following:

```
GQL:
LET date1 = ZONED_DATETIME ("2024-11-01T12:00:00"),
    date2 = ZONED_DATETIME("2024-09-30T10:58:50")
LET duration1 = DURATION_BETWEEN(date1, date2)
RETURN duration1
```

The result is P32D1H1M10S, representing a duration of 32 days, 1 hour, 1 minute, and 10 seconds.

Note that duration results can vary by time zones:

- In UTC, which does not observe **Daylight Saving Time** (**DST**), the duration is 32 days, 1 hour, 1 minute, and 10 seconds.

- In time zones observing DST, such as **Central European Time** (**CET**), the duration is 32 days, 0 hours, 1 minute, and 10 seconds due to DST ending on Sunday, October 27 at 01:00 UTC, when clocks will be set back by 1 hour.

> If no duration unit is specified, durations default to the *DAY to SECOND* unit. Specifying a unit, such as *YEAR to MONTH*, can change the result, potentially discarding values for days, hours, minutes, and seconds.
>
> *DAY to SECOND* durations are not comparable to *YEAR to MONTH* durations because not all months (and not all years) have the same number of days.

Valid temporal operations

Valid operations between temporal instants (date, time, and datetime) and durations are summarized in *Table 5.18*:

Operand 1	Operator	Operand 2	Result
instant	-	instant	duration
instant	+ or -	duration	instant
duration	+	instant	instant
duration	+ or -	duration	duration
duration	* or /	number	duration
number	*	duration	duration

Table 5.18: Valid operations between temporal instants and durations

If an invalid operation is attempted, an exception will arise.

List expressions

Define a list using a constructor or list function. You can concatenate two lists with the || operator.

Here's an example of concatenating two lists:

```
GQL:
LET list1 = ["a", "b"], list2 = ["b", "c", "d"]
RETURN list1 || list2
```

The query returns ["a", "b", "b", "c", "d"].

Path expressions

Path values, similar to lists, consist of sequences of nodes or edges and support concatenation. Two paths can be concatenated if they form a valid continuous path in the graph.

Here's an example of concatenating two paths:

```
GQL:
MATCH p1 = ({name: "GQL"})->(n), p2 = (n)<-()
RETURN p1 || p2
```

This query concatenates p1 and p2, returning the new path.

> ✏️ The end node of the first path must match the start node of the second path or an error will arise.

Other expressions

GQL also provides other expressions, such as value query expressions, which generate values from query blocks.

Value query expressions

A value query expression assigns the result of a query to a variable.

Here's an example:

```
GQL:
LET v = VALUE { MATCH (n) RETURN n LIMIT 1 }
RETURN v
```

In this query, `VALUE { MATCH (n) RETURN n LIMIT 1 }` assigns a node result to the v variable.

The return value must not be empty, only one `<return item>` is allowed, and the variable type must accommodate the result.

LET value expressions

The `LET` expression defines local variables, uses them within a specific scope, and returns the final result.

Here's an example of using a `LET` value expression to generate a value:

```
GQL:
LET v = LET a = 1, b = 2 IN a + b END
RETURN v
```

This query creates local a and b variables, which are used in the a + b expression and return the result to the v variable.

> If you try to return a or b, an error will be raised because they can only be accessed within the scope of the LET expression.

CASE expressions

The CASE expression produces values based on conditions.

CASE WHEN

GQL supports utilizing the CASE expression with CASE WHEN syntax:

```
GQL:
MATCH (g:Lang)
RETURN
    CASE g.name
      WHEN "GQL" THEN "Graph Query Language"
      WHEN "Cypher" THEN "Neo4J's Query Language"
      WHEN "UQL" THEN "Ultipa Query Language"
      ELSE "Other Languages"
    END
```

This query specifies a value based on the value of g.name. If g.name matches a WHEN condition (equivalence), it returns the corresponding THEN value. Otherwise, it returns the ELSE value.

Alternatively, you can write filter conditions explicitly after each WHEN:

```
GQL:
MATCH (g:Lang)
LET language =
CASE WHEN g.name = "GQL" THEN "Graph Query Language"
     WHEN g.name = "Cypher" THEN "Neo4J's Query Language"
     WHEN g.name = "UQL" THEN "Ultipa Query Language"
     ELSE "Other Languages"
END
RETURN DISTINCT "(" || g.name || ") " || language
```

NULLIF and COALESCE, commonly used in SQL, have been added to the GQL standard as shorthand for certain CASE expressions.

NULLIF

This function returns NULL if two specified expressions are equal; otherwise, it returns the first expression. This function is particularly useful for handling situations where you want to avoid specific values (often zeros) and replace them with NULL, which can simplify data processing and analysis.

NULLIF(v1, v2) is equivalent to the following CASE WHEN expression:

```
GQL:
...
CASE
    WHEN v1 = v2 THEN NULL
    ELSE v1
END
...
```

When v1 equals v2, the CASE expression returns NULL; otherwise, it returns v1

Here are some examples:

- NULLIF("a", "a") returns NULL, v1 "a" equals to v2 "a"
- NULLIF("a", "b") returns v1 "a", v1 "a" is not equal to "b"
- NULLIF(NULL, "b") returns v1 NULL, v1 NULL is not equal to "b"
- NULLIF(NULL, NULL) returns v1 NULL, v1 NULL is not equal to v2 NULL

COALESCE

COALESCE returns the first non-NULL value among the given values. If all values are NULL, it returns NULL.

COALESCE(v1, v2) is equivalent to the following CASE WHEN expression:

```
GQL:
...
CASE
    WHEN v1 IS NOT NULL THEN v1
    ELSE v2
END
...
```

When v1 is not NULL, the CASE expression returns v1; otherwise, it returns v2.

Here are some examples:

- COALESCE("a", "b") returns "a"; the v1 "a" is not null
- COALESCE(NULL, "b") returns "b"; the v1 is null, so it returns v2 "b"
- COALESCE(NULL, NULL, "a") returns "a"; the v1 and v2 are both null, so it returns v3 "a"

Summary

In this chapter, we covered various operators for comparing values, calculating numeric values, composing value expressions, and obtaining truth values using Boolean operators. We explored value expressions and learned how to specify values through operators and expressions. Finally, we discussed the CASE expression, which is valuable for defining values based on conditions.

With a solid understanding of GQL operators and value expressions, we are ready to move to the next chapter, on GQL functions, which offer robust capabilities for use in GQL value expressions.

Get This Book's PDF Version and Exclusive Extras

UNLOCK NOW

Scan the QR code (or go to packtpub.com/unlock). Search for this book by name, confirm the edition, and then follow the steps on the page.

Note: Keep your invoice handy. Purchases made directly from Packt don't require an invoice.

6

Working With GQL Functions

In the previous chapter, we explored GQL value expressions, which enable us to derive values tailored to user requirements. To further enhance this capability, this chapter introduces a variety of essential functions for effective data manipulation and analysis. These functions can be employed for aggregating records such as counting the total number of entries or determining the maximum value, performing scientific calculations such as computing the logarithm of a number, or constructing values such as generating a `Time` value using the `DateTime` function. Graph database providers may offer more functions to facilitate system usability.

In this chapter, we will cover the following functions:

- Numeric functions
- String functions
- Temporal functions
- Aggregation functions
- Other functions

Technical requirements

All the queries are located in the repository at `https://github.com/PacktPublishing/Getting-Started-with-the-Graph-Query-Language-GQL/tree/main/Ch06`.

Numeric functions

Numeric functions in GQL provide a robust set of operations for performing calculations on numerical data and deriving computed numerical values. This section explores the following categories:

- *Mathematical functions*: Including rounding, absolute value, modulus, logarithmic, and exponential functions, as well as functions for determining the length of values
- *Trigonometric functions*: Covering operations involving radians, degrees, basic, and inverse trigonometric functions

Let's begin with mathematical functions.

Mathematical functions

GQL offers a range of mathematical functions, such as rounding, absolute value, modulus, logarithmic, and exponential functions.

Rounding, absolute value, and modulus functions

The following table illustrates essential functions related to rounding, absolute values, and modulus:

Function	Description	Example
FLOOR	Rounds down to the nearest integer	FLOOR(1.8) returns 1
CEIL or CEILING	Rounds up to the nearest integer	CEIL(1.2) returns 2
ABS	Returns the absolute value of a number	ABS(-1) returns 1
MOD	Returns the remainder of a division	MOD(10, 3) returns 1
ROUND	Returns the nearest number at a specific decimal position	ROUND(1.567,2) returns 1.57

Table 6.1: Rounding, absolute, and modulus functions

For example, use GQL Playground to run all the examples in *Table 6.1*:

```
GQL:
RETURN FLOOR(1.8),
       CEIL(1.2),
       ABS(-1),
       MOD(10, 3),
       ROUND(1.567,2)
```

The query returns 1, 2, 1, 1, and 1.57 as results.

Logarithmic and exponential functions

GQL provides functions for logarithmic and exponential calculations, as shown here:

Function	Description	Example
POWER	Raises a number to the power of another number	POWER(2, 4) returns 16
SQRT	Computes the square root of a given number	SQRT (16) returns 4
EXP	Computes the value of Euler's number raised to the power of a given number, where is approximately equal to 2.71828	EXP(2) returns 7.38905609893065
LOG	Computes the logarithm of a number with a specified base	LOG(2, 8) returns 3
LOG10	Computes the Base-10 logarithm of a number	LOG10(100) returns 2
LN	Computes the natural logarithm (base) of a number	LN(100) returns 4.60517018598809

Table 6.2: Logarithmic and exponential functions

Here is an example running all the functions in *Table 6.2*:

```
GQL:
RETURN POWER(2, 4), SQRT(16), EXP(2), LOG(2, 8), LOG10(100), LN(100)
```

This query returns the results shown in *Table 6.2*.

Length of values

GQL provides the CARDINALITY function to calculate the length of strings, paths, lists, and records. It also offers dedicated LENGTH functions for each type.

List length

To calculate the length of a list, use the following code:

```
GQL:
RETURN CARDINALITY([1,2,3])
```

Alternatively, here's how you can use the SIZE() function:

```
GQL:
RETURN SIZE([1,2,3])
```

The SIZE() function can only be used for list values.

Moving forward, LENGTH is also a proposed feature of GQL and may be included in future versions.

> Nowadays, new languages usually support multi-type parameters instead of multi-type functions. In GQL Playground, the LENGTH function can be a generic function to get the length of strings, lists, bytes, and so on. Users don't need to remember different length functions anymore.

String length

GQL provides functions to calculate the length of string types, including character and binary strings. You can use CHAR_LENGTH and BYTE_LENGTH as alternatives. These can also be expressed in their full forms: CHARACTER_LENGTH and OCTET_LENGTH.

To calculate the length of character strings, you can use the following code:

```GQL
GQL:
RETURN CHAR_LENGTH ("Graph Query")
```

The query results in 11.

LENGTH("Graph Query") and CHARACTER_LENGTH("Graph Query") yield the same result.

For calculating the length of byte strings, here's the code:

```GQL
GQL:
RETURN LENGTH(x'1F')
```

The query results in 1.

BYTE_LENGTH(x'00') and OCTET_LENGTH(x'00') yield the same result.

Path length

The length of a path is determined by the number of edges it contains. GQL offers the PATH_LENGTH function to return this length. Alternatively, LENGTH functions can be used.

Here is an example:

```GQL
GQL:
MATCH p=()-[]-()-[]-() LIMIT 1 RETURN PATH_LENGTH(p)
```

With this code, the query returns 2, as the path contains two edges. LENGTH(p) yields the same result.

The cardinality of a path value has different definitions compared to other value types. The cardinality of a path value is the number of path elements, which includes both nodes and edges in the path.

Therefore, replace `PATH_LENGTH` with `CARDINALITY` in the previous example:

```
GQL:
MATCH p=()-[]-()-[]-() LIMIT 1 RETURN CARDINALITY(p)
```

This query returns 5, as the path contains three nodes and two edges.

Record length

The length of a record is determined by the number of its fields. You can calculate the record length using the `CARDINALITY` or `LENGTH` function.

Here is an example:

```
GQL:
RETURN LENGTH({name : "GQL", year: 2024})
```

The query returns 2, as the record contains two fields.

Trigonometric functions

GQL provides essential functions for working with angles and periodic patterns. The parameter of trigonometric functions should be a numeric expression.

Radians and degrees

Let's learn about two fundamental functions used to convert between radians and degrees.

`RADIANS` helps convert degrees to radians. For example, the radians of 180° is , which is approximately 3.14159267:

$$radians \ = \ degree \times \frac{\pi}{180}$$

Here is an example:

```
GQL:
RETURN RADIANS(60)
```

The query returns 1.0471975511966, which is the radians value of 60 degrees.

DEGREES helps convert radians to degrees. For example, the degree of is 180°:

$$degrees = radians \times \frac{180}{\pi}$$

Here is an example:

```
GQL:
RETURN DEGREES(pi())
```

The query returns 180, as corresponds to 180 degrees.

With these two functions, we can compute the parameters for other trigonometric functions.

Basic trigonometric functions

Basic trigonometric functions include SIN, COS, TAN, and COT, which derive corresponding angle values from radians.

Table 6.3 illustrates the basic trigonometric functions:

Function	Description	Range	Example
SIN	Sine	[-1, 1]	SIN(radians(30)) = 0.5
COS	Cosine	[-1, 1]	COS(radians(60)) = -0.5
TAN	Tangent	$(-\infty, +\infty)$	TAN(radians(45)) = 1
COT	Cotangent	$(-\infty, -1] \cup [1, +\infty)$	COT(radians(45)) = 1

Table 6.3: Basic trigonometric functions

Inverse trigonometric functions

Inverse trigonometric functions include ASIN, ACOS, ATAN, and ACOT, which derive corresponding angle values from radians.

Table 6.4 illustrates the inverse trigonometric functions:

Function	Description	Example
ASIN	Calculates sine	SIN(radians(30)) = 0.5
ACOS	Calculates cosine	COS(radians(60)) = -0.5
ATAN	Calculates tangent	TAN(radians(45)) = 1
ACOT	Calculates cotangent	COT(radians(45)) = 1

Table 6.4: Inverse trigonometric functions

Hyperbolic trigonometric functions

Hyperbolic trigonometric functions include SINH, COSH, and TANH.

Table 6.5 illustrates the hyperbolic trigonometric functions:

Function	Description	Example
SINH	Calculates hyperbolic sine	`SINH(radians(30)) =` `0.54785347388804`
COSH	Calculates hyperbolic cosine	`COSH(radians(60)) =` `1.60028685770239`
TANH	Calculates hyperbolic tangent	`TANH(radians(45)) =` `0.655794202632672`

Table 6.5: Hyperbolic trigonometric functions

String functions

GQL offers string functions to perform operations such as extracting substrings, trimming, folding, and normalizing strings. Let's look at them in detail.

Substring functions

GQL allows the extraction of substrings from either the left or right side, with a specified length.

For example, here's how you can obtain the first five letters of a sentence:

```
GQL:
RETURN LEFT("Hello GQL", 5)
```

The query returns "Hello".

This is how to extract GQL using the RIGHT function:

```
GQL:
RETURN RIGHT("Hello GQL", 3)
```

The query returns "GQL" as the result, which is the last three characters.

The LEFT and RIGHT functions also can be applied to a sub-byte string:

```
GQL:
RETURN LEFT(x'1F2F3F', 2)
```

The query returns x'1F2F', extracting a byte string with a length of 2 bytes.

Uppercase and lowercase

To convert all letters to uppercase or lowercase, GQL provides the UPPER and LOWER functions.

Here is an example:

```
GQL:
LET s = "Hello GQL"
RETURN UPPER(s), LOWER(s)
```

The query returns "HELLO GQL" and "hello gql".

Trimming strings

GQL provides functions to trim strings by removing specified characters from either the leftmost, rightmost, or both ends of a string.

Single-character trim

The TRIM function removes occurrences of a specified character.

The trim specifications can be LEADING, TRAILING, or BOTH. If no specification is set, BOTH is used by default.

For example, trimming spaces from both sides is done with the following:

```
GQL:
RETURN TRIM(BOTH " " FROM "  Hello GQL  ")
```

This query removes spaces from both sides, returning "Hello GQL".

Since the space and BOTH parameters are defaults, they can be omitted:

```
GQL:
RETURN TRIM("  Hello GQL  ")
```

Both queries yield the same result.

To remove a different character and use LEADING and TRAILING specifications, use the following:

```
GQL:
RETURN TRIM(LEADING "_" FROM "__Hello GQL"),
       TRIM(TRAILING "_" FROM "Hello GQL__")
```

These queries remove underscores from the left and right sides, returning "Hello GQL".

Single-character trim for byte strings

The TRIM function can be applied to byte strings.

Here is an example:

```
GQL:
RETURN TRIM(BOTH x'1F' FROM x'1F2F1F1F')
```

The query removes all x'1F' from both sides and returns x'2F'. The output may display "/", which is the corresponding code.

Multiple-character trim

To trim multiple characters, GQL provides the BTRIM, LTRIM, and RTRIM functions, which remove substrings from both, left, and right sides, respectively.

Here is an example:

```
GQL:
RETURN BTRIM("123123Hello GQL123123", "123")
```

This query removes all occurrences of "123" from the left and right sides of the source string, returning "Hello GQL".

Using LTRIM would return "Hello GQL123123", and RTRIM would return "123123Hello GQL".

Normalizing strings

GQL provides the NORMALIZE function to convert strings into a consistent format, based on the specified normalization form. This adheres to the Unicode Standard Annex #15 (https://www.unicode.org/reports/tr15/).

For example, to retrieve the equivalent regular digit of ① with the normalization function:

```
GQL:
RETURN NORMALIZE("①", NFKC)
```

The query returns the digit 1, which is the regular equivalent of ①.

The following table illustrates the behavior of the normalization function:

Form	Behavior	Input example	Output example
NFC	Canonical composition	A (U+0041) + ○˚ (U+030A)	Å(U+00C5)
NFD	Canonical decomposition	Å (U+00C5)	A (U+0041) + ○˚ (U+030A)
NFKC	Compatibility composition	2⁵A○˚	25Å
NFKD	Compatibility decomposition	2⁵Å	25A○˚

Table 6.6: Normalization forms

Temporal functions

GQL provides temporal functions for constructing and manipulating DateTime and duration values. We covered the construction functions in *Chapter 2, Key Concepts of GQL*, which you may refer to for more detailed information.

The following table illustrates the available temporal functions:

Functions	Description	Example
CURRENT_DATE	Returns the current date, equivalent to DATE()	CURRENT_DATE
DATE(<>)	Generates a Date value	DATE("2019-03-17")
CURRENT_TIME	Returns the current time, equivalent to ZONED_TIME()	CURRENT_TIME
ZONED_TIME(<>)	Returns the time with time zone information	ZONED_TIME("T12:00:01+1:00")
LOCAL_TIME	Returns the time without time zone information	LOCAL_TIME | LOCAL_TIME("T12:00:01")
CURRENT_TIMESTAMP	Returns the current timestamp, equivalent to ZONED_DATETIME()	CURRENT_TIMESTAMP
LOCAL_TIMESTAMP	Returns the current timestamp without a time zone, equivalent to LOCAL_DATETIME	LOCAL_TIMESTAMP

Functions	Description	Example
ZONED_DATETIME(<>)	Returns a DateTime value with time zone information	ZONED_DATETIME("2019-01-01T12:00:01+01:00")
LOCAL_DATETIME(<>)	Returns a DateTime value without time zone information	LOCAL_DATETIME("2019-01-01T12:00:01))

Table 6.7: Temporal functions

The <> temporal parameter should be either a DateTime string that complies with ISO 8601 standards or a record value containing the following fields: Year, Month, Day, Hour, Minute, Second, and Timezone.

For example, to obtain the current DateTime with and without time zone information, use the following:

```
GQL:
RETURN CURRENT_TIMESTAMP, LOCAL_TIMESTAMP
```

The query returns two DateTime values, one with and one without time zone information.

For example, to specify a local DateTime using a record, use the following:

```
GQL:
RETURN LOCAL_DATETIME({
    year: 2024, month: 5, day: 15,
    hour: 10, minute: 30, second: 0
})
```

This query returns a DateTime value of '2024-05-15 10:30:00'.

Aggregating values

GQL aggregation functions are provided to compute values from a set of records, offering a range of operations to handle diverse data aggregation requirements. The basic functions include COUNT, which counts the number of records; AVG, for calculating averages, MAX and MIN, for obtaining the maximum and minimum values, respectively; and SUM, for totaling the values. Advanced functions encompass COLLECT_LIST, which aggregates values into a list, and statistical functions such as STDDEV_SAMP and STDDEV_POP for sample and population standard deviation calculations. Additionally, GQL supports binary set functions such as PERCENTILE_CONT and PERCENTILE_DISC, which are used for continuous and discrete percentile calculations, respectively.

Set quantifiers: DISTINCT and ALL

Before stepping into aggregation examples, it is crucial to understand set quantifiers in GQL.

DISTINCT removes duplicates from results, while ALL (applied implicitly when DISTINCT is omitted) includes all records.

For example, to count the number of distinct target nodes in paths, use the following:

```
GQL:
MATCH (n:Lang)-(target:Category)
RETURN COUNT(DISTINCT target)
```

This query returns the count of unique target nodes. If DISTINCT is omitted, the ALL quantifier is implicitly applied.

> All aggregation functions support the use of DISTINCT and ALL quantifiers.

Counting records

The first aggregation function to discuss is the COUNT function. As explained in *Chapter 2, Key Concepts of GQL*, the records stored in the binding table drive the query statement, and the COUNT function is used to count these records.

Here is an example of counting the number of Category nodes:

```
GQL:
MATCH (c:Category) RETURN COUNT(c)
```

In this query, the MATCH statement produces the Category nodes and binds them to the c variable. The COUNT function takes c as a parameter and returns the number of Category nodes.

The COUNT function supports using an asterisk (*) as the parameter to count all records in the working table:

```
GQL:
MATCH (c:Category)-(n) RETURN COUNT(*)
```

The DISTINCT and ALL quantifiers are not allowed to be used with an asterisk.

Numeric aggregation functions

GQL provides numeric aggregation functions. Here is the list of numeric aggregation functions:

- MAX: Returns the maximum value from all records
- MIN: Returns the minimum value from all records
- AVG: Returns the average value from all records
- SUM: Returns the sum value from all records
- STDDEV_SAMP: Calculates the sample standard deviation from the values of records
- STDDEV_POP: Calculates the population standard deviation from the values of records
- PERCENTILE_CONT: Calculates a continuous percentile from the values of records
- PERCENTILE_DISC: Calculates a discrete percentile from the values of records

MAX, MIN, AVG, and SUM

To calculate the maximum, minimum, average, and sum of ages for the query languages, use the following:

```
MATCH (g:Lang)
LET age = `YEAR`(CURRENT_DATE) - g.year
RETURN MAX(age) as maxAge,
       MIN(age) as minAge,
       AVG(age) as averageAge,
       SUM(age) as sumAge
```

This query returns the maximum, minimum, average, and summed total ages of query languages.

Standard deviation

Standard deviations are widely used to measure statistical dispersion. GQL offers functions for sample and population standard deviation.

To calculate sample and population standard deviations, use the following:

```
GQL:
FOR v IN [1, 2, 3, 10, 29, 30]
RETURN STDDEV_SAMP(v) as sample_deviation,
       STDDEV_POP(v)  as population_deviation
```

To derive a value by the percentile of the values' position (normally ordered values), we can use the PERCENTILE_CONT and PERCENTILE_DISC percentile functions.

PERCENTILE_CONT

PERCENTILE_CONT calculates the value at a specific percentile, using interpolation if needed. Here are the detailed calculation steps:

- Let POSITION start from 1; POSITION is 1+ <percentile> * (<number_of_values> - 1)
- If POSITION is an integer, then the result is the value at the position
- If POSITION is not an integer, then the formula to calculate PERCENTILE_CONT is floor_pos_value * (POS - position_index) +
- ceil_pos_value * (ceil_position - POS)

This example shows how to use PERCENTILE_CONT:

```
GQL:
FOR v IN [10, 20, 30]
RETURN PERCENTILE_CONT(v, 0.5)
```

In the query, POSITION is calculated by 1 + 0.5 * (3 - 1), which is 2 and it's an integer; therefore, the result is the second value in the list, which is 20.

Let's give 0.25 as the percentile in the function:

```
GQL:
FOR v IN [10, 20, 30]
RETURN PERCENTILE_CONT(v, 0.25)
```

POSITION is calculated by 1 + 0.25 * (3 - 1), which is 1.5 and it's not an integer. So, the Floor value is 10 and the Ceiling value is 20, which are the values from POSITION 1 and 2; therefore, the result is 10 * (1.5 - 1) + 20 * (2 - 1.5), which is 15.

> If the value is empty, the PERCENTILE_CONT and PERCENTILE_DISC functions will return NULL as the result.

PERCENTILE_DISC

PERCENTILE_DISC calculates the value at a specific percentile but only uses discrete positions.

POSITION can be calculated by a Round or floor numeric function. In GQL Playground, we will use the floor function to calculate the position of the values.

Let's look at this example:

```
GQL:
FOR v IN [10, 20, 30]
RETURN PERCENTILE_DISC(v, 0.25)
```

The percentile is 0.25 and the number of values is 3, so POSITION is

floor(1 + 0.25 * (3 - 1)), which is 1. Therefore, the result is 10 from the first position.

Collect list

GQL offers a collection function to aggregate the values into a list.

Here is an example:

```
GQL:
MATCH (n:Lang)
RETURN COLLECT_LIST(n.name)
```

This query returns the names of query languages into a list value.

Other functions

In this section, we will explore the additional functions provided by GQL.

Trimming a list

As discussed earlier, the TRIM function can be used to trim strings; it can also be applied to trim a list value.

The trim list function removes a specified number of elements from the right end of the list.

Here is an example:

```
GQL:
RETURN TRIM([1,2,3,4,5], 2)
```

The query returns a new list with [1, 2, 3], with the last 2 elements from the right side of the list removed.

Converting a path to a list

The ELEMENTS function converts a path value to a list value.

Here is an example:

```
GQL:
MATCH p=()-[]-() RETURN ELEMENTS(p) LIMIT 1
```

The query returns a list containing two nodes and one edge, instead of a path value.

Converting a data type with CAST

GQL supports using the CAST function to convert data to a target type explicitly.

The syntax of the CAST function is CAST (<value> AS <target type>).

For example, to convert a "-123a" string to an integer, use the following:

```
GQL:
RETURN CAST("-123" AS INT)
```

The query returns -123.

To convert a list to a string, use the following:

```
GQL:
RETURN CAST([1,2,3] AS STRING)
```

The query returns "[1,2,3]".

If the value cannot be converted to the target type, an exception is raised, as in this example:

```
GQL:
RETURN CAST("a123" AS INT)
```

This query returns an exception as "a123" cannot be converted to an integer.

Extra functions

GQL Playground provides additional functions beyond the GQL standard. Here are some widely used functions.

Function name	Description
pnodes(<path>)	Returns the nodes as a list
pedges(<path>)	Returns the edges as a list
append(<list>, <value>)	Adds a new value to the end of the list
difference(<list_1>, <list_2>)	Returns the difference between two lists
intersection(<list_1>, <list_2>)	Returns the intersections from two lists
head(<list>)	Returns the first value in a list
listContains(<list>, <value>)	Returns a truth value to check whether the value exists in the list
listUnion(<list_1>,<list_2>)	Returns the union of two lists
reduce(<reduce parameter>)	Performs a calculation iteratively using each element in a list

Table 6.8: Additional functions

Example: The reduce function

The reduce function is used to perform iterative calculations over list elements.

To calculate the total of the elements in a list, use the following:

```
GQL:
LET v = [1,3,5]
RETURN reduce(_sum = 0, item in v | _sum + item)
```

The query returns 9, which is the sum of each item in the v list.

Summary

In this chapter, we covered string, mathematical, and aggregation functions, as well as conversion and additional functions. GQL's functions equip the language with powerful capabilities to process data to meet a wide range of requirements. These functions can be extended within graph database systems, allowing for enhanced usability as you continue working with GQL.

By the end of this chapter, you should have acquired the essential skills for using GQL, including working with values and value types, combining statements and clauses, and using GQL functions.

In the next chapter, we'll explore advanced queries and dive deeper into GQL's capabilities.

Get This Book's PDF Version and Exclusive Extras

UNLOCK NOW

Scan the QR code (or go to packtpub.com/unlock). Search for this book by name, confirm the edition, and then follow the steps on the page.

Note: Keep your invoice handy. Purchases made directly from Packt don't require an invoice.

7

Delve into Advanced Clauses

In previous chapters, you explored the basics of GQL, including statements, clauses, functions, operators, and value expressions. This knowledge will help you work with graph data for most requirements. In the *Retrieving Graph Data* section in *Chapter 4*, *GQL Basics*, you briefly touched on advanced queries such as returning path results.

In this chapter, you will delve into more advanced usages of GQL that allow for more sophisticated graph queries and operations. These advanced clauses enable users to construct more intricate and efficient queries, which are pivotal when tackling complex datasets and scenarios in real-world applications. Before diving into this chapter, it is crucial that you have a solid understanding of the fundamental concepts, especially the MATCH statement. The MATCH statement is the starting point for pattern matching in GQL and is essential for grasping the more advanced querying techniques discussed in this chapter.

This chapter will cover four primary topics:

- GQL path modes and edge modes
- Shortest-path finding
- GQL procedures
- Optional statements

Technical requirements

All the example queries used in this chapter are available in the GitHub repository: https://github.com/PacktPublishing/Getting-Started-with-the-Graph-Query-Language-GQL/tree/main/Ch07.

Traversing modes

One of GQL's key strengths lies in its flexible graph traversal capabilities, allowing you to precisely control how queries navigate through graph paths. GQL provides path modes and match modes that let you control traversal behavior and set constraints on the paths returned.

Path modes

Path modes are designated as the addition of a path search prefix in the path pattern. GQL supports four path modes: WALK, TRAIL, SIMPLE, and ACYCLIC.

To set the path mode as TRAIL, do the following:

```
GQL:
MATCH p= TRAIL PATHS ()-() RETURN p
```

Alternatively, the PATHS keyword can be omitted:

```
GQL:
MATCH p= TRAIL()-() RETURN p
```

> GQL defines WALK as the default path mode. However, based on usage metrics in Ultipa, TRAIL is the most frequently used mode. Therefore, GQL Playground defaults to TRAIL.

Let's delve into each path mode with examples.

WALK mode

WALK mode permits the repetition of both nodes and edges, offering maximum flexibility in path pattern matching. This mode is particularly beneficial when exploring all possible routes within a graph, regardless of repetition, such as in exhaustive search scenarios or when modeling scenarios that require revisiting nodes and edges.

Figure 7.1 illustrates a graph with three nodes and three edges.

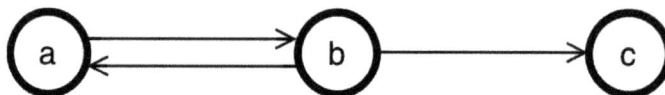

Figure 7.1: Example graph for testing walk mode

Take the following example:

```
GQL:
MATCH p = WALK ({_id: "a"})->{1,4}() RETURN p
```

The query traverses the path starting with node a, exploring potential routes up to four steps and returning the following paths:

- a->b
- a->b->c
- a->b->a
- a->b->a->b
- a->b->a->b->a
- a->b->a->b->c

With WALK mode, the path-finding query returns all possible paths by the specified depth, allowing nodes and edges to be revisited.

WALK mode is useful for analyzing all possible routes and identifying critical nodes. This makes it particularly suitable for scenarios such as maze games, where the goal is to explore every possible path, including those that revisit nodes or edges, to find all solutions or the most optimal one.

TRAIL mode

TRAIL mode ensures paths do not have repeated edges, making it suitable for scenarios where traversing the same edge multiple times is undesirable. This mode is commonly used to meet specific graph requirements.

The following is how to use TRAIL mode for the graph in *Figure 7.1*:

```
GQL:
MATCH p = TRAIL ({_id: "a"})->{1,4}() RETURN p
```

The query returns the following paths:

- a->b
- a->b->c
- a->b->a

Compared to WALK mode, TRAIL mode excludes paths that contain duplicate edges, such as the a->b->a->b path, where the edge a->b is traversed more than once.

TRAIL mode is widely used and resembles the Euler path concept. In this book, TRAIL mode is the default for query examples.

ACYCLIC mode

ACYCLIC mode ensures paths do not have repeated nodes. It's ideal for scenarios requiring a straightforward, non-repetitive path. This mode is useful when ensuring each node is visited only once.

The following is an example of using ACYCLIC path mode for the graph in *Figure 7.1*:

```
GQL:
MATCH p = ACYCLIC ({_id: "a"})->{1,4}() RETURN p
```

The query returns the following paths:

- a->b
- a->b->c

Compared to TRAIL mode, the path a->b->a is excluded in ACYCLIC mode because it contains a duplicate node a.

SIMPLE mode

SIMPLE mode is similar to ACYCLIC mode, ensuring paths do not have repeated nodes unless they are the start and end nodes. This mode allows acyclic paths, or cyclic paths where only the start and end nodes are the same. SIMPLE mode is useful for detecting cyclic behavior without repeating intermediate nodes and edges.

The following is an example of using SIMPLE mode for the graph in *Figure 7.1*:

```
GQL:
MATCH p = SIMPLE ({_id: "a"})->{1,4}() RETURN p
```

The query returns the following paths:

- a->b
- a->b->c
- a->b->a

SIMPLE mode includes all ACYCLIC mode results, with the addition of a cyclic path, a->b->a, as the duplicated node a appears only as the first and last node.

To conclude, TRAIL mode prevents a single path pattern from repeating edges, while the ACYCLIC and SIMPLE modes prevent a single path pattern from repeating nodes. Consider this question: How can we prevent repeating elements in multiple path patterns specified in a MATCH statement?

The answer is revealed in the next section.

MATCH modes

GQL provides two MATCH modes: REPEATABLE ELEMENTS and DIFFERENT EDGES. If no match mode is specified explicitly, the GQL implementer can decide which one to use as default. In GQL Playground, the default is the DIFFERENT EDGES match mode.

REPEATABLE ELEMENTS

REPEATABLE ELEMENTS gives no restrictions on repeating nodes and edges in all path patterns contained in a MATCH statement.

To specify REPEATABLE ELEMENTS match mode explicitly, use the following:

```
GQL:
MATCH REPEATABLE ELEMENTS p=(a)-(),(b)->(a) RETURN p
```

The query is equivalent to MATCH p=(a)-(), (b)->(a) RETURN p in GQL Playground.

Figure 7.2 illustrates a graph with five people and four friendship relationships:

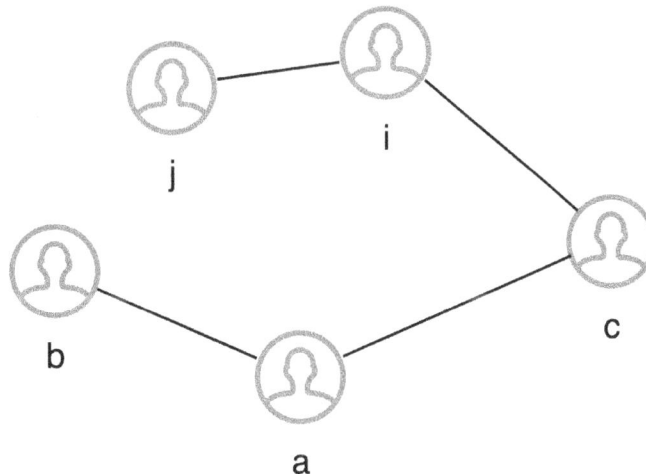

Figure 7.2: Example graph for testing REPEATABLE ELEMENTS

The following is the query to insert the nodes and edges for the graph:

```
GQL:
INSERT (a:Node {_id: 'a'}),
       (b:Node {_id: 'b'}),
       (c:Node {_id: 'c'}),
       (i:Node {_id: 'i'}),
       (j:Node {_id: 'j'}),
       (b)-[:Edge]->(a),
       (a)-[:Edge]->(c),
       (c)-[:Edge]->(i),
       (i)-[:Edge]->(j)
```

To find the friends of a and determine how many people can be reached in two steps for each friend, use the following:

```
GQL:
MATCH (a {_id: "a"})
MATCH REPEATABLE ELEMENTS p1=TRAIL (a)-(x),
                          p2=TRAIL (x)-()-(f)
RETURN count(f), x._id
GROUP BY x
```

This query returns two rows:

- 1, b
- 2, c

Let's break down the second MATCH statement.

The statement uses the REPEATABLE ELEMENTS match mode and two path patterns with the TRAIL path mode, ensuring there are no duplicate edges in individual path patterns.

The following are possible results from path patterns:

- p1=a-b, p2=b-a-c, combined as a-b-a-c
- p1=a-c, p2=c-a-b, combined as a-c-a-b
- p1=a-c, p2=c-i-j, combined as a-c-i-j

These combinations illustrate how path sequences can include repeated nodes or even repeat edges across different path patterns. Based on these combinations, we can observe the following effects of the REPEATABLE ELEMENTS mode and how it interacts with the MATCH clause:

1. The combined result of p1 and p2 contains repeated edges; REPEATABLE ELEMENTS allows repeatable edges for the MATCH statement

2. GROUP BY is applied to the x variable, which are b and c

3. Return the number of f in each group

Thus, REPEATABLE ELEMENTS affects the results after matching all specified path patterns, which is useful for matching subgraphs without duplicate edges in each path pattern but allowing them in the combined graph.

DIFFERENT EDGES

The DIFFERENT EDGES mode restricts duplicate edges after path patterns.

Replacing the match mode in the previous REPEATABLE ELEMENTS example looks as follows:

```
GQL:
MATCH (a {_id: "a"})
MATCH DIFFERENT EDGES p1=TRAIL (a)-(x),
                      p2=TRAIL (x)-()-(f)
RETURN count(f), x._id
GROUP BY x
```

Only one path is matched by the MATCH statement: a-c-i-j.

Therefore, the query returns the following: 1, c

Other potential paths, a-b-a-c and a-c-a-b, contain duplicated edges and do not meet the DIFFERENT EDGES mode requirement.

> DIFFERENT EDGES match mode and TRAIL path mode are used as the defaults in GQL Playground.

We've explored GQL path modes and match modes. The path mode acts as a prefix to the path pattern and the match mode acts as a prefix to the graph pattern.

In the next section, we'll cover other prefixes related to path searching.

Restrictive path search

GQL provides path search prefixes to restrict the number of paths and assist in finding the shortest path.

In this section, we introduce the fundamental path search prefixes – ALL and ANY. In the next section, we will explore another set of path search prefixes that facilitate shortest path discovery.

ALL path prefix

The ALL path prefix is used to return all matching paths. If omitted, the ALL prefix is applied by default.

You can create the graph shown in *Figure 7.3* by using the following queries:

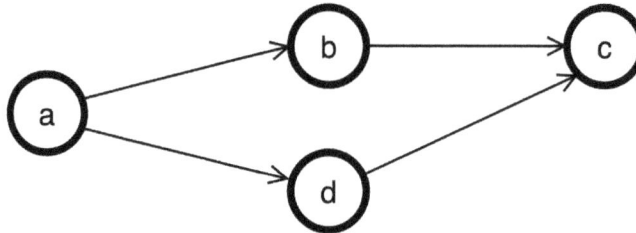

Figure 7.3: Example graph for testing the ALL path prefix

Here is the query to create the graph:

```
GQL:
CREATE GRAPH Ch07_3 {
    NODE Node ({}),
    EDGE Edge ()-[{}]->()
}
```

Here is the query to insert all nodes and edges:

```
GQL:
INSERT (a:Node {_id: "a"}), (b:Node {_id: "b"}),
       (c:Node {_id: "c"}), (d:Node {_id: "d"}),
       (a)-[:Edge]->(b), (b)-[:Edge]->(c),
       (a)-[:Edge]->(d), (d)-[:Edge]->(c)
```

With the Ch07_3 graph, you can retrieve the paths using the ALL path prefix.

For example, to find the paths between the a and c nodes in the graph, use the following:

```
GQL:
MATCH (a {_id: "a"}), (c {_id: "c"})
MATCH p = ALL (a)-()-(c)
RETURN p
```

The query returns two paths:

- a->b->c
- a->d->c

The second MATCH statement is equivalent to MATCH p = (a)-()-(c).

ANY path prefix

In GQL, all path search prefixes work by partitioning the paths by their starting and ending nodes, which are the first and last nodes in each path. The ANY path prefix limits the maximum number of paths to return for each partition.

We will update the graph shown in *Figure 7.3* to *Figure 7.4* by adding a new node, e, and an edge from node d to e.

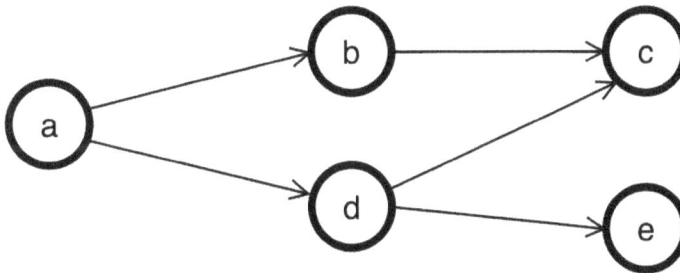

Figure 7.4: Example graph for testing the ANY path prefix

The following is the query to add a new node and edge:

```
GQL:
MATCH (d:Node {_id: "d"})
INSERT (d)-[r:Edge]->(e:Node {_id: "e"})
RETURN d, r, e
```

This query updates the graph from *Figure 7.3* to look like *Figure 7.4*.

In the updated graph, find the paths between node a and node c or e with the ANY prefix:

```
GQL:
MATCH (a {_id: "a"}),
      (ce WHERE ce._id = "c" OR ce._id = "e")
MATCH p = ANY 1 (a)-()-(ce)
RETURN p
```

This query returns two paths:

- a->d->c
- a->d->e

In the ANY 1 (a)-()-(ce) path pattern, the starting node is a and the end nodes are c and e. This means there are two partitions for the ANY prefix to work: (a, c) and (a, e). The query will return at most one path for each pair of endpoints.

The ANY and ANY 1 path prefixes are equivalent:

```
GQL:
MATCH (a {_id: "a"}), (ce WHERE ce._id = "c" OR ce._id = "e")
MATCH p = ANY (a)-()-(ce)
RETURN p
```

The query returns the same results as previously.

If the number is larger than or equal to the number of all possible paths for the groups, the query will return the same results as using the ALL prefix:

```
GQL:
MATCH (a {_id: "a"}), (ce WHERE ce._id = "c" OR ce._id = "e")
MATCH p = ANY 2 (a)-()-(ce)
RETURN p
```

The query returns three paths, two from the (a, c) partition and another one from the (a, e) partition:

- a->b->c
- a->d->c
- a->d->e

The ANY path prefix is useful for limiting the number of paths retrieved between each distinct pair of start and end nodes. This can reduce computational costs, especially in scenarios where the user only needs singular paths to connect all target nodes. In Ultipa, this feature is commonly referred to as the autonet function.

Searching shortest paths

Shortest-path search is extensively utilized across various scenarios such as route optimization, driving navigation, electrical network optimization, and even path planning in electronic games.

GQL offers a robust shortest-path search feature.

Specifying a shortest-path search

To specify a shortest-path query, the SHORTEST keyword can be incorporated into the path pattern.

Additionally, the shortest-path search supports the use of the ALL and ANY prefixes.

> The SHORTEST prefix also follows the partition rules like other path search prefixes. It groups paths based on their starting and ending nodes, which are the first and last nodes in each path.

ALL SHORTEST

ALL SHORTEST path search returns all of the shortest paths with the same minimum length for each pair of endpoints.

For practice, we will update the graph shown in *Figure 7.4* to the one in *Figure 7.5* by adding an f node and its related edges.

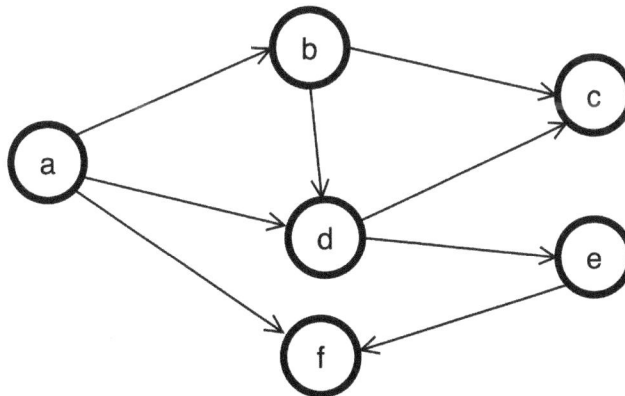

Figure 7.5: Example graph for testing shortest prefix

To add a new node, f, use the following:

```
GQL:
INSERT (n:Node {_id: "f"}) RETURN n
```

To insert new edges (b->d, a->f, e->f), use the following:

```
GQL:
MATCH (b {_id: "b"}), (d {_id: "d"}), (a {_id: "a"}),
      (f {_id: "f"}), (e {_id: "e"})
INSERT (b)-[:Edge]->(d), (a)-[:Edge]->(f), (e)-[:Edge]->(f)
```

With the updated graph, find the shortest paths from node a to node c or f:

```
GQL:
MATCH (a WHERE a._id = "a"),
      (cf WHERE cf._id IN ["c", "f"])
MATCH p = ALL SHORTEST (a)->{1,5}(cf)
RETURN p
```

The query returns three shortest paths:

- a->b->c
- a->d->c
- a->f

Here is an explanation of the path pattern with the shortest prefix:

- ALL SHORTEST specifies to return all of the shortest paths for each partition. In the (a, c) partition, two shortest paths are found with a length of 2; in the (a, f) partition, one shortest path is found with a length of 1.
- -> indicates the directions of all edges in the path as outgoing.
- {1,5} is a path pattern quantifier, seeking the shortest path within 1 to 5 steps.

You can update the quantifier to {3,5}:

```
GQL:
MATCH (a WHERE a._id = "a"),
      (cf WHERE cf._id IN ["c", "f"])
MATCH p = ALL SHORTEST (a)->{3,5}(cf)
RETURN p
```

This query returns two shortest paths within the length of 3 to 5 steps:

- a->b->d->c
- a->d->e->f

The shortest-path length between nodes (a, c) and nodes (a, f) is 3 when setting the path quantifier to 3 to 5 steps.

ANY SHORTEST

The ANY prefix can also be used with the SHORTEST prefix. The ANY SHORTEST path prefix allows the return of any one shortest path for each partition.

For example, to find one shortest path from node a to c in *Figure 7.5*, use the following:

```
GQL:
MATCH (a {_id: "a"}), (c {_id: "c"})
MATCH p = ANY SHORTEST (a)->{1,5}(c)
RETURN p
```

This query returns one shortest path:

- a->b->c

The result could also be a->d->c, depending on the data storage position. Both results are valid.

Updating the end nodes to c and f looks as follows:

```
MATCH (a WHERE a._id = "a"),
      (cf WHERE cf._id IN ["c", "f"])
MATCH p = ANY SHORTEST (a)->{1,5}(cf)
RETURN p
```

This query returns two shortest paths, one for each partition:

- a->b->c
- a->f

The ANY prefix cannot be used with SHORTEST. An error will arise in the following query:

```
GQL:
MATCH (a {_id: "a"}), (c {_id: "c"})
MATCH p = ANY 2 SHORTEST (a)->{1,5}(c)
RETURN p
```

Note that the shortest-path search prefixes are typically used with quantified path patterns that specify variable-length paths. If you use a shortest-path search prefix with a fixed-length path pattern, it won't technically find the "shortest" paths but the paths that match the pattern. For example, the following query applies ANY SHORTEST to a fixed-length path pattern:

```
GQL:
MATCH (a WHERE a._id = "a"), (c WHERE c._id = "c")
MATCH p = ANY SHORTEST (a)->()->()->(c)
RETURN p
```

This query is equivalent to the following:

```
GQL:
MATCH (a WHERE a._id = "a"), (c WHERE c._id = "c")
MATCH p = ANY (a)->()->()->(c)
RETURN p
```

Counted shortest search

GQL provides a counted shortest search prefix, SHORTEST N, to specify the maximum number of shortest paths to be returned in a path pattern.

For example, to return one shortest path for each pair of endpoints in the graph illustrated in *Figure 7.5*, use the following:

```
GQL:
MATCH (a WHERE a._id = "a"),
      (cf WHERE cf._id IN ["c", "f"])
MATCH p = SHORTEST 1 (a)->{1,5}(cf)
RETURN p
```

This query returns two shortest paths, one for each partition:

- a->b->c
- a->f

ANY SHORTEST is an alternative to SHORTEST 1.

In the previous example, the query returns one shortest path for each partition.

By changing the number of shortest paths to 2, the query will return a maximum of two shortest paths for each partition:

```
GQL:
MATCH (a WHERE a._id = "a"),
      (cf WHERE cf._id IN ["c", "f"])
MATCH p = SHORTEST 2 (a)->{1,5}(cf)
RETURN p
```

The query returns four shortest paths:

- a->d->c
- a->b->c
- a->f
- a->d->e->f

It is easy to understand that there are two shortest paths for the (a, c) partition. However, for the (a, f) partition, there are two shortest paths found with different lengths.

This is because the counted shortest path prefix aims to return the specified number of shortest paths for each partition. If there aren't enough shortest paths, it continues searching for the second shortest paths, third shortest paths, and so on, until the desired count is met.

This prefix is useful for retrieving a specified number of shortest paths from the query, irrespective of their varying lengths.

Counted shortest group search

GQL provides the GROUP specification in counted shortest-path searching, which groups the matched paths by path lengths in ascending order.

Take the following example:

```
GQL:
MATCH (a {_id: "a"}), (c {_id: "c"})
MATCH p = SHORTEST 1 GROUP (a)->{1,5}(c)
RETURN p
```

The query returns all shortest paths from the first group (i.e., the group of shortest paths):

- a->d->c
- a->b->c

`SHORTEST 1 GROUP` is an alternative to `ALL SHORTEST`.

Replace the number with 2:

```
GQL:
MATCH (a {_id: "a"}), (c {_id: "c"})
MATCH p = SHORTEST 2 GROUPS (a)->{1,5}(c)
RETURN p
```

The query returns all shortest paths from the first group (i.e., the group of shortest paths) and the second group (i.e., the group of second shortest paths):

- a->d->c
- a->b->c
- a->b->d->c

To explain the presence of two groups, consider the following query:

```
GQL:
MATCH (a {_id: "a"}), (c {_id: "c"})
MATCH p = (a)->{1,5}(c)
LET pathLength = LENGTH(p)
RETURN count(p), pathLength
GROUP BY pathLength
```

The following is the result:

count(p)	pathLength
1	3
2	2

Table 7.1: Result showing count (p) and pathLength

The query retrieves all paths from node a to node c within 1 to 5 steps, and returns the count of paths that are of the same length. From the result, we can see there are two paths with a length of 2 and one path with a length of 3.

Counted shortest group search also follows the partition rules for each pair of endpoints.

For example, updating the end nodes to c and f is done as follows:

```
GQL:
MATCH (a WHERE a._id = "a"),
      (cf WHERE cf._id IN ["c", "f"])
```

```
MATCH p = SHORTEST 1 GROUP (a)->{1,5}(cf)
RETURN p
```

This query returns three paths, two for the (a, c) partition and one for the (a, f) partition:

- a->b->c

- a->d->c

- a->f

Counting K-hop neighbors by shortest group

K-kop query refers to retrieving the neighbors of a target node that are located exactly *K* steps away, based on the shortest distance, or the length of the shortest paths.

For example, when *K* is 2, the shortest distance between the 2-hop neighbors of the target node must be 2.

To count the 2-hop neighbors of the target node, a, in *Figure 7.6*, which is the same as *Figure 7.5*:

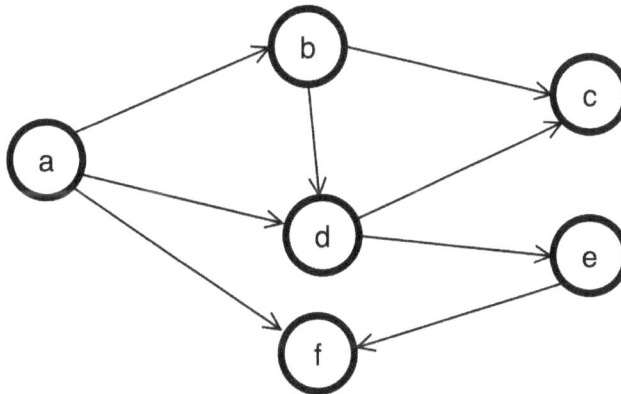

Figure 7.6: Example graph for a K-hop query

This can be implemented using GQL as follows:

```
GQL:
MATCH (a {_id: "a"})
MATCH p = ANY SHORTEST (a)->{1,2}(n)
RETURN n
EXCEPT DISTINCT
MATCH (a {_id: "a"})
MATCH p = ANY SHORTEST (a)->{1}(n)
RETURN n
```

This query returns two nodes: c and e. Here is how this composite query operates:

1. The first sub-query identifies all nodes that node a can reach with one- or two-step shortest paths, which are nodes b, d, f, c, and e.

2. The second sub-query identifies all nodes that node a can reach with one-step shortest paths, which are nodes b, d, and f.

3. The EXCEPT DISTINCT conjunction returns a result set that includes distinct records from the first query that are not present in the second query, which are nodes c and e.

Using the TEMP variable

GQL allows the use of TEMP to declare temporary variables within a graph pattern. The temporary variables are discarded once the MATCH statement concludes.

Take the following example:

```
GQL:
MATCH (TEMP c:Category WHERE c.name = "Graph")-[]->(g:Lang)
RETURN g.name
```

In this query, a temporary variable, c, and a general variable, g, are declared in the MATCH statement. The c.name is used to filter the Graph category in the WHERE clause, which is part of the MATCH statement.

Attempting to use the c variable in the subsequent statements will result in an exception:

```
GQL:
MATCH (TEMP c:Category)-[]->(g:Lang)
FILTER c.name = "Graph"
RETURN g.name
```

The query will raise an exception because the temporary variable, c, is removed after the execution of the MATCH statement.

CALL procedures

GQL provides an inline procedure and a named procedure. Both procedures are invoked by the CALL keyword.

Inline procedures

GQL inline procedures are query blocks that can be called in another query.

They are particularly useful for handling complex data processes that cannot be managed with a simple linear query.

Example: Using CALL to count grouped neighbors

To determine the number of neighbors for each node, an aggregate function can be used.

For example, to calculate the number of neighbors for each node from the graph in *Figure 7.5*, use the following:

```
GQL:
MATCH (start)
MATCH (start)-(end)
RETURN start._id as startNode, COUNT(end) as total
GROUP BY startNode
```

The query returns each startNode and its total number of neighbors:

startNode	total
a	3
b	3
f	2
c	2
d	4
e	2

Alternatively, using CALL to initiate an inline procedure can enhance the clarity:

```
GQL:
MATCH (start)
CALL {
    MATCH (start)-(end)
    RETURN COUNT(end) as total
}
RETURN start._id as startNode, total
```

Both queries yield identical results.

While there are no differences in the output of these queries, the use of a CALL procedure block can simplify query execution.

For instance, to retrieve nodes with more than two neighbors, use the following:

```
GQL:
MATCH (start)
CALL {
    MATCH (start)-(end)
    RETURN COUNT(end) as total
}
FILTER total > 2
RETURN start._id as startNode, total
```

It is important to note that GQL only allows us to use the GROUP BY clause in the RETURN statement, which means FILTER cannot be used after the grouping operation.

The CALL procedure is beneficial for breaking down complex statements into sub-query blocks, thereby facilitating the combination of the entire query.

Example: Aggregating values in paths

Previously, you explored using CALL to aggregate results with the COUNT function. In this example, let's use CALL to aggregate values within a path.

In the graph shown in *Figure 7.7*, the numbers on the edges indicate the rank property values:

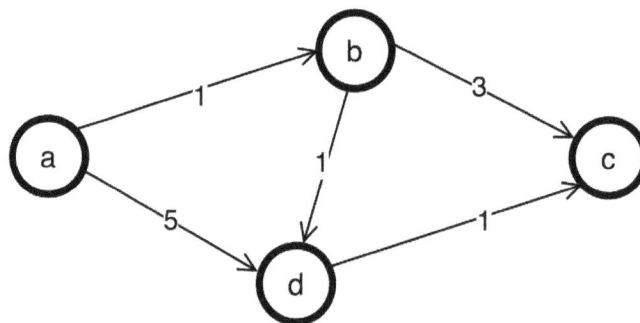

Figure 7.7: Example graph for testing aggregating path data

To create the graph, you can use the following queries.

The following is the query to create the graph shown in *Figure 7.7*:

```
GQL:
CREATE GRAPH Ch07_7 {
    NODE Node ({}),
    EDGE Edge ()-[{rank float}]->()
}
```

The following is the query to insert the nodes and edges:

```
GQL:
INSERT (a:Node {_id: "a"}),
       (b:Node {_id: "b"}),
       (c:Node {_id: "c"}),
       (d:Node {_id: "d"}),
       (a)-[:Edge{rank: 1}]->(b),
       (b)-[:Edge{rank: 3}]->(c),
       (a)-[:Edge{rank: 5}]->(d),
       (d)-[:Edge{rank: 1}]->(c),
       (b)-[:Edge{rank: 1}]->(d)
```

In this graph, the following query finds all shortest paths between nodes a and c within five steps:

```
GQL:
MATCH (a {_id: "a"}), (c {_id: "c"})
MATCH p = ALL SHORTEST (a)-[e]->{1,5}(c)
RETURN p
```

This query returns two paths:

- a->d->c
- a->b->c

If our goal is to identify the cheapest paths, or weighted shortest path, which finds the paths between nodes a and c with the minimum sum of edge rank, we can aggregate the edge ranks in each path:

```
GQL:
MATCH (a {_id: "a"}), (c {_id: "c"})
MATCH p = SHORTEST 10 (a)-[e]->{1,5}(c)
CALL {
    FOR edge IN e
```

```
    RETURN SUM(edge.rank) as weight
}
RETURN p, weight
ORDER BY weight ASC
LIMIT 1
```

The query returns the a->b->d->c shortest path stored in the p variable, with the lowest-weight value of 3.

By using the CALL statement, variables can be unfolded and aggregated during query execution.

Alternatively, the REDUCE function in GQL Playground can address this requirement:

```
GQL:
MATCH (a {_id: "a"}), (c {_id: "c"})
MATCH p=SHORTEST 10 (a)-[e]->{1,5}(c)
let weight = REDUCE(weight=0, edge in e | weight + edge.rank)
RETURN p, weight
ORDER BY weight ASC
LIMIT 1
```

The REDUCE function aggregates the ranks for each path effectively.

> SHORTEST 10 identifies the shortest paths between nodes based on the fewest number of steps. In many cases, it can also be used to calculate weighted shortest paths, though this is not always guaranteed.
>
> For example, consider a path with a single hop and an edge weight of 100, versus another path with 50 hops where each edge has a weight of 1. Although the first path is shorter in terms of steps, the second path has a lower total weight (50 versus 100), making it the true weighted shortest path.
>
> Handling such scenarios—especially those involving negative edge weights—often requires specialized algorithms. Many graph database vendors provide dedicated solutions for this purpose.
>
> For Ultipa Graph, you can visit the UQL documentation on weighted shortest paths: https://www.ultipa.com/docs/uql/ab#Finding-Weighted-Shortest-Paths.

While inline procedures are useful, they have limitations, especially when tackling complex graph algorithms or specific business models, which may exceed GQL's core capabilities.

For more advanced industry challenges, such as calculating intricate financial indicators or executing graph community detection algorithms, GQL supports calling named procedures to extend beyond the constraints of inline procedures.

Named procedures

Named procedures are predefined functions, queries, or operations. The GQL standard supports calling named procedures but does not define any specific named procedures. This allows the implementation to include named procedures that are extensions of the standard. Here, we will look into procedures related to a graph algorithm available in GQL Playground.

To execute a built-in graph algorithm, you can utilize a GQL procedure. Before executing a named procedure, let's briefly introduce a renowned graph algorithm: PageRank.

PageRank is an algorithm developed by Google co-founders Larry Page and Sergey Brin. It measures the importance of web pages by analyzing both the quantity and quality of links pointing to them. It is used to determine the ranking of nodes within a network.

Before executing PageRank in GQL Playground, run the following query:

```
GQL:
CREATE HDC GRAPH Ch07_7_hdc ON "hdc-server" OPTIONS {
    nodes: { "*" : ["*"]},
    edges: { "*" : ["*"]}
}
```

This query creates an HDC graph, Ch07_7_hdc, by loading data from the current graph, Ch07_7, for executing algorithms. You will learn more about HDC graphs in *Chapter 11, Beyond GQL*.

With the HDC graph created by this query, you can use it to execute the PageRank algorithm:

```
GQL:
CALL algo.page_rank("Ch07_7_hdc", {
    params: { order: "DESC" }
}) YIELD rank
MATCH (n {_uuid: rank._uuid})
RETURN n LIMIT 10
```

The query returns the top 10 nodes with the highest ranks.

Here's a breakdown of the query:

1. The CALL statement calls a named procedure, which is the PageRank algorithm provided by Ultipa.

2. The procedure produces results, represented by the variable named rank, declared in the YIELD clause.

3. The MATCH statement finds nodes whose _uuid values match those contained in the rank variable.

4. It returns the information of the top 10 nodes.

For more detailed information about the PageRank algorithm, visit Ultipa's documentation: https://www.ultipa.com/docs/graph-analytics-algorithms/pagerank.

Named procedures enhance GQL by providing additional capabilities, such as the PageRank algorithm. Ultipa Graph offers a comprehensive collection of graph algorithms as named procedures that can be called within GQL. You can view them all by visiting https://www.ultipa.com/docs/graph-analytics-algorithms.

Using OPTIONAL

GQL provides the OPTIONAL keyword to ensure the statements execute continuously even when no data is available to drive subsequent statements.

In general, OPTIONAL assigns a NULL value when the statement cannot produce any result.

OPTIONAL MATCH

The MATCH statement in GQL supports the OPTIONAL keyword.

For example, to retrieve nodes with some IDs from the graph shown in *Figure 7.5*, use the following:

```
GQL:
FOR id in ["a", "b", "z"]
OPTIONAL MATCH (n {_id: id})
RETURN n
```

The query returns the following:

- a
- b
- NULL

Since the node z does not exist, the result corresponding to the ID z is NULL. If the query is executed without the OPTIONAL keyword, it will return only the matched results:

```
GQL:
FOR id in ["a", "b", "z"]
MATCH (n {_id: id})
RETURN n
```

This query returns the following:

- a
- b

Another example is to retrieve optional values from multiple MATCH statements, using braces or parentheses to encapsulate the MATCH statements:

```
FOR id in ["a", "b", "z"]
OPTIONAL {
    MATCH (start {_id: id})
    MATCH (start)->(end)
}
RETURN end._id
```

This query returns the following:

- b
- d
- f
- c
- d
- NULL

The NULL result is produced from the ID z, as a node with that ID does not exist.

Alternatively, parentheses can be used to replace the braces:

```
FOR id in ["a", "b", "z"]
OPTIONAL (
    MATCH (start {_id: id})
    MATCH (start)->(end)
)
RETURN end._id
```

The query returns the same data as the previous example.

OPTIONAL CALL

The OPTIONAL keyword can also be used with CALL procedures to ensure the query continues and assigns a NULL value when the procedures do not return any results.

For example, to get the neighbor list for the source nodes from the graph in *Figure 7.5*, use the following:

```
GQL:
FOR id in ["a", "b", "z"]
OPTIONAL CALL {
    MATCH (start {_id: id })
    MATCH (start)-(end)
    RETURN COLLECT_LIST(end._id) as neigbours
}
RETURN id, neigbours
```

The query returns the following:

id	neighbors
a	["b","d","f"]
B	["a","c","d"]
z	null

If the OPTIONAL keyword is removed, the last row will not be returned.

To improve the return values, you use CASE WHEN or COALESCE to set a default value when NULL is encountered.

For example, replacing NULL with an empty list for the node with ID z:

```
GQL:
FOR id in ["a", "b", "z"]
OPTIONAL CALL {
    MATCH (start {_id: id })
    MATCH (start)-(end)
    RETURN COLLECT_LIST(end._id) as neigbours
}
LET neigbours = COALESCE(neigbours, [])
RETURN id, neigbours
```

The query returns the following:

id	neighbors
a	["b","d","f"]
b	["a","c","d"]
z	[]

Alternatively, we can use a CASE WHEN expression:

```
FOR id in ["a", "b", "z"]
OPTIONAL CALL {
    MATCH (start {_id: id })
    MATCH (start)-(end)
    RETURN COLLECT_LIST(end._id) as neigbours
}
LET neigbours = CASE WHEN neigbours IS NULL
                     THEN []
                     ELSE neigbours
            END
RETURN id, neigbours
```

The query returns the same results as the previous query.

Summary

This chapter explores various aspects of advanced traversing and querying graphs using GQL. We explored different path modes such as WALK, TRAIL, and ACYCLIC, each offering unique traversal methods. MATCH modes were discussed next, highlighting the importance of repeatable elements and differentiating edges. The chapter also covered constraint path patterns, including ALL and ANY, which help to limit the number of query results returned for each partition.

Additionally, the chapter delved into searching for the shortest path, including specifying shortest search criteria and counted shortest search. The CALL procedure was also explained. Finally, the chapter concluded with a look at OPTIONAL MATCH and OPTIONAL CALL, providing flexibility in query execution.

Get This Book's PDF Version and Exclusive Extras

UNLOCK NOW

Scan the QR code (or go to packtpub.com/unlock). Search for this book by name, confirm the edition, and then follow the steps on the page.

Note: *Keep your invoice handy. Purchases made directly from Packt don't require an invoice.*

8

Configuring Sessions

A GQL session is initiated by a GQL client, such as GQL Playground, and a GQL service, such as a graph database. It maintains parameters for communication between the GQL client and the service, efficiently managing requests and responses.

In this chapter, you will delve into session management, exploring the creation, modification, and termination of sessions. The chapter presents a detailed overview of the session context, commands for setting session parameters, and resetting and closing sessions.

This chapter will cover the following topics:

- The concept of a GQL session
- Setting a session context
- Closing a session

Technical requirements

All the queries are located in the repository at https://github.com/PacktPublishing/Getting-Started-with-the-Graph-Query-Language-GQL-/tree/main/Ch08.

What is a GQL session?

A GQL session can be initiated from a GQL client, such as GQL Playground, or a graph database driver. Sessions can be created either explicitly or implicitly, depending on the context and the actions taken by the client.

Explicit session creation

A session is explicitly created when the GQL client sends a specific command to initiate a session. This is often used in scenarios where precise control over session management is required.

Implicit session creation

For instance, in GQL Playground, a session is automatically created whenever a query is executed. This implicit creation ensures that users can seamlessly interact with the graph database without needing to manually manage session initiation.

Session management

The context of sessions can be managed by GQL or the settings from a GQL client. In this book, we will explore how to manage sessions with GQL queries.

A GQL session is capable of handling multiple consecutive requests. The session context maintains essential data, such as the following:

- *Authorization identifier:* Ensures that the session is securely linked to the correct user or agent.
- *Time zone information:* Adjusts query results and operations according to the relevant time zone.
- *Session schema:* Identifies the working schema reference.
- *Session graph:* Identifies the current working graph.
- *Session parameters:* A possible empty dictionary with corresponding parameters. For instance, in GQL Playground, a timeout can be set in the session parameters.
- *Transactions:* Sets to start, commit, or roll back a transaction. A detailed exploration will be provided in *Chapter 9, Graph Transactions*.
- *Termination flag:* Sets a truth value to close the session.
- *Current graph context:* Keeps track of the specific graph or subgraph being interacted with during the session.

In this chapter, we will explore how to utilize SESSION SET clauses to manage the session context.

Setting sessions

GQL provides the SESSION SET statement to modify the session settings.

Setting a GQL schema

In *Chapter 2*, *Key Concepts of GQL*, and *Chapter 4*, *GQL Basics*, you have already explored the concept of a GQL schema and its operation. Additionally, the current working schema can be set in the session settings.

You can use `SESSION SET SCHEMA` to specify a GQL schema reference within the session.

For example, to set a session schema, use the following:

```
GQL:
SESSION SET SCHEMA /root/mySchema
```

This query adjusts the default GQL schema context for all requests within the session. Consequently, operations such as `CREATE GRAPH` and `DROP GRAPH` will automatically apply within the `/root/mySchema` context.

> **Note:** At the time of writing, some features are not yet supported in the GQL Playground or on Cloud. These features are planned for future releases.

Setting the current graph

Like the GQL schema session setting, the current working graph can also be set in the session settings.

You can use `SESSION SET PROPERTY GRAPH` to set a GQL graph reference in the session.

For example, to set a session graph, use the following:

```
GQL:
SESSION SET PROPERTY GRAPH myGraph
```

The query sets `myGraph` as the current graph in the session. The `PROPERTY` keyword is optional:

```
GQL:
SESSION SET GRAPH myGraph
```

Setting the time zone

GQL session management allows setting the time zone using a time zone string that is compliant with ISO 8601-1:2019 "time shift" standards.

For example, to change the session time zone to +1:00, use the following:

```
GQL:
SESSION SET TIME ZONE "+01:00"
```

Configuring session parameters

Within a session, GQL enables the configuration of parameters, which can be utilized in subsequent queries within the same session.

There are three types of parameters:

- Graph parameters
- Binding table parameters
- Value parameters

Setting a graph parameter

A graph parameter acts as a graph initializer. Similar to the CREATE GRAPH statements discussed in *Chapter 3, Getting Started with GQL*, we can use a graph expression to declare the graph parameter.

The syntax is as follows:

```
SESSION SET GRAPH $<parameter name> = <graph expression>
```

For example, to set a graph parameter named mainGraph to CURRENT GRAPH, do the following:

```
GQL:
SESSION SET GRAPH $mainGraph = CURRENT_GRAPH
```

You can also utilize a graph reference to set the graph parameter:

```
GQL:
SESSION SET GRAPH $mainGraph = QueryLanguage
```

To use the graph parameter in a focused linear query, use the following:

```
GQL:
USE $mainGraph
MATCH (n) RETURN n LIMIT 10
```

This query executes the MATCH statement on the $mainGraph graph.

If $mainGraph points to QueryLanguage, the query is equivalent to the following:

```
GQL:
USE QueryLanguage
MATCH (n) RETURN n LIMIT 10
```

Setting a binding table parameter

GQL supports defining a binding table session parameter for use in queries.

The syntax is as follows:

```
SESSION SET TABLE $<parameter name> = <table expression>
```

To set a binding table parameter using the result of a subquery, use the following:

```
GQL:
SESSION SET TABLE $table1 = { MATCH (n:Lang) RETURN n }
```

The query declares the table parameter named $table1, which is a reference to the binding table, and contains all Lang nodes.

A binding table can be iterated using a FOR statement:

```
GQL:
FOR row IN $table1
LET n = row.n
RETURN COUNT(n), AVG(n.year)
```

The query returns the total number of rows from the $table1 table parameter and the average release year from the n column.

A binding table reference can also be assigned to a table parameter; however, this book does not cover using binding table references.

Setting a value parameter

GQL allows the assignment of values to a value parameter.

The syntax is as follows:

```
SESSION SET VALUE $<parameter name> = <value expression>
```

For example, to set a query language name, use the following:

```
GQL:
SESSION SET VALUE $query = "GQL"
```

To use the value parameter in a MATCH statement, use the following:

```
GQL:
MATCH (n:Lang WHERE n.name = $query) RETURN n
```

This query employs the $query parameter to locate Lang nodes with the specified name.

Setting all parameters

Let's consolidate all the session-setting statements in one request:

```
GQL:
SESSION SET SCHEMA /
SESSION SET $graph = QueryLanguage
SESSION SET TIME ZONE "+02:00"
SESSION SET $query = "GQL"
```

This query configures multiple session settings in a single request.

Resetting a session

The session can be restored to its default settings, clearing any customized session settings, by using the SESSION RESET clause.

Resetting all session settings

To reset all parameters, including graph, schema, and time zone, use the following:

```
GQL:
SESSION RESET
```

Alternatively, use the ALL PARAMETERS keywords:

```
GQL:
SESSION RESET ALL PARAMETERS
```

Alternatively, you can use the ALL CHARACTERISTICS keywords:

```
GQL:
SESSION RESET ALL CHARACTERISTICS
```

Resetting a single setting

The SESSION RESET clause also allows resetting individual settings.

To reset the schema, use the following:

```
GQL:
SESSION RESET SCHEMA
```

This query resets the schema session setting. If no default setting exists, the schema will remain unset.

To reset the graph, use the following:

```
GQL:
SESSION RESET GRAPH
```

The query resets the graph to a default graph. If no default setting exists, the graph will remain unset.

To reset the time zone, use the following:

```
GQL:
SESSION RESET TIME ZONE
```

This query resets the time zone to its default setting.

> SCHEMA, GRAPH, and TIME ZONE can be reset to a default value or a non-value that is designed by the graph database providers.

To reset a parameter, use the following:

```
GQL:
SESSION RESET $graph
```

Alternatively, use the following:

```
GQL:
SESSION RESET PARAMETER $graph
```

This query removes the $graph parameter.

> If the graph database has a default parameter setting, such as a default value for
> $graph, using SESSION RESET $graph will set $graph to the default value instead
> of removing it.

Closing a session

A GQL session can be closed using the SESSION CLOSE clause.

To close the session, use the following:

```
GQL:
SESSION CLOSE
```

This query closes the session. When SESSION CLOSE is executed, the session termination flag is set to TRUE.

Summary

In this chapter, we delved into the concept of GQL sessions, in particular, introducing session creation. We then demonstrated how to set and reset the session schema, graph, time zone, and various parameters, including graph, binding table, and value parameters. Finally, we covered the process of closing the session.

The session settings are instrumental for queries involving common parameters.

Understanding GQL sessions is crucial, as they are fundamental for executing transactions, which we will explore in the next chapter.

9

Graph Transactions

In the previous chapter, you explored sessions that connect the GQL client and service, providing the environment to manage transactions. In this chapter, you will explore transaction management, including an overview of the fundamental concepts, their characteristics, and their lifecycle states. The chapter then delves into the specifics of initiating transactions using the START TRANSACTION command, detailing the syntax, usage, and conditions for starting a transaction. Finally, it explains how to effectively terminate transactions with COMMIT and ROLLBACK commands to maintain data integrity and consistency.

This chapter will cover the following main topics:

- Concept of transactions
- Starting a transaction
- Committing a transaction
- Rolling back a transaction

Technical requirements

All the queries are located in the repository at https://github.com/PacktPublishing/Getting-Started-with-the-Graph-Query-Language-GQL/tree/main/Ch09.

What is a transaction?

A GQL transaction is a sequence of operations that either all succeed or all fail as a unit, ensuring no partial changes are made to the GQL catalog or graph data.

Types of transactions in databases

Databases offer various transaction types:

- *Serializable transactions*: Only one transaction executes at a time in a strict serial order. This ensures data consistency and prevents issues such as dirty reads and phantom reads. Due to their strict requirements, they come with higher performance costs. They are commonly used in banking systems to prevent problems such as double-spending.

- *Concurrent transactions*: Multiple transactions run simultaneously, offering better performance. They rely on different concurrency control mechanisms to maintain data correctness based on the scenarios. For example, in banking transactions, the database should enforce a serializable isolation level to ensure correctness when multiple operations attempt to modify the same data at the same time. In other scenarios, where users access non-conflicting data, a weaker isolation level may be sufficient.

- *Single-node transactions*: Transactions are confined to a single server node, ensuring consistency at the node level but not across clusters. These transactions can be either serializable or concurrent.

- *Distributed transactions*: Transactions span multiple servers or clusters, ensuring consistent changes across the distributed system. Like single-node transactions, they can be serializable or concurrent.

- *Read or write transactions*: These involve operations limited to either reading or writing. GQL provides standard definitions for READ and WRITE modes, which help ensure users can only read or modify data within a transaction.

- *Batch transactions*: These handle a group of operations within a single transaction, such as batch data imports. This is useful when importing, for example, 10,000 nodes or edges in one operation, ensuring that all succeed or fail together.

> Ultipa's GQL Playground uses a serializable isolation level as the default for transactions. All users have both read and write access privileges within a transaction. Since each user can only access their own data, transactions are typically non-conflicting, allowing them to run concurrently across the entire system.

ACID rules

Transactions typically adhere to ACID principles (*ACID* stands for *Atomicity*, *Consistency*, *Isolation*, and *Durability*).

A transaction may comply with all or some of these rules:

- *Atomicity* ensures that a transaction either fully succeeds or fails.

- *Consistency* guarantees that a transaction brings the database from one valid state to another, according to rules such as constraints and triggers. In graph databases, constraints often mean that deleting nodes requires deleting related edges. In distributed graph databases, it's crucial to ensure complete insertion of nodes or edges across the cluster consistently. In high-availability systems, data changes must be reflected in all copies.

- *Isolation* ensures that incomplete transactions are not visible to others in systems supporting concurrent transactions.

- *Durability* ensures that once a transaction is committed, it remains so even in the event of system failures such as power outages.

Fully supporting ACID can significantly impact transaction performance due to the additional operations required, such as extensive logging and creating multiple data versions and snapshots.

This performance cost leads many databases to adopt alternative implementations, such as ensuring ACID compliance during writes but not reads, to enhance performance under high loads. Some products forego ACID entirely for optimal performance, particularly in offline analysis and big data processing.

As graph databases evolve to handle both online and offline, real-time, and long-term scenarios, users must judiciously decide when to use ACID transactions for business purposes. For example, avoid using ACID for executing entire graph algorithms or deep traversals, but enable it for critical operations such as recording cash transfers.

Finding the optimal solution for achieving specific goals is more important than demanding every feature a vendor offers, regardless of their utility.

Remember the saying "Jack of all trades, master of none."

With these transaction concepts in mind, let's explore how to manage transactions effectively.

Initializing a transaction

A GQL transaction can be initialized either implicitly or explicitly, depending on the implementation and method of invocation.

Implicit transaction initialization

If there is no explicit transaction declaration when executing GQL, the transaction is implicitly initialized by the GQL client.

For example, when using the GQL Playground without an explicit transaction statement, an implicit transaction is automatically declared.

For example, to retrieve nodes by MATCH statement, the following is used:

```
GQL:
MATCH (n) RETURN n LIMIT 10
```

The process for sending this query is illustrated in *Figure 9.1.*

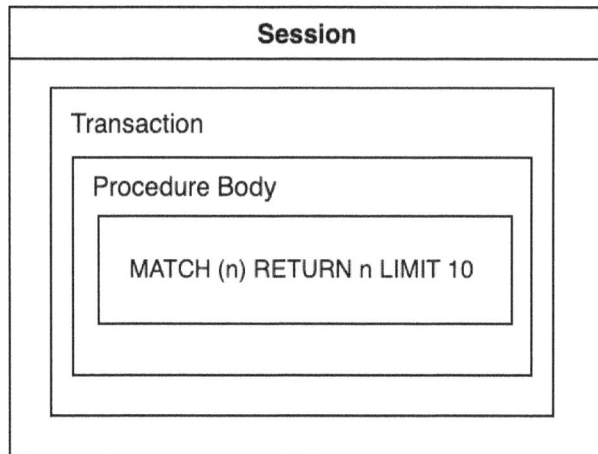

Figure 9.1: Session, transaction, and procedure

Let's walk through the steps in the process:

1. The GQL Playground, acting as a GQL client, creates a session to connect to the GQL service (the graph database).

2. Within this session, the GQL Playground initiates a transaction.

3. An inline procedure body is created as part of the transaction.

4. The query, including MATCH, RETURN, and LIMIT statements, is incorporated into the procedure body.

5. The GQL Playground sends the query along with the transaction request and commits it.

6. The transaction is closed upon completion.

7. The session is closed.

In a production environment, the session may remain active as long as the application exits, allowing users to send multiple transactions within the same session.

In implicit transactions, the system automatically initiates and manages transaction lifecycles behind the scenes. This allows users to focus on executing queries and operations without the need to manually open or close transactions, reducing boilerplate code and simplifying the development experience. By abstracting transaction handling, implicit transactions lower the barrier to entry, especially for newcomers to the database.

However, this convenience comes with trade-offs. Because users have no control over transaction boundaries, they cannot group multiple queries into a single atomic operation or implement recovery mechanisms for partial failures. In high-throughput environments, implicit transactions may also introduce performance overhead, as each small operation triggers its own transaction lifecycle. These limitations can be effectively addressed by using explicit transactions.

Explicit transaction initialization

To explicitly initialize a transaction, GQL provides comprehensive syntax such as START, COMMIT, and ROLLBACK for a transaction.

Creating a transaction

To create a new transaction, the START statement is used in GQL:

```
GQL:
START TRANSACTION
```

This query initiates a new transaction in the current session.

Attempting to execute this query again will result in an error, as a session typically supports only one transaction at a time.

Some systems may support concurrent transactions.

Specifying the transaction mode

When creating a transaction, different modes can be specified, including access modes and implementation-defined modes.

GQL defines two access modes:

- `READ ONLY`: This mode allows the transaction to read data but not modify it
- `READ WRITE`: This mode permits both reading and modifying data

Most databases use `READ WRITE` as the default access mode.

For example, to set transaction mode to `READ ONLY`, the following is used:

```
GQL:
START TRANSACTION READ ONLY
```

Users can define only one access mode, either `READ ONLY` or `READ WRITE`.

Let's say a transaction is set to `READ ONLY` mode and the following query is executed:

```
GQL:
MATCH (n) FILTER n.name = "GQL" SET n.name = "gql"
```

An error will occur because the transaction is restricted to reading data only.

The user can use the `READ WRITE` mode to solve this problem, as follows:

```
GQL:
START TRANSACTION READ WRITE
```

Or they could simply use the following:

```
GQL:
START TRANSACTION
```

The queries set the access mode to `READ WRITE`, which allows modifying GQL data and GQL catalogs.

Customized modes

GQL allows implementers to offer additional access modes, which can be used alongside standard modes.

For instance, to enhance transaction isolation, you might specify the following:

```
GQL:
START TRANSACTION READ ONLY, SNAPSHOT
```

In this example, SNAPSHOT is not a standard GQL feature but can be provided by graph database vendors. SNAPSHOT typically requests the system to create a snapshot for the transaction, preventing dirty reads during execution.

> A dirty read, also known as a read-write conflict, occurs when a transaction reads data that has been modified but not yet committed by another transaction.

Once the transaction is initialized, all queries are executed within the context of the created transaction.

Committing the transaction

GQL provides a COMMIT statement to finalize and submit all modifications made within a transaction.

To commit a transaction and apply all changes, use the following:

```
GQL:
COMMIT
```

The COMMIT command finalizes a transaction by applying all changes made to the graph database.

If an error occurs during the commit process, the operation fails, and all changes to the graph data and catalog are discarded. Otherwise, the commit is successful, and the transaction is concluded.

Here is a complete example of committing a transaction:

1. Start a transaction:

    ```
    GQL:
    START TRANSACTION
    ```

    This query initiates a transaction.

2. Modify the data:

    ```
    GQL:
    MATCH (n) FILTER n.name = "GQL"
    SET n.name = "gql"
    ```

    This query finds nodes named GQL and changes the name to lowercase, gql.

3. Commit the transaction:

    ```
    GQL3:
    COMMIT
    ```

This query commits the transaction, permanently changing the name of the GQL node to gql.

Other transactions will see the updated value after this transaction is committed. The transaction is terminated upon commitment.

Rolling back a transaction

In a transaction, all modifications can be rolled back if needed.

To roll back modifications in a transaction, use the following:

```
GQL:
ROLLBACK
```

This query undoes all modifications and terminates the transaction.

Here is a complete example of rolling back a transaction:

1. Start a transaction:

    ```
    GQL:
    START TRANSACTION
    ```

    The query initiates a transaction.

2. Modify the data:

    ```
    GQL2:
    MATCH (n) FILTER n.name = "GQL"
    SET n.year = 2025
    ```

    This query finds a node named GQL and sets its year property to 2025.

3. Roll back the transaction:

```
GQL3:
ROLLBACK
```

This query rolls back all modifications, reverting the year property of the GQL node to its previous value.

The transaction is terminated upon rollback.

Summary

In this chapter, we explored how GQL transactions ensure that all procedures are either completed successfully or fail without affecting the GQL catalog and graph data partially.

A transaction can be serializable, concurrent, single-node, distributed, or read/write. Adhering to ACID rules is essential.

Transactions can be initialized implicitly or explicitly, with modes such as READ ONLY or READ WRITE, along with vendor-specific modes.

Committing a transaction applies all changes, and rolling back reverts them, maintaining data integrity and consistency across the system.

Transactions in GQL are a powerful tool for making operations clear and resettable. However, it's important to assess whether ACID compliance is necessary for your scenarios. In many graph computing situations, ACID is not essential, and users often forgo it to enhance performance and save time.

10

Conformance to the GQL Standard

Conformance to the GQL standard pertains to how closely a **graph database management system (GDBMS)** adheres to the features, syntax, and semantics defined by the official specification, which is maintained by the **International Organization for Standardization (ISO)** and is formally designated as ISO/IEC 39075.

Ensuring GQL conformance is critical for fostering compatibility and portability across graph database platforms. When applications are built using standardized GQL, they can be easily migrated between different compliant systems, allowing developers and analysts to design graph structures and execute queries with a consistent experience.

Given its significance, most database vendors explicitly document their level of GQL conformance, stating which standard features are fully supported, partially supported, or extended beyond the specification.

This chapter covers the following topics:

- Required capabilities, which are mandatory features that a conforming GQL implementation must support
- Optional features, which are extensions defined within the standard that vendors may choose to implement

- Implementation-defined elements, which are aspects that require explicit documentation by each GDBMS vendor to specify their behavior

- Implementation-dependent elements, which are features whose behavior is not strictly defined by the standard and may vary across implementations

By understanding these dimensions, users can ensure that their queries are portable across compliant GQL systems while also leveraging additional vendor-specific enhancements where applicable. This knowledge is essential for both developers aiming for broad interoperability and organizations seeking to adopt graph database technology with confidence. Additionally, vendors should provide detailed documentation on their GQL implementations, outlining supported features, extensions, and limitations. This documentation helps developers make informed decisions when choosing and implementing GQL-compliant systems.

To fully benefit from a standard, it is essential to choose technologies that clearly specify their level of conformance. This is particularly important for new standards such as that of GQL, especially in the early stages of compliant releases.

As the publication of this book, only Neo4j and Ultipa have shared information about the conformance of their implementations to the GQL standard. Here's where you can learn more about it:

- *Neo4j*: `https://neo4j.com/docs/cypher-manual/current/appendix/gql-conformance`
- *Ultipa*: `https://www.ultipa.com/document/gql/gql-conformance`

Minimum conformance

To achieve minimum conformance with the GQL standard, a GDBMS must meet the requirements of the data model and mandatory features.

Requirements of the data model

A claim of minimum conformance shall include the following:

1. *Graph type support*: At least one of the following features must be implemented:

    a. Feature GG01, *Graph with an open graph type*

    b. Feature GG02, *Graph with a closed graph type*, and at least one of the following:

        - Feature GG20, *Explicit element type names*

        - Feature GG21, *Explicit element type key label sets*

        - Feature GG22, *Element type key label set inference*

        - Feature GG23, *Optional element type key label sets*

2. ***Unicode Compliance***: A claim of conformance to a specific version of The Unicode® Standard and the synchronous versions of Unicode Technical Standard #10, Unicode Standard Annex #15, and Unicode Standard Annex #31. The claimed version of The Unicode Standard shall not be less than 13.0.0.

A claim of conformance to the set of all value types that are supported as the types of property values. A conforming GQL implementation must support a specified set of property value types, including at least the following:

a. The character string type specified by `STRING` or `VARCHAR`

b. The Boolean type specified by `BOOLEAN` or `BOOL`

c. The signed regular integer type specified by `SIGNED INTEGER`, `INTEGER`, or `INT`

d. The approximate numeric type specified by `FLOAT`

Let's review the definitions of closed and open graphs.

A graph that has a constraining graph type is said to be **closed** (also known as **schema-full**). A closed graph cannot contain nodes and edges that are instances of node types and edge types, respectively, that are not specified in the graph's constraining graph type. A graph that does not have a constraining graph type is said to be **open** (also known as **schemaless**). An open graph does not restrict the types of nodes and edges it can contain.

Here is a graph creation example to further explain the aforementioned features (GG20, GG21, GG22, and GG23) related to a closed graph type. Note that this example cannot be executed successfully in the GQL Playground, because, so far, it only conforms to Features GG20 and GG23:

```
GQL:
CREATE GRAPH myGraph {
    NODE TYPE Person (:Employee&Shareholder {name string}),
    NODE TYPE (:Company IMPLIES {name string}),
    EDGE TYPE ()-[:WorksIn {startOn datetime}]->(),
    EDGE TYPE ()-[IMPLIES :Invests {amount int64}]->()
}
```

With Feature GG20, *Explicit element type names*, you can specify the node or edge type names. The graph has a node type named `Person`; other node and edge types are unnamed.

Features GG21, GG22, and GG23 are related to the key label set, the implied label set, and the label set of node and edge types. Let's understand these sets:

- *Key label set*:

    a. If a node or edge type has the **key label set** definition, its key label set is the labels specified by the definition. The second node type has the key label set definition of :Company IMPLIES, and its key label set contains :Company. The second edge type has the key label set definition of IMPLIES, and its key label set is empty.

    b. If a node or edge type has an explicit type name, it cannot contain the key label set definition. In this case, its key label set is specified by the type name. The key label set of the Person node type contains :Person.

    c. Otherwise, the key label set is omitted. This is the case for the first edge type.

- *Implied label set*: If a node or edge type has the implied content, its implied label set is the labels involved in it:

    a. The Person node type has the implied content of :Employee&Shareholder {name string}, and its implied label set contains :Employee and :Shareholder

    b. The second node type has the implied content of {name string}, and its implied label set is empty

    c. The first edge type has the implied content of :WorksIn {startOn datetime}, and its implied label set is empty

    d. The second edge type has the implied content of :Invests {amount int64}, and its implied label set contains :Invest

- *Label set*: The label set of a node or edge type is the union of its key label set and the implied label set.

You can refer to the following table to see the key label set, implied label set, and label set of the node and edge types defined in the example:

Type	Node/Edge Type Name	Key Label Set	Implied Label Set	Label Set

NODE	Person	`:Person`	`:Employee,`
			`:Shareholder`
				`:Person,`
				`:Employee,`
				`:Shareholder`

		`:Company`	Empty	`:Company`
EDGE		Omitted	`:WorksIn`	`:WorksIn`
		Empty	`:Invests`	`:Invests`

With Feature GG21, *Explicit element type key label sets*, a node or edge type may contain a key label set. Feature GG22, *Element type key label set inference*, is related to how an effective key label set is inferenced when the key label set is *omitted*:

- If this feature is supported, the effective key label set for a node or edge type consists of all labels in its implied label set, excluding those found in the label sets of any other node or edge types

- Without this feature, the effective key label set of a node type is the same as the label set of that node type

With Feature GG23, *Optional element type key label sets*, the key label set of a node or edge type can be omitted.

Mandatory features

All syntax and semantics not explicitly identified as belonging to an optional feature are considered **mandatory features**. Since the GQL standard does not provide an explicit list of mandatory features, this section explores how to identify and interpret the mandatory features embedded within the standard.

In a typical subclause of the GQL standard, such as subclause *14.9*, *<order by and page statement>*, which defines the *<order by and page statement>* syntax element, the *Syntax Rules* and *General Rules* sections specify the requirements for this element. All such requirements are considered mandatory, unless selected and relaxed in the *Conformance Rules* section. Each conformance rule begins with the phrase: *Without Feature <Feature ID>, <Feature Name>, ...*

Subclause 14.9 includes the following conformance rules:

1. *"Without Feature GQ12, ORDER BY and page statement: OFFSET clause, in conforming GQL language, an <order by and page statement> shall not contain an <offset clause>."*

2. *"Without Feature GQ13, ORDER BY and page statement: LIMIT clause, in conforming GQL language, an <order by and page statement> shall not contain a <limit clause>."*

These rules designate the OFFSET clause and LIMIT clause contained in the ORDER BY and page statement as optional features, meaning their implementation is not required. However, the other part of the statement, the ORDER BY clause, remains a mandatory feature in GQL.

In some cases, the conformance rules imply mandatory features. An example can be found in the conformance rules of subclause *21.3, <token>, <separator>, and <identifier>*:

"Without Feature GB01, Long identifiers, in conforming GQL language, the maximum length in characters of the representative form of a <non-delimited identifier> or a <delimited identifier> shall be 2⁷ – 1 = 127."

This optional feature (GB01) corresponds to the syntax rule *(5).b* of subclause *21.3*, which states that the maximum length in characters of the representative form of a non-delimited identifier or a delimited identifier shall be $2^{14} - 1 = 16{,}383$. Consequently, the presence of Feature GB01 implies that the maximum supported length of characters in identifiers in a conforming GQL implementation should be no less than 127.

One way for the graph database vendors to declare their conformance to mandatory features is by referencing the substantial subclauses of the GQL standard and indicating whether each is fully or partially supported. Since the GQL standard does not explicitly list mandatory features, vendors must carefully analyze the standard's *Syntax Rules*, *General Rules*, and *Conformance Rules* sections to determine which aspects are essential for compliance.

For examples of how vendors document their conformance to mandatory GQL features, refer to Neo4j and Ultipa:

- *Neo4j*: https://neo4j.com/docs/cypher-manual/current/appendix/gql-conformance/supported-mandatory/

- *Ultipa*: https://www.ultipa.com/document/gql/gql-conformance

Optional features

As discussed in the mandatory features of GQL, most optional features are explicitly specified by the *Conformance Rules* sections in subclauses. In the meantime, a few are specified implicitly elsewhere in the standard. For example, subclause *4.16.8, Immaterial value types: null type and empty type*, includes the following statements:

"The immaterial value types are only provided by GQL-implementations that support the Feature GV70, "Immaterial value types". In such GQL-implementations, the null type provides a portable most specific value type for various values (e.g., certain constructed values such as empty list values or the null value)."

This passage designates the immaterial value types, including null types and empty types, as optional rather than mandatory.

In the ISO/IEC 39075:2024 version of the GQL standard, every optional feature is clearly referenced by a feature ID (formatted as "G" followed by three digits) and a feature name. You can find the full list of 228 optional features in Ultipa GQL conformance in *Chapter 14, Glossary and Resources*.

> Some optional features are independent. If a GQL implementation claims to support a feature, it must also support all features it implies. Example dependencies are Feature GA04, *Universal comparison implies*, Feature GA09, *Comparison of paths*. Feature GV46, *Closed record types implies*, and Feature GV45, *Record types*.

Implementing optional features in a GQL-compliant graph database requires a strategic approach that balances user expectations and system capabilities. Vendors should prioritize features that enhance their product's usability and competitiveness.

High-demand optional features include the following:

- Feature G017, *All shortest path search*, supports efficient shortest path discovery. It's a fundamental operation in graph analytics.
- Feature GQ20, *Advanced linear composition with NEXT*, enables the composition of multiple linear query statements, which is necessary for users to achieve more comprehensive querying purposes in a single GQL query.

Although these features are optional in the GQL standard, they address critical use cases and should be prioritized by vendors aiming to align with market needs and outperform competitors.

Some optional features require significant engineering effort and may introduce performance trade-offs. A thorough cost-benefit analysis is essential before determining whether an optional feature is worth implementing.

For example, Feature GP01, *Inline procedure*, allows users to invoke procedural logic within queries, enabling modular and reusable computations in queries. However, achieving efficient support for inline procedures is not trivial but requires careful consideration of query optimization, transaction management, and compatibility handling. Vendors should evaluate whether their query execution engine can efficiently handle procedural execution before committing to this feature.

If an optional feature conflicts with the existing system architecture, vendors may choose not to implement it. An example is Feature GQ01, *USE graph clause*, which makes querying multiple graphs in a single GQL query possible. However, some vendors opt not to offer it, as supporting it would lead to great changes to the system's core design. For vendors, such decisions must weigh the technical feasibility against the potential value it adds to users.

While optional features allow vendors to differentiate their graph database offerings, selecting which ones to implement is important. By prioritizing user needs, performance considerations, and system compatibility, vendors can make informed decisions.

Implementation-defined elements

The term *implementation-defined* refers to characteristics that may vary across different GQL implementations but must be explicitly documented by each vendor. These elements provide necessary flexibility while ensuring transparency, clarity for users, and interoperability across different platforms.

The GQL standard specifies 172 implementation-defined features, each assigned a five-character ID and a descriptive name. You can view them all in *Chapter 14, Glossary and Resources*.

Next, we will highlight some representative examples.

Most implementation-defined elements are related to the value types and the various handling of values, such as computation, ordering, approximation, comparison, and so on:

1. IA011, *Whether rounding or truncating is used on division with an approximate mathematical result*:

    ```
    GQL:
    RETURN 5/3
    ```

In the GQL Playground, this query returns 1.66666666666667, meaning that rounding is used on division with an approximate mathematical result. If truncating is used, it will return 1.66666666666666 instead.

2. ISO01, *The implicit ordering of NULLs*:

```
GQL:
MATCH (n:Person)
ORDER BY n.name DESC
RETURN n.name
```

This query specifies the results ordered by n.name in descending order but lacks the explicit null ordering specification. In the GQL Playground, the NULL FIRST implicit null ordering is applied when ordering in the DESC order, and NULL LAST is applied when ordering in the ASC order. Therefore, if any n.name is null in the returns, it appears at the top.

Some are related to the type of returns for statements, expressions, specifications, and functions:

1. ID076, *The declared type of results of the ELEMENT_ID function*:

```
GQL:
MATCH (n:User)
RETURN ELEMENT_ID(n)
```

The ELEMENT_ID function generates unique identifiers for nodes and edges. In the GQL Playground, this function returns the _uuid values of nodes and edges, which are of the UINT64 type.

The graph pattern matching also has implementation-defined elements:

1. ID086, *The default graph pattern match mode*:

```
GQL:
MATCH
    p1 = ({_id: "Comp1"})->({_id: "comp2"}),
    p2 = ({_id: "Comp1"})->()
RETURN p1, p2
```

The graph pattern does not explicitly specify a match mode; in this case, the default match mode is implicitly applied. In the GQL Playground, the default match mode is designated as `DIFFERENT EDGES`. Thus, the preceding query is equivalent to the following:

```
GQL:
MATCH DIFFERENT EDGES
    p1 = ({_id: "Comp1"})->({_id: "comp2"}),
    p2 = ({_id: "Comp1"})->()
RETURN p1, p2
```

2. IL018, *The maximum value of the upper bound of a general qualifier:*

```
GQL:
MATCH p = ({_id: "U8561"})->{2,5}(n)
RETURN p
```

Both the lower bound and upper bound in a quantifier should be set as an unsigned integer. This query matches a path containing quantified edges with a lower bound of 2 and an upper bound of 5. In the GQL Playground, the upper bound can be set to a positive infinite integer.

There are implementation-defined elements regarding transactions and sessions:

1. IW004, *The alternative mechanism for starting and terminating transactions*

2. ID049, *The default session parameters*

Implementation-dependent elements

The term *implementation-dependent* is used to identify characteristics that may differ between GQL implementations and are not strictly defined by the standard. Implementation-dependent elements allow for variations across vendors and even variations between executions with the same implementation. Since their behavior is not mandated by the GQL standard, vendors are not required to document them, making them inherently unpredictable for users.

A common example of an implementation-dependent element is the order of results in a query without the `ORDER BY` clause. The database is not required to explain how it determines the order, and the behavior may change across versions or depend on factors such as indexing.

Implementation-dependent elements introduce flexibility in areas where strict standardization is impractical or unnecessary. This allows vendors to optimize their systems based on performance, scalability, or architectural considerations while maintaining overall GQL compliance.

The GQL standard specifies 20 implementation-dependent features, each assigned a 5-character ID and a descriptive name. You can view them all in *Chapter 14, Glossary and Resources*. Next, we will discuss one example: UA005, *Which path bindings are retained in an any paths search if the number of candidates exceeds the required number*.

The following query evaluates a selective path pattern with the path search prefix ANY 10:

```
GQL:
MATCH p = ANY 10 ({_id: "U8561"})-[]->(v{_id: "U2023"})
RETURN p
```

If exactly 10 or fewer than 10 paths exist from U8561 to U8561, the entire path bindings will be returned. Otherwise, it's implementation-dependent (UA005) which path bindings are retained if the number of candidates exceeds the required number. The GQL Playground retained the 10 paths that are first returned.

Future of GQL conformance

As an emerging standard, GQL continues to evolve, with new features, refinements, and best practices shaping its trajectory. As more vendors adopt GQL, real-world usage patterns will also influence the standard, leading to improvements driven by practical needs.

Future versions of the GQL standard ISO/IEC 39075 may introduce changes that impact conformance. Syntax and semantics may be adjusted, some current optional features could become mandatory, new optional features may be introduced, and certain features may be deprecated. These changes could affect both query behavior and implementation requirements.

To maintain compliance and take advantage of advancements, vendors should stay informed about GQL's development roadmap, participate in standardization discussions, and proactively update their implementations.

Summary

This chapter explored GQL conformance and the key requirements for vendors to achieve GQL compliance. Before adopting a graph database, users should evaluate its GQL conformance to ensure compatibility, portability, and alignment with industry standards. Verifying conformance helps protect investments and ensures seamless integration with other GQL-compliant systems.

Get This Book's PDF Version and Exclusive Extras

UNLOCK NOW

Scan the QR code (or go to packtpub.com/unlock). Search for this book by name, confirm the edition, and then follow the steps on the page.

Note: Keep your invoice handy. Purchases made directly from Packt don't require an invoice.

11

Beyond GQL

You have nearly covered all the features outlined in the GQL standard. As the second database query language standard since SQL's debut in 1987, GQL addresses the challenges posed by various graph database languages. It introduces innovative and comprehensive syntax for ease of use, enhancing both functionality and user experience. Although many useful ideas did not make it into the initial version, there is plenty of room for future enhancements in a GQL sequel.

As mentioned in *Chapter 10*, *Conformance to the GQL standard*, GQL allows implementers to tailor their support of some features based on product characteristics.

To boost usability in real-world applications, you will move beyond the standard and explore additional syntax with the GQL style provided by Ultipa Graph Database.

In this chapter, we will explore the extensions of GQL provided by Ultipa Graph to learn about the following:

- Enhancing query performance
- Property constraints
- Access controls
- Other operations

Technical requirements

All the queries are located in the repository at https://github.com/PacktPublishing/Getting-Started-with-the-Graph-Query-Language-GQL/tree/main/Ch11.

Graph operations

Managing a graph database often requires a variety of operations to fulfill specific needs. GQL covers essential actions, such as creating and dropping graphs. Apart from that, graph database vendors may offer further commands to modify graphs, display graph lists, and implement advanced options when working with graphs.

In this section, we'll explore the capabilities beyond the basic GQL graph statements using GQL Playground, powered by Ultipa Graph.

Showing the list of graphs

To perform further operations, users may need to view the complete list of graphs stored in the database. This can be done by executing the following query in GQL Playground:

```
GQL:
SHOW GRAPH
```

Alternatively, execute the following:

```
GQL:
SHOW GRAPHS
```

These queries return a list of graphs containing the graph ID, name, number of nodes and edges, description, and current status.

Options for creating a graph

Standard GQL provides the CREATE GRAPH statement to define a graph with specific node and edge types.

In Ultipa, you can create a graph along with additional options, including constraints, distributed storage configuration, and comments.

Consider the following query:

```
GQL:
CREATE GRAPH userBehaviors {
    NODE Person (:Person {name string, age int32}),
    EDGE Follows ()-[:Follows]->()
}
```

```
EDGE KEY id string
ON SHARDS [1]
PARTITION BY CRC32
COMMENT 'a graph stores user behavior'
```

This query creates a graph named userBehaviors with a descriptive comment. It configures the graph to be stored on shard 1 and partitions it with the CRC32 hash algorithm. The EDGE KEY clause sets the id property as a unique key for all edges. This option automatically creates the id property with the string type for each edge.

> Shards are horizontal partitions stored across multiple servers in distributed databases. A user can set multiple shards to store a single graph. GQL Playground provides one shard for each user.

The ON SHARDS, PARTITION BY, and COMMENT clauses are optional for standard compliance.

If these options are not specified, the following will occur:

- The system will automatically select all the shards
- CRC32 will be used as the default partition algorithm
- Comments will be set to empty

Altering a graph

During development, users may need to modify the name or comments of a graph—for example, renaming the graph from TransactionGraph to TransactionGraph2024 or adding a comment such as the backup transaction graph for 2024.

Ultipa GQL offers the ALTER GRAPH statement to rename and set comments on an existing graph.

Renaming a graph

To rename a graph, use the ALTER GRAPH statement, as follows:

```
GQL:
ALTER GRAPH userBehaviors RENAME TO SocialNetwork
```

This query renames the graph from userBehaviors to SocialNetwork.

> Graph names must adhere to the following rules:
>
> - Begin with a letter
> - Contain 2 to 127 characters
> - Allow the following characters:
> - a-z, A-Z, 0-9, and underscore

Updating comments on a graph

To update comments on a graph, use the following:

```GQL
ALTER-GRAPH SocialNetwork COMMENT 'a social network.'
```

Ultipa GQL also allows adding comments to a node type, an edge type, or properties. You will explore these syntaxes later in this chapter.

Next, you will learn how to modify node and edge types.

Node and edge schema operations

In Ultipa GQL, node and edge types are referred to as node and edge schemas. Thus, we have GQL-Schema, Node-Schema, and Edge-Schema.

In this section, you will learn how to list and modify these schemas and their properties.

> For consistency and better practice, we will use the terms *node schema* and *edge schema* instead of *node type* and *edge type* in this chapter.

Showing node and edge schemas

The syntax to show schemas is as follows:

```
SHOW { NODE | EDGE } SCHEMA
```

To list all node schemas in the graph, you can run the following query:

```GQL
SHOW NODE SCHEMA
```

This query returns a list of node schemas, including the following:

- Schema name
- Status
- Description
- Properties

The following is a list of node schemas from the graph named myGraph, which can be created using the example queries provided in GQL Playground.

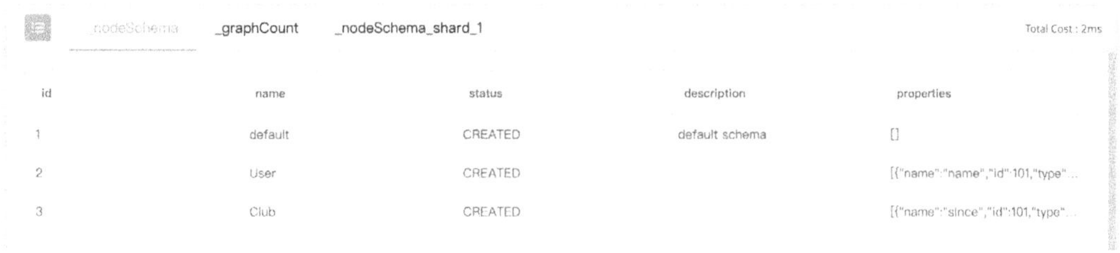

id	name	status	description	properties
1	default	CREATED	default schema	[]
2	User	CREATED		[{"name":"name","id":101,"type"...
3	Club	CREATED		[{"name":"since","id":101,"type"...

_nodeSchema   _graphCount   _nodeSchema_shard_1   Total Cost : 2ms

Figure 11.1: Node schema list

Additionally, the query returns two other special records:

- _graphCount
- _nodeScema_shard_1

You can click on them and explore these records.

For example, this is what the _graphCount record looks like:

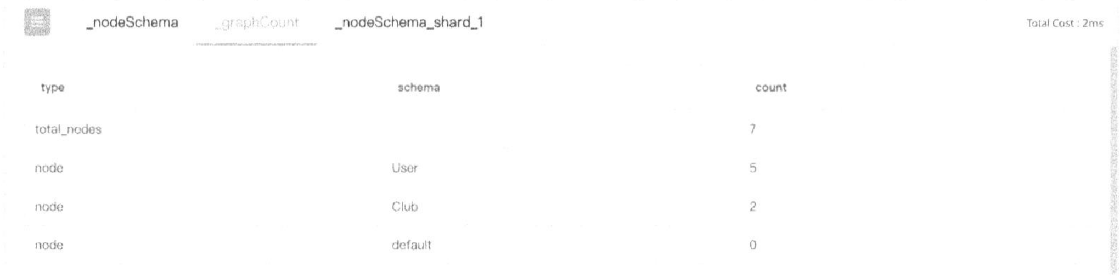

_nodeSchema   _graphCount   _nodeSchema_shard_1   Total Cost : 2ms

type	schema	count
total_nodes		7
node	User	5
node	Club	2
node	default	0

Figure 11.2: Statistics of nodes

It provides the count of nodes for each schema, which is useful for understanding the overall structure and distribution of your graph.

The following query is used to list the edge schema for a better understanding of the graph:

```GQL
GQL:
SHOW EDGE SCHEMA
```

This query returns a list of edge schemas, as well as graph count records:

type	schema	from_schema	to_schema	count
total_edges				7
edge	Follows	User	User	4
edge	Joins	User	Club	3

_edgeSchema   _graphCount   _edgeSchema_shard_1   Total Cost : 2ms

Figure 11.3: Statistics of edges

The _graphCount record includes statistical data such as the following:

- Total number of edges: Seven
- Edge types:
  - Four follow edges from User to User
  - Three join edges from User to Club

These statistics provide a quick overview of the graph structure, helping you understand the relationships and interactions between entities.

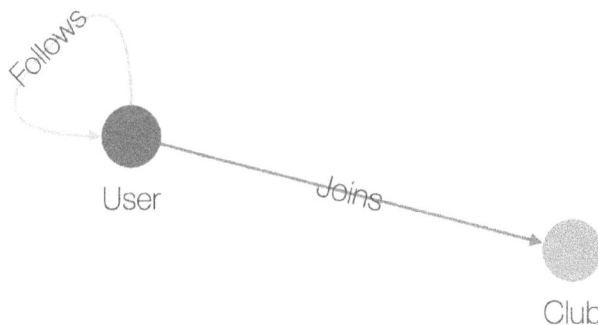

Figure 11.4: Graph overview

You may notice that there is a default schema. Ultipa automatically creates default schemas for both nodes and edges. These serve as foundational structures and are present in every graph by default.

Modifying the node or edge schema

The graph structure often evolves over time, and it needs to be modified without recreating the graph. Ultipa GQL provides extended statements to add, drop, and modify node and edge schemas within an existing graph.

Adding a new schema

To add a new Node or Edge schema, use the ALTER statement.

The syntax is as follows:

```
[ALTER [PROPERTY] GRAPH <graph name>]
ADD {NODE | EDGE} <schema name> <specifications>
```

For example, to add new node schemas, User and Product, to the SocialNetwork graph, do the following:

```
GQL:
ALTER GRAPH SocialNetwork
ADD NODE {
    User ({name string, age int32}),
    Product ({name string, price float})
}
```

This query adds two new node schemas, User and Product.

Dropping a schema

To remove unused schemas, use the following syntax:

```
[ALTER [PROPERTY] GRAPH <graph name>]
DROP {NODE | EDGE} <schema names>
```

For example, to drop the User and Product node schemas from the SocialNetwork graph, use the following:

```
GQL:
ALTER GRAPH SocialNetwork DROP NODE User, Product
```

This query deletes the User and Product node schemas along with all nodes associated with them. Since the nodes are removed, edges connected to these nodes are also automatically deleted.

> When a graph is created using a graph type—via the TYPED keyword or the : : operator—Ultipa treats the new graph as an instance of that graph type.
>
> This means the following:
>
> - The new graph inherits all structural definitions (schemas, relationships, etc.) from the graph type
> - Any modifications made to the instance graph do not affect the original graph type
> - This separation allows users to experiment or customize instance graphs without altering the foundational structure defined by the graph type

Renaming a schema and updating its comment

You can modify the names and comments of node and edge schemas.

The syntax to rename a node and edge schema is as follows:

```
ALTER {NODE | EDGE} <name> RENAME TO <new_name>
```

For example, to rename the Person node schema, do the following:

```
GQL:
ALTER NODE Person RENAME TO User
```

This query renames the node schema from Person to User.

You can update the comment of a node or edge type by following this syntax:

```
ALTER {NODE | EDGE} <name> COMMENT '<comment>'
```

For example, to update the comment of the User node schema, use the following:

```
GQL:
ALTER NODE User COMMENT 'user details'
```

Property operations

Just like node and edge schemas, node and edge properties in Ultipa GQL can be listed, modified, and removed. This flexibility allows users to maintain and evolve the graph structure dynamically, ensuring that property definitions stay aligned with the graph's data model and analytical needs.

Listing properties

Ultipa GQL allows users to display properties for all node and edge schemas, or just for a specific one. This is useful for inspecting the structure and metadata associated with graph elements.

The following is the syntax for listing properties:

```
SHOW { NODE | EDGE } [<schema name>] PROPERTY
```

For example, to show all node properties, use the following:

```
GQL:
SHOW NODE PROPERTY
```

This query shows a list of properties, including the following:

- Property name
- Property type
- Schema name
- Current privileges, such as read and write

Load to Engine (LTE) enables properties to be filtered in a more efficient way during graph traversals.

name	type	lte	read	write	. schema
_id	string	false	1	1	default
_id	string	false	1	1	User
age	int32	false	1	1	User
name	string	false	1	1	User

Figure 11.5: Node property list

For LTE operations, you can visit `https://www.ultipa.com/docs/uql/lte` for details.

If you want to check the properties of just the User node schema, use the following:

```
GQL:
SHOW NODE User PROPERTY
```

This query returns a list of properties from just the User node:

name	type	lte	read	write	schema
_id	string	false	1	1	User
age	int32	false	1	1	User
name	string	false	1	1	User

Figure 11.6: User node property list

The SHOW PROPERTY statements are very useful. In the following section, we will look at statements for verifying the changes made to the graph after adding and removing properties.

Adding and dropping a property

To add or remove properties for nodes and edges, use the following syntax:

```
ALTER {NODE | EDGE} { <schema name> | * }
{ ADD PROPERTY <property> | DROP <property name> }
```

For example, to add properties to the User node, do the following:

```
GQL:
ALTER NODE User ADD PROPERTY {gender string, email string}
```

This query adds two properties to the User node.

> These two properties will be added to all existing User nodes with a default NULL value.

To remove properties from the User node, do the following:

```
GQL:
ALTER NODE User DROP PROPERTY gender, email
```

This query removes the two properties from all existing User nodes.

Sometimes, different node schemas in a graph may have properties with the same name, such as a rank property calculated by a graph algorithm. You can add or remove properties for all schemas with a single query.

For instance, to add a rank property to all node schemas, use the following:

```
GQL:
ALTER NODE * ADD PROPERTY {rank float}
```

This query adds a rank property to all node schemas in the current graph.

The property can be removed from all node schemas with a single query as well.

To remove the property from all schemas, use the following:

```
GQL:
ALTER NODE * DROP PROPERTY rank
```

This query removes the rank property from all node schemas.

Renaming a property

Properties can be renamed.

The following is the syntax to do so:

```
ALTER { NODE | EDGE } <schema name>
RENAME PROPERTY <name> TO <new name>
```

For example, to rename a property, use the following:

```
GQL:
ALTER NODE User RENAME PROPERTY name TO username
```

This query renames the name property to username in the User node schema. It will also affect all existing User nodes.

You explored how to create graphs with additional options and modify the structure of an existing graph. In the next section, you will explore how to set constraints on properties to ensure they are NOT NULL or UNIQUE or designated as an edge key.

Constraining properties

To ensure data quality in graph databases, constraints are often employed. Ultipa GQL provides capabilities to manage constraints for node or edge properties.

Creating constraints

Constraints can be created when defining a new graph or added to an existing graph.

The syntax for adding constraints is as follows:

```
ALTER {NODE | EDGE} <name | *> ADD CONSTRAINT [IF NOT EXISTS] <constraint
name>
{UNIQUE | NOT NULL | EDGE KEY} (<property list>)
[OPTIONS <a key value record>]
```

Ultipa currently supports three types of constraints:

Type	Supported Property	Support Multi-Properties
UNIQUE	Node or edge property	Yes
NOT NULL	Node or edge property	No
EDGE KEY	Edge property	Yes

Table 11.1: Overview of Constraint Types Supported in Ultipa GQL

The following table summarizes the types of constraints currently supported in Ultipa, along with their applicable properties and whether they support multi-properties:

- UNIQUE ensures that property values in the target node schema are non-duplicative
- NOT NULL ensures that property values are NOT NULL
- EDGE KEY specifies the primary key for all edges within a graph

For example, to add constraints to the current graph, use the following:

```
GQL:
ALTER NODE User ADD CONSTRAINT NOT NULL ON username
```

This query adds a NOT NULL constraint to the username property of the User node. As you might expect, there is a way to retrieve the list of all constraints, on both node and edge schemas:

```
GQL:
SHOW NODE CONSTRAINT
```

The preceding query returns the list of node constraints.

```
GQL:
SHOW EDGE CONSTRAINT
```

The preceding query returns the list of edge constraints.

Deleting constraints

Constraints can be deleted to reduce performance costs.

The syntax is as follows:

```
ALTER {NODE | EDGE} <schema name>
DROP CONSTRAINT [IF EXISTS] <constraint name>
```

For example, to drop a constraint, use the following:

```
GQL:
ALTER NODE User DROP CONSTRAINT NOT NULL ON username
```

This query removes the NOT NULL constraint.

Managing EDGE KEY

EDGE KEY is a graph-level constraint that designates the primary key for edges across all edge schemas. A graph can only have one EDGE KEY constraint.

This constraint is useful for efficiently overwriting edges and serves as a primary index for all edges.

For example, to create an EDGE KEY constraint for the current graph, use the following:

```
GQL:
ALTER EDGE * ADD CONSTRAINT EDGE KEY id string
```

This query adds an EDGE KEY constraint based on the id property.

> The id properties associated with each edge schema in the graph must be of the same type.

EDGE KEY can be utilized during the batch insertion of edges, allowing the insertion mode to overwrite existing edges.

Removing EDGE KEY can improve the performance when inserting edges by avoiding checking for edge keys. You can remove EDGE KEY with the following query:

```
GQL:
ALTER EDGE * DROP CONSTRAINT EDGE KEY
```

This query removes EDGE KEY from the current graph.

Improving query performance

Most databases offer various indexing systems to enhance query performance. Ultipa GQL can be used to manage indexes within a graph.

Additionally, Ultipa supports **high-density computing** (**HDC**) graphs. More details will be provided later in this section.

Managing the property index

Property indexes can significantly improve the query performance.

Users can create and drop indexes. Ultipa supports individual, compound, full-text, and vector indexes.

Creating an index

To create an index, use the following syntax:

```
CREATE {INDEX | FULLTEXT} <index name> ON {NODE | EDGE} <node/edge type
name> ( <property names> )
```

The following is an example:

```
GQL:
CREATE INDEX name ON NODE User ( username(10) )
```

This query creates an index named name using the username property of User nodes, indexing the first 10 bytes of username values. This index could speed up the searching performance when filtering with the username property.

The length of indexing bytes can be omitted:

```
GQL:
CREATE INDEX name ON NODE User ( username )
```

This query creates the name index, for the username property. As the data type of this property is string and the length is not specified in the index definition, the system will take a maximum of 1,024 bytes by default.

You can also create a compound index with multiple properties, which helps improve performance when filtering by multiple properties.

To create a compound index using username and age, use the following:

```
GQL:
CREATE INDEX nameWithAge ON NODE User ( username, age )
```

This query creates a compound index with two properties.

Ultipa offers a built-in full-text index for searching large volumes of text data, such as articles, documents, or descriptions.

To create a full-text index for the string-type username property, use the following:

```
GQL:
CREATE FULLTEXT name ON NODE User ( username )
```

This query creates a full-text index on username of User nodes.

You can find more details by visiting https://ultipa.com/docs/gql/full-text-index.

Nowadays, leveraging the power of graph databases and **large language models** (LLMs) can generate exciting and innovative AI solutions. For example, when creating a chat robot to identify key knowledge from a knowledge graph, vector search can help with finding the most relevant nodes based on the questions.

Therefore, Ultipa introduces the vector search capability based on the GQL style, to search embedded entities.

To search nodes by vectors and similarity algorithms, you need to create a vector index.

Here is an example of creating a vector index:

```
GQL:
CREATE VECTOR INDEX factor ON NODE User (embedding) OPTIONS {
    dimensions: 128,
    similarity_function: "COSINE"
}
```

This query creates a vector index on the embedding property of the User node. The embedding property must be a list of float numbers, which forms a vector. The new vector index uses 1,024 dimensions to represent the nodes and employs cosine similarity to search for similar nodes.

You can find more details by visiting https://ultipa.com/docs/gql/vector-index.

Showing the index

You can list all indexes for nodes or edges using the following syntax:

```
SHOW {NODE | EDGE} {INDEX | FULLTEXT | VECTOR INDEX}
```

To display the indexes created in the previous section, use the following:

```
GQL:
SHOW NODE INDEX
```

This query shows all node indexes in the current graph.

> Index creation is an asynchronous process. If the index does not appear, you can use the SHOW JOB statement to check the status of the creation.

To show the full-text indexes, use the following:

```
GQL:
SHOW NODE FULLTEXT
```

The preceding query shows the full-text indexes of nodes.

Dropping an index

Ultipa GQL allows dropping indexes to manage performance costs associated with updating, inserting, or deleting property values.

To avoid unnecessary costs from unused indexes, consider removing them:

```
DROP {NODE | EDGE} {INDEX | FULLTEXT | VECTOR INDEX} <index name>
```

For example, to drop a node index, use the following:

```
GQL:
DROP NODE INDEX name
```

This query drops the node index named name.

In this section, we explored managing the index system to optimize query performance. Ultipa Graph supports advanced graph computing features, such as warming up and in-memory computing engines. Visit https://www.ultipa.com/docs/gql/indexing-and-caching for more information.

Ultipa's HDC graph

Ultipa offers the HDC engine to accelerate complex graph computing tasks.

Within the Ultipa Graph Database cluster, the HDC is also known as the HDC server. These servers provide high-performance elastic computing resources.

The performance of HDC is derived from a unique data structure created by Ultipa that fully leverages multi-threaded CPU capabilities and in-memory data interactions.

Increasing the number of CPUs and memory within an HDC server can enhance its performance.

> Some queries in the following sections may not be executable in GQL Playground due to permission restrictions. Instead, you can try them in Ultipa Cloud.
>
> A GPU is not required for graph computing on an HDC server, but it can be integrated for additional tasks, such as matrix computing and embedding tasks.

HDC graph

An HDC graph is a virtual graph created from data persisted in Ultipa Graph. It is stored and processed on the HDC server. It supports both general and customized graph structures to meet various business needs:

- A **general graph structure** ensures that most queries, including pathfinding, shortest paths, k-hops, and all graph algorithms, can be executed.
- A **customized graph structure** is optimized for specific purposes, potentially offering the highest performance for dedicated algorithms. In practice, customized graph structures can reduce memory and time costs for large graphs containing tens of billions of nodes and edges.

You can choose to use the general or customized graph structure offered by Ultipa.

Managing an HDC graph

Ultipa GQL provides capabilities for the operations of an HDC graph, such as creating, dropping, and querying.

Listing HDC graphs

You can show all the HDC graphs and view details such as the HDC graph name, creation parameters, and status.

For example, to list all HDC graphs, use the following:

```
GQL:
SHOW HDC GRAPHS
```

This query lists all HDC graphs, including detailed information.

Creating an HDC graph

The syntax for creating an HDC graph is as follows:

```
CREATE HDC GRAPH [IF NOT EXISTS] <hdc graph name>
ON "<hdc server name>"
OPTION[S] {<hdc options>}
```

Options for creating an HDC graph include the following:

Option	Example	Description
nodes	* {"*": "*"} {Lang: "*"} {Lang: ["name", "year"]}	Defines the scope of nodes loaded in the HDC graph.
edges	Same as the previous example	Defines the scope of edges loaded in the HDC graph.
query	<GQL>	Defines the scope of nodes and edges loaded in the HDC graph by query. Cannot be used with the nodes and edges options.
direction	undirected / in / out	Specifies whether to load only incoming edges, outgoing edges, or both for each node. The default is undirected.
load_id	TRUE / FALSE	Determines whether to load the _id value of nodes into the HDC graph. The default is TRUE.
update	static / async / sync	Specifies the update strategy, with the static, async, and sync options. The default is static.

Next, you will explore the details of the node and edge scope from the options to create an HDC graph.

Data scope

The following are details of the node and edge scope options:

- "*" loads all nodes or edges with all properties. It is equivalent to
- {"*": "*"}.
- {User: "*"} loads User nodes with all properties.
- {User: ["name", "age"]} loads User nodes with the name and age properties. Multiple node or edge schemas can be set, such as
- {User: ["name", "age"], Product: ["name"]}.

For example, to create an HDC graph, use the following:

```
GQL:
CREATE HDC GRAPH HDCSocialGraph ON "hdc-1"
OPTIONS {
    nodes: {
        User: "*"
    },
    edges: "*"
}
```

This query creates a new HDC graph named HDCSocialGraph on the hdc-1 HDC server. The options ensure that HDCSocialGraph contains data with User nodes and all edges.

Alternatively, you can use this query to create an HDC graph:

```
GQL:
CREATE HDC GRAPH HDCSocialGraph ON "hdc-1"
OPTIONS {
    queries: ["MATCH (source:User)-[edge]->(target:User)
                RETURN source, edge, target"]
}
```

This query creates a similar HDC graph using a GQL query.

> The HDC graph created by the query may not be identical to the one created using the nodes and edges options because the query will not return isolated nodes, that is, nodes without neighbors.

You can configure the update option when creating an HDC graph to control whether the graph can be updated dynamically.

Update option

The update option controls whether the nodes and edges of the HDC graph are updated when the source data changes.

There are three update methods available:

- `static` ensures the data remains unchanged when the sources change. The HDC graph remains static until removed.
- `sync` keeps the data consistent with the source data. Modifying the source graph will simultaneously update the related HDC graphs.
- `async` is similar to `sync`, but the HDC graph updates with a delay after modifying the source data, providing better performance without blocking other requests.

For example, to change the update option, use the following:

```
GQL:
CREATE HDC GRAPH HDCSocialGraph ON "hdc-1"
OPTIONS {
    nodes: {
        User: "*"
    },
    edges: "*",
    update: "sync"
}
```

This query initiates the creation of a dynamic HDC graph using the sync update method. It returns a job ID that can be used to track the creation status.

To check the job status, use the following GQL statement:

```
GQL:
SHOW JOB
```

The `SHOW JOB` statement returns details such as job status, start and end time, the original query, and other relevant metadata.

Dropping an HDC graph

An HDC graph can be removed when no longer needed.

In graph analysis and feature engineering scenarios, graphs are often dropped after completing tasks to free up memory and CPU resources for other tasks.

The syntax to remove an HDC graph is the following:

```
DROP HDC GRAPH <hdc graph name>
```

An example is as follows:

```
GQL:
DROP HDC GRAPH HDCSocialGraph
```

This query drops the `HDCSocialGraph` HDC graph. This operation will not affect the source data.

Querying an HDC graph

To execute an algorithm on an HDC graph, you can call a procedure using GQL.

For example, to run an HDC algorithm, use the following:

```
CALL algo.degree.stream("HDCSocialGraph ", {
    direction: "out",
    order: "desc",
    limit: 10
}) YIELD topDegree
MATCH (n WHERE n._uuid = topDegree._uuid)
RETURN n, topDegree
```

This query executes the degree centrality algorithm on the `HDCSocialGraph` HDC graph and returns the top 10 records with the highest degrees. The details of nodes are then retrieved using a `MATCH` statement.

For more information about the degree algorithm, you can visit

`https://www.ultipa.com/docs/graph-analytics-algorithms/degree-centrality`.

You can also execute the **Ultipa Query Language** (**UQL**) on an HDC graph. However, this book does not cover UQL. If you are interested in it, you can visit

`https://www.ultipa.com/docs/uql`.

Next, you will explore access controls with Ultipa's GQL.

Access controls

In a graph database, security is paramount for production environments. Access control is a critical aspect of this security, ensuring that only authorized users can access or manipulate data. Effective access control mechanisms help protect sensitive information, maintain data integrity, and comply with regulatory requirements. Ultipa GQL enhances security by providing robust access control features. It allows administrators to define fine-grained privileges for different roles, ensuring that users have the appropriate level of access to perform their tasks. With Ultipa GQL, you can manage graph, system, and property privileges, making it easier to enforce security policies and protect your data.

User management

The user system forms the foundation of access control mechanisms. Ultipa's GQL provides capabilities to create, modify, and delete users, ensuring effective management of user access and permissions.

Listing users

To list all users, you can use the following query:

```
GQL:
SHOW USERS
```

The query lists all the users in the graph database system.

Creating users

Users can be created with a password.

The syntax to create a user is as follows:

```
CREATE USER <username> WITH PASSWORD '<password>'
```

For example, to create the user user001, use the following:

```
GQL:
CREATE USER user001 WITH PASSWORD '@passwor6'
```

This query creates a new user with the username user001 and sets the password to @passwor6.

Deleting users

Users can be deleted when they are no longer needed.

The syntax to delete a user is as follows:

```
DROP USER <username>
```

Take the following example:

```
GQL:
DROP USER user001
```

This query deletes the user user001.

Updating users

Usernames and passwords can be modified using the ALTER statement.

The syntax to rename a user is as follows:

```
ALTER USER <username> RENAME TO <new name>
```

For example, to update a username, do the following:

```
GQL:
ALTER USER user001 RENAME TO user1
```

This query renames user001 to user1.

The syntax to reset a password is the following:

```
ALTER USER <username> SET PASSWORD '<new password>'
```

The following is an example:

```
GQL:
ALTER USER user1 SET PASSWORD 'New@Passwor5'
```

This query sets a new password for user1.

Once a user is created, you can manage their privileges.

Granting and revoking privileges

Privileges, such as the ability to create or drop graphs, can be granted to and revoked from a user. By using the granting and revoking operations, you can customize the list of accessible options for each user and update them according to your needs.

Understanding the privilege system

In Ultipa Graph, the privilege system is organized into three levels with different scopes:

- **System level**: Privileges independent of specific graphs, such as managing users, creating graphs, and configuring systems
- **Graph level**: Privileges related to specific graphs, such as creating node or edge schemas and reading graph status
- **Property level**: Controls the read and write privileges for specific node or edge schemas and their properties

Next, let's learn how to manage privileges.

Managing privileges

To assign privileges to a user, Ultipa GQL provides GRANT and REVOKE statements.

Here's how to manage privileges at each level.

Managing system privileges

To grant system-level privileges, do the following:

```
GQL:
GRANT ['CREATE_USER', 'DROP_USER'] TO user1
```

This query grants two system-level privileges to user1.

To grant all system privileges to a user, use the following:

```
GQL:
GRANT * TO user1
```

To revoke privileges, replace GRANT with REVOKE:

```
GQL:
REVOKE ['CREATE_USER', 'DROP_USER'] FROM user1
```

This query revokes two privileges from user1.

> For more information on system-level privileges, go to `https://www.ultipa.com/docs/gql/privilege#System-Privileges`.

Managing graph privileges

Graph privileges can also be granted and revoked.

To grant graph privileges, use the following:

```
GQL:
GRANT ['INSERT', 'DELETE'] ON SocialNetwork TO user1
```

This query grants two privileges to user1 for the SocialNetwork graph.

To grant all privileges on a graph, use the following:

```
GQL:
GRANT * ON SocialNetwork TO user1
```

This query grants all privileges to user1 for the SocialNetwork graph.

To grant all graph-level privileges on all graphs, use the following:

```
GQL:
GRANT * ON * TO user1
```

This query grants all privileges on all graphs to user1. The first asterisk (*) denotes all available privileges, while the second asterisk represents all graphs.

If you want to revoke all privileges from the SocialNetwork graph, use the following:

```
GQL:
REVOKE * ON SocialNetwork FROM user1
```

This query revokes all privileges on the SocialNetwork graph from user1.

Managing property privileges

Ultipa GQL supports the management of privileges for node and edge schemas, including both READ and WRITE access controls.

For example, to grant the READ privilege, use the following:

```
GQL:
GRANT ['READ'] ON NODE User(name, age) TO user1
```

This query grants READ privilege to user1 on the name and age properties of the User node schema.

To grant all property privileges on User nodes, use the following:

```
GQL:
GRANT * ON NODE User * TO user1
```

This query grants READ and WRITE privileges on all properties of the User node schema. The first asterisk (*) denotes all privileges, which are READ and WRITE, and the second represents all properties of the User node schema.

To grant all READ and WRITE privileges for all node schemas and properties, use the following:

```
GQL:
GRANT * ON NODE * * TO user1
```

This query grants user1 full READ and WRITE access to all node schemas. The first asterisk (*) denotes all privileges, and the second and third represent all node schemas and properties.

To revoke privileges, replace GRANT with REVOKE:

```
GQL:
REVOKE ['WRITE'] ON NODE User * FROM user1
```

This query revokes WRITE privileges from user1 for all properties of the User node.

Managing a huge number of individual user privileges can be challenging, so creating roles and assigning them to users can simplify the process.

In the next section, you will explore how to apply privileges with roles.

Role management

In Ultipa Graph, roles encapsulate a set of privileges that can be assigned to users.

You can list roles using the following query:

```
GQL:
SHOW ROLES
```

This query lists all the roles created in the current graph database.

Creating and dropping roles

The syntax to create a role is `CREATE ROLE <role name>`.

For example, to create a new role, use the following:

```
GQL:
CREATE ROLE readOnly
```

This query creates a role named `readOnly`, intended for granting only read privileges.

The syntax to drop a role is `DROP ROLE <role name>`.

The following is an example:

```
GQL:
DROP ROLE readOnly
```

This query removes the `readOnly` role, and it will be unassigned from all users who have this role.

Granting and revoking privileges

Managing roles is similar to granting and revoking privileges for users.

For example, to grant system-level privileges, do the following:

```
GQL:
GRANT ['SHOW_GRAPH','SHOW_USER'] TO ROLE readOnly
```

This query grants the `readOnly` role the `SHOW_GRAPH` and `SHOW_USER` system privileges, enabling any user with this role to list graphs and users.

Graph privileges can also be granted to a role:

```
GQL:
GRANT ['READ','SHOW_SCHEMA'] ON SocialNetwork
TO ROLE readOnly
```

This query grants the `readOnly` role the READ and SHOW SCHEMA graph privileges on the `SocialNetwork` graph. These privileges allow users with this role to use the MATCH and SHOW SCHEMA statements to retrieve data.

In Ultipa Graph, privileges can be set at the property level for roles as well.

Take the following example:

```
GQL:
GRANT ['READ', 'WRITE'] ON NODE User *
TO ROLE readOnly
```

This query grants the readOnly role the READ and WRITE privileges on all properties of the User node schema in the current graph. This allows users with this role to read and modify the properties.

All privileges granted to a role can be revoked by replacing the GRANT keyword with REVOKE:

```
GQL:
REVOKE ['WRITE'] ON NODE User * FROM ROLE readOnly
```

This query revokes the WRITE privilege on the User node schema in the current graph from the =readOnly role.

Assigning roles

Roles can be assigned to users and other roles.

To assign a role with the GRANT syntax, use the following:

```
GRANT ROLE <role> TO { <user> | ROLE <role> }
```

For example, to assign roles to a user, use the following:

```
GQL:
GRANT ROLE readOnly TO user1
```

This query assigns the readOnly role to user1.

A role can also be a subordinate role to another role.

First, create a parent role:

```
GQL:
CREATE ROLE admin
```

Add the readOnly role as the subordinate role for admin:

```
GQL:
GRANT ROLE readOnly TO ROLE admin
```

This query assigns the readOnly role as a child role of admin.

Other operations

Ultipa GQL offers other useful statements for interacting with a graph database, such as managing background jobs and truncating data.

Checking background jobs

Graph management and analysis tasks can be time-consuming, so requests can be executed as background jobs.

Tasks such as creating indexes, rebalancing graphs, and running high-cost algorithms can be processed in the background.

Listing job records

To display all jobs, use the following:

```
GQL:
SHOW JOB
```

This query lists all jobs, including those that are finished, in progress, or failed.

Stopping and clearing jobs

Ultipa GQL allows users to stop an in-progress job and delete records of completed jobs.

To stop an in-processing job, use the following:

```
GQL:
STOP JOB 1
```

This query stops the job with ID 1.

To delete a job record if it is completed or failed, use the following:

```
GQL:
DELETE JOB 1
```

This query removes the job record with ID 1.

Deleting an in-progress job is not permitted.

Truncating a graph

Ultipa GQL allows the use of TRUNCATE GRAPH to efficiently remove graph data.

Truncating an entire graph

To truncate all graph data for nodes and edges in a graph, use the following:

```
GQL:
TRUNCATE GRAPH SocialNetwork
```

This query deletes all nodes and edges from the SocialNetwork graph, but retains the definition of node and edge schemas and properties.

Alternatively, you can omit the GRAPH keyword:

```
GQL:
TRUNCATE SocialNetwork
```

Using the TRUNCATE statement will lead to better performance as graph data is removed.

Truncating a node and an edge

Ultipa GQL allows truncating specific nodes and edges.

The syntax to truncate node and edge data is as follows:

```
TRUNCATE { NODE EDGE }
{ <node or edge schema name> | * } ON <graph>
```

For example, to truncate all node data, use the following:

```
GQL:
TRUNCATE NODE * ON SocialNetwork
```

This query deletes all node data from the SocialNetwork graph.

To truncate a specified node schema, use the following:

```
GQL:
TRUNCATE NODE User ON SocialNetwork
```

This query deletes all nodes of the User type.

It is equivalent to the following:

```
GQL:
MATCH (p:User) DETACH DELETE p
```

This query deletes all User nodes. With the Ultipa GQL optimizer, it is recognized as a truncation operation. Note that truncating nodes will also lead to the deletion of their connected edges.

Summary

We explored numerous valuable query extensions for GQL, which are crucial for solving real-world problems and maintaining a graph database. GQL provides a foundational standard for querying graphs, and Ultipa GQL, along with other graph vendors, extends this standard with advanced features to meet industry requirements.

Having learned about GQL and Ultipa GQL extensions, we will now apply this knowledge to tackle a real-world challenge in the next chapter: identifying suspicious transactions in money transfers for anti-fraud analysis.

Get This Book's PDF Version and Exclusive Extras

UNLOCK NOW

Scan the QR code (or go to packtpub.com/unlock). Search for this book by name, confirm the edition, and then follow the steps on the page.

Note: Keep your invoice handy. Purchases made directly from Packt don't require an invoice.

12

A Case Study — Anti-Fraud

In earlier chapters, we explored how to efficiently use GQL for graph and data manipulation. These skills enable us to create meaningful insights, as graph data mirrors real-world scenarios and reflects human-like thinking by naturally connecting information. With a strong grasp of data, graph models, and the robust GQL standard, we are well-equipped to address complex challenges intuitively and effectively.

In this chapter, we will move from theory to practice by tackling a common issue with GQL: identifying suspicious transactions in bank accounts. While a basic understanding of banking concepts such as accounts, cards, and loans is beneficial, rest assured—this book will guide you through the process.

We will cover the following topics:

- Case introduction
- Data preparation
- Establishing the transaction graph
- General query techniques
- Anti-fraud graph model

By the end of the chapter, you will be equipped to implement an anti-fraud solution.

Technical requirements

Before stepping into this chapter, you should have acquired the skills to use GQL and learned how to create graphs and execute queries with it. For further resources, you can visit the repository at `https://github.com/PacktPublishing/Getting-Started-with-the-Graph-Query-Language-GQL/tree/main/Ch12`.

Case introduction

In today's digital age, doing transactions online has become incredibly convenient, with most banks offering online banking services that allow you to manage your money and make payments in just a few seconds. However, this convenience also comes with risks. Not all transactions are legal; some are the result of fraudulent activities, such as identity theft, phishing, and loan fraud. Fraudsters continuously evolve their tactics, exploiting technological advancements and security loopholes to deceive both businesses and consumers and dodge regulations.

Understanding transaction fraud

Transaction fraud encompasses various deceptive activities, including identity theft, phishing, money laundering, and misuse of loan funds. Graph technology can effectively analyze complex transaction patterns to better address money laundering, loan misuse, and other fraud.

Here's a brief overview of money laundering and loan misuse:

Money Laundering	Misuse of Loans
This involves concealing the origins of money acquired through illegal activities, such as drug trafficking or terrorism, to make it appear legitimate. The process generally includes three stages: placement, layering, and integration.	This occurs when loan funds are employed for purposes not specified in the loan agreement. Examples include using business loans for personal expenses or providing false information to secure loans. Misuse of loan funds can result in severe legal repercussions.

Fraudulent transactions can result in substantial financial losses, harm to business reputation, and erosion of customer trust. In 2024, the total losses exceeded 1 trillion dollars globally: `https://www.gasa.org/post/global-state-of-scams-report-2024-1-trillion-stolen-in-12-months-gasa-feedzai`. Graph technology can significantly mitigate the costs associated with fraud.

In this chapter, we will learn how to use GQL to detect loan misuse effectively.

Data preparation

To enhance our understanding of the cash flow graph and demonstrate the implementation method, we will use a small graph consisting of hundreds of nodes and edges to simulate a transactional network.

> In real-world scenarios, analyzing billions of transactions within a single graph may be necessary.

These are the nodes in the transaction network:

Node Schema Name	Properties	Description
Account	id, balance, name	Stores details of a bank account
Loan	id, payment_method, amount, time,	Stores details of a loan
Corporation	id, name	Stores corporate account information

These are the edges in the transaction network:

Node Schema Name	Properties	Description
Transfer	id, time, type, amount	Connects accounts; loans can transfer money to accounts.
Own	/	Connects a corporation to an account.
Related	/	Indicates relationships among corporations.
Apply	/	Connects a corporation to a loan.

Figure 12.1 illustrates the graph model:

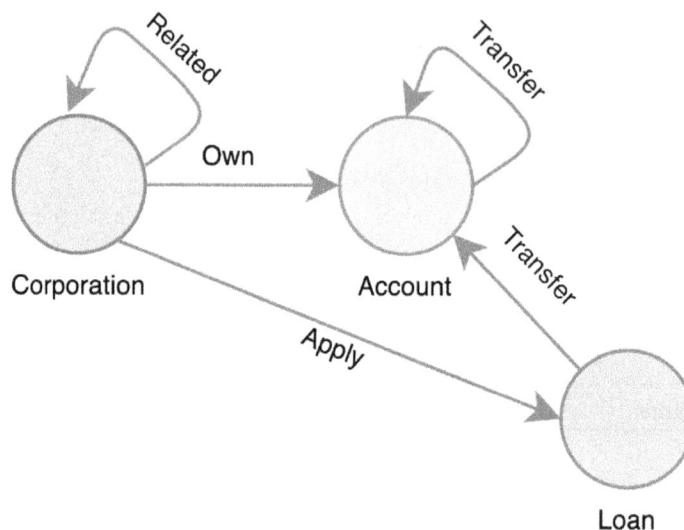

Figure 12.1: Transaction graph model

Corporations own accounts, and these accounts can transfer money to other accounts. When a corporation applies for a loan, the bank transfers the loan amount to the corporation's account. This transaction graph stores all necessary data for subsequent analysis.

Establishing the transaction graph

In this section, we will construct the graph by adding all the necessary nodes and edges. Let's open GQL Playground and begin building the solution.

Visit https://www.ultipa.com/gql-playground to get started.

Creating the graph

To construct the graph depicted in *Figure 12.1*, we will utilize the CREATE statement.

```
GQL:
CREATE GRAPH TransactionGraph{
    NODE Account ({ name string, balance double }),
    NODE Loan ({ payment_method string, amount double, time datetime }),
    NODE Corporation ({ name string }),
    EDGE Transfer ()-[{amount double, time datetime}]->(),
    EDGE Own ()-[{}]->(),
```

```
    EDGE Related ()-[{}]->(),
    EDGE Apply ()-[{}]->()
} PARTITION BY HASH(Crc32) SHARDS [1]
```

This query establishes the graph according to the transaction graph model, creating three types of nodes and four types of edges with specified properties. Additionally, it sets the partition method and shard IDs for use in a distributed graph system.

Once the graph is created, you can use the following commands to list the node and edge types:

GQL:

SHOW NODE SCHEMA

id	name	status	description	properties
1	default	CREATED	default schema	[]
2	Account	CREATED		[{"name":"name","id":101,"type...
3	Loan	CREATED		[{"name":"payment_method","i...
4	Corporation	CREATED		[{"name":"name","id":101,"type...

Figure 12.2: Node schema list

GQL:

SHOW EDGE SCHEMA

id	name	status	description	properties
1	default	CREATED	default schema	[]
2	Transfer	CREATED		[{"name":"amount","id":102,"type":"double","description":"","index...
3	Own	CREATED		[]
4	Related	CREATED		[]
5	Apply	CREATED		[]

Figure 12.3: Edge schema list

You can also list the graph to verify its creation:

GQL:

SHOW GRAPH

id	name	total_nodes	total_edges	description	status
8	TransactionGraph	0	0		NORMAL

Figure 12.4: Graph list

This command displays the graph name, total number of nodes and edges, descriptions, and status.

> 📝 The IDs of the graph and schema may differ from your results, as they are automatically generated by the database.

Next, let's proceed to create all the nodes and edges.

Inserting data

Transactions occur continuously, and in a production environment, data is generated in real time from message queues or loaded from data warehouses daily or more frequently. Given the potentially large volume of data, efficient import tools are essential. Ultipa Graph offers Ultipa Transporter, which supports various data sources and facilitates rapid data importation.

In this section, we will use a small dataset to explore the case study. To insert all the nodes and edges, use the following GQL:

```
GQL:
INSERT
(loan3:Loan { _id: 'loan3', amount: 400000.0, payment_method: 'Hybrid
Payment' }),
(loan16:Loan { _id: 'loan16', amount: 200000.0, payment_method: 'Hybrid
Payment' }),
(loan18:Loan { _id: 'loan18', amount: 200000.0, payment_method: 'Hybrid
Payment' }),
......
(account12o:Account {_id: 'account12o', balance: 0.0, name: 'Green,
Guerrero and Silva' }),
(account18o:Account {_id: 'account18o', balance: 0.0, name: 'Cortez-
Mullins' }),
(account16o:Account {_id: 'account16o', balance: 0.0, name: 'Nguyen Group'
}),
......
(corp13:Corporation {_id: 'corp13', name: 'Ferrell Inc' }),
(corp19:Corporation {_id: 'corp19', name: 'Austin Inc' }),
```

```
(corp17:Corporation {_id: 'corp17', name: 'Butler-Lopez' }),
......
(corp13)-[:Own]->(account13i),
(corp13)-[:Own]->(account13o),
(corp19)-[:Own]->(account19i),
......
(account3i)-[:Transfer {amount : 198601.0, time: '2024-01-01 13:00:36'
}]->(account6i),
(account3i)-[:Transfer {amount : 56106.0, time: '2024-01-01 13:01:04'
}]->(account6i),
(account3i)-[:Transfer {amount : 191806.0, time: '2024-01-04 13:27:14'
}]->(account2i),
......
```

This GQL snippet demonstrates how to insert nodes and edges into the graph.

For the complete code, please visit Ch12/Ch12-insert.gql in the repository.

Once the data is inserted, you can use the SHOW GRAPH command again to verify the graph's structure and contents.

```
GQL:
SHOW GRAPH
```

id	name	total_nodes	total_edges	description	status
17	TransactionGraph	81	103		NORMAL

Figure 12.5: Graph list

The total nodes and edges are updated to 81 and 103.

You can use a MATCH statement to retrieve the entire graph:

```
GQL:
MATCH p=()->() RETURN p
```

This query will retrieve all the one-hop paths, excluding isolated nodes.

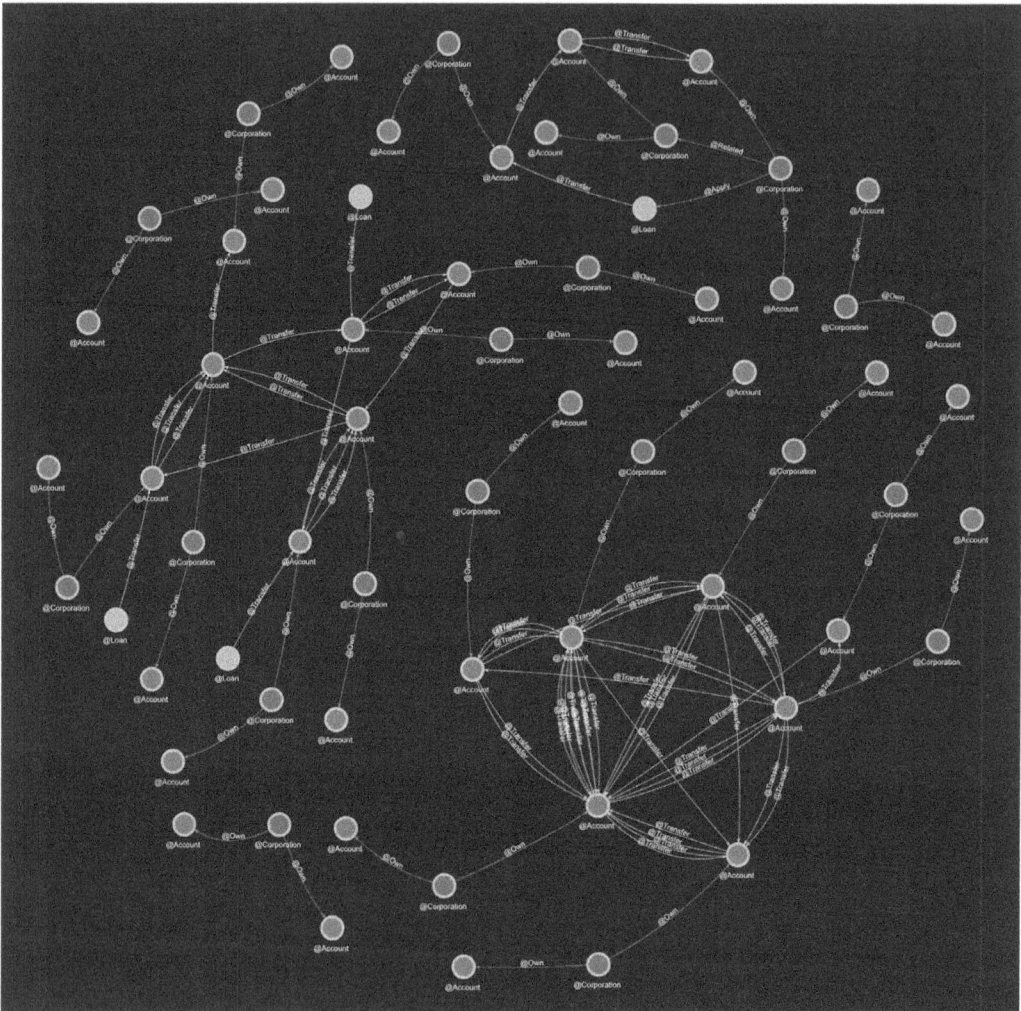

Figure 12.6: Transaction graph

Let's enhance the graph's visualization by adding icons, colors, and different node types.

The customized styling feature is available in Ultipa Manager. For more information, please visit `https://www.ultipa.com/document/ultipa-manager-user-guide`.

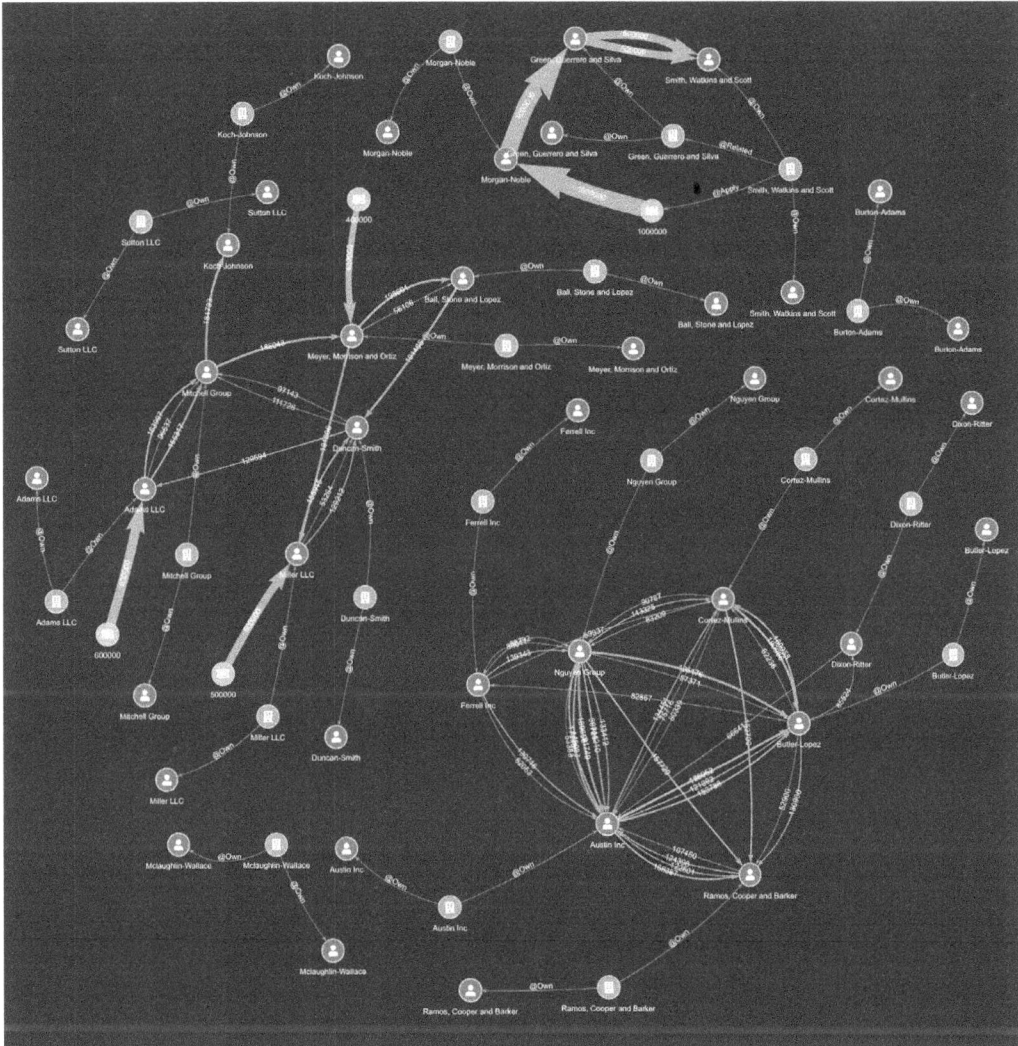

Figure 12.7: Styled transaction graph

To verify the number of nodes and edges, use the following query:

```
GQL:
MATCH (n) RETURN count(n) as totalNodes
```

This query returns the total number of nodes.

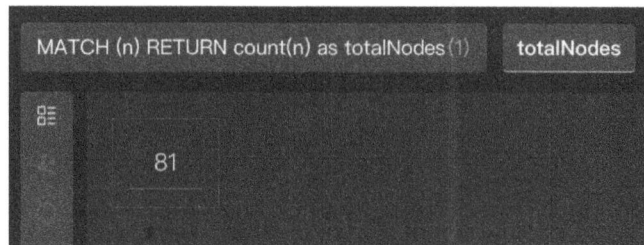

Figure 12.8: Total number of nodes

```
GQL:
MATCH ()-[e]->() RETURN count(e) as totalEdges
```

This query returns the total number of edges.

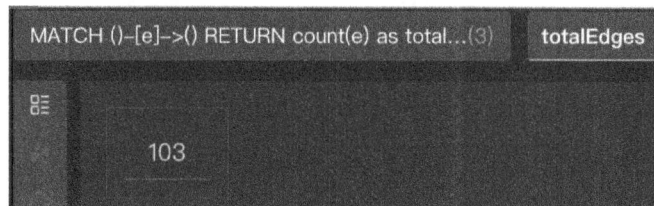

Figure 12.9: Total number of edges

These queries should yield the same values as the SHOW GRAPH command.

Querying the graph

With the transaction graph established, we can begin using GQL to execute various operations.

GQL can perform queries to retrieve nodes and edges based on specified conditions.

Here's an example:

```
GQL:
MATCH (a:Account WHERE a.balance > 50000) RETURN a
```

This query retrieves all `Account` nodes with a balance exceeding 50,000.

_id	_uuid	name	balance
account3i	2954363554578301285	Meyer, Morrison and Ortiz	69226
account10i	3458766712843796851	Smith, Watkins and Scott	51743
account14i	37469970889955508591	Ramos, Cooper and Barker	97331
account6i	7782222355119473021	Ball, Stone and Lopez	84301
account11i	8142510325309112708	Morgan-Noble	52915
account9i	11745390027205509484	Mitchell Group	61693
account1i	12321850779508932976	Mclaughlin-Wallace	79625
account5i	12610081155660644721	Burton-Adams	82541
account16i	13114484313926140263	Nguyen Group	92859

Figure 12.10: List of Account nodes with a balance over 50,000

UUIDs may vary as they are generated randomly.

Count the number of accounts and sum their balances:

```
GQL:
MATCH (a:Account WHERE a.balance > 50000)
RETURN count(a) as total, sum(a.balance)
```

This query returns the total number of `Account` nodes with a balance over 50,000 and the sum of their balances.

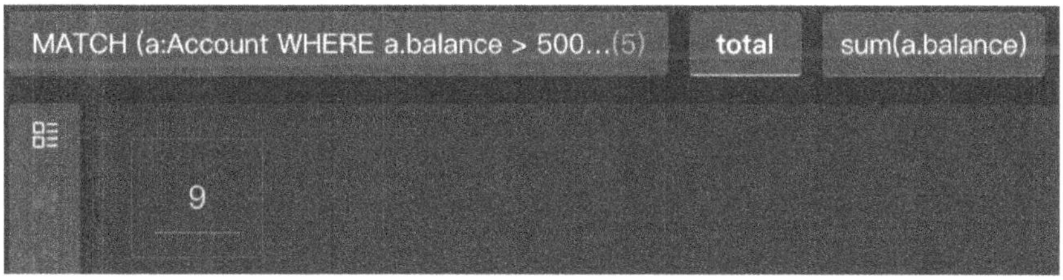

Figure 12.11: Total number of accounts with balance over 50,000

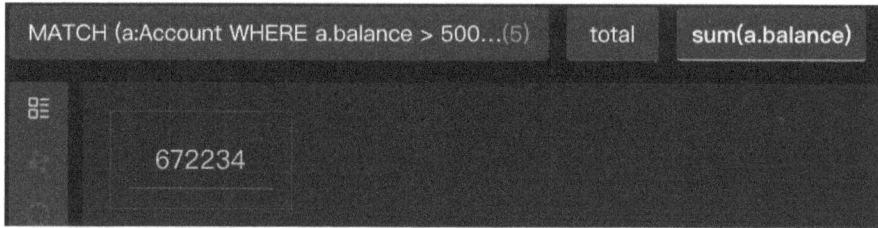

Figure 12.12: Total of balance

Find all transaction details from a specific account:

```
GQL:
MATCH p=(n:Account {_id : "account14i"})-[t:Transfer]->()
RETURN t, p
```

This query returns paths and edges originating from account account14i.

_uuid	_from	_to	_from_uuid	_to_uuid	amount	time
39	account14i	account19i	37469970889955...	8718971077612535...	107450	2024–01–01 13:41:...
40	account14i	account19i	37469970889955...	8718971077612535...	122801	2024–01–01 13:43...
41	account14i	account19i	37469970889955...	8718971077612535...	124398	2024–01–06 13:34...

Figure 12.13: List of transfers from account14i

You can view the transactions by switching the return item to p for a graph and list view, illustrated in *Figure 12.4*.

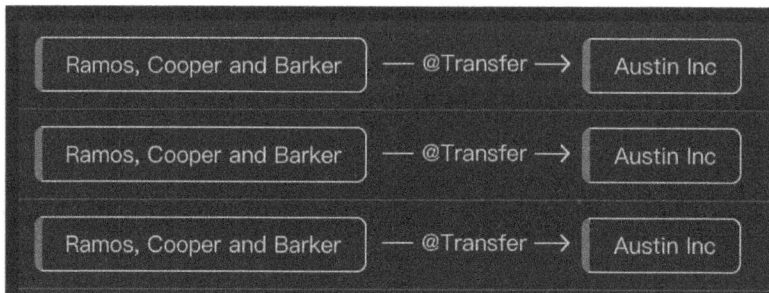

Figure 12.14: Transfer Paths from account14i

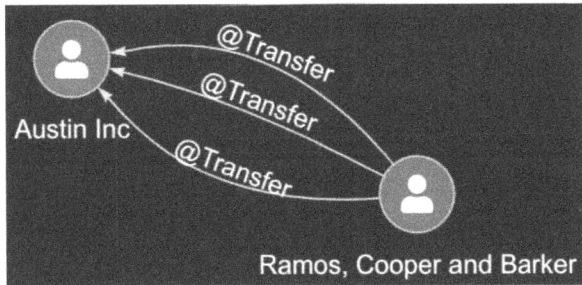

Figure 12.15: Graph of transfers from account14i

Find transactions from account14i to other accounts in two steps:

```
GQL:
MATCH p=(n:Account {_id : "account14i"})-[:Transfer]->{2}()
RETURN p
```

This query returns two-step paths with transfer relations.

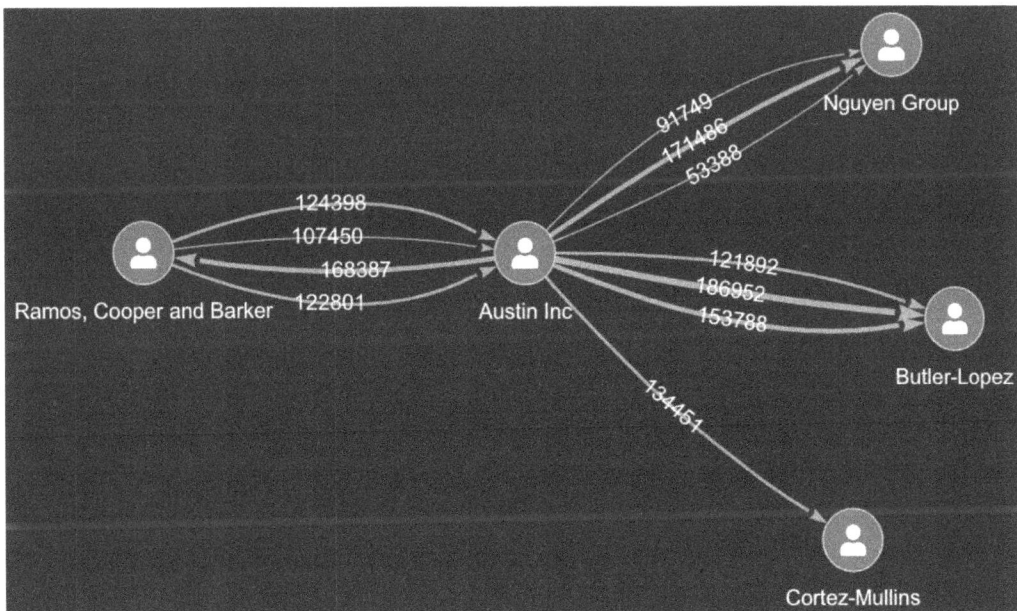

Figure 12.16: Two-hop transaction paths from account14i

If you notice a cyclic transaction, such as `Ramos` `-> Austin` `-> Ramos`, you can set conditions to avoid loops:

```
GQL:
MATCH p=(
    n:Account {_id : "account14i"}
)-[t:Transfer]->{2}(m WHERE m._id <> n._id)
RETURN p
```

This query returns two-hop transaction paths, excluding loop transactions.

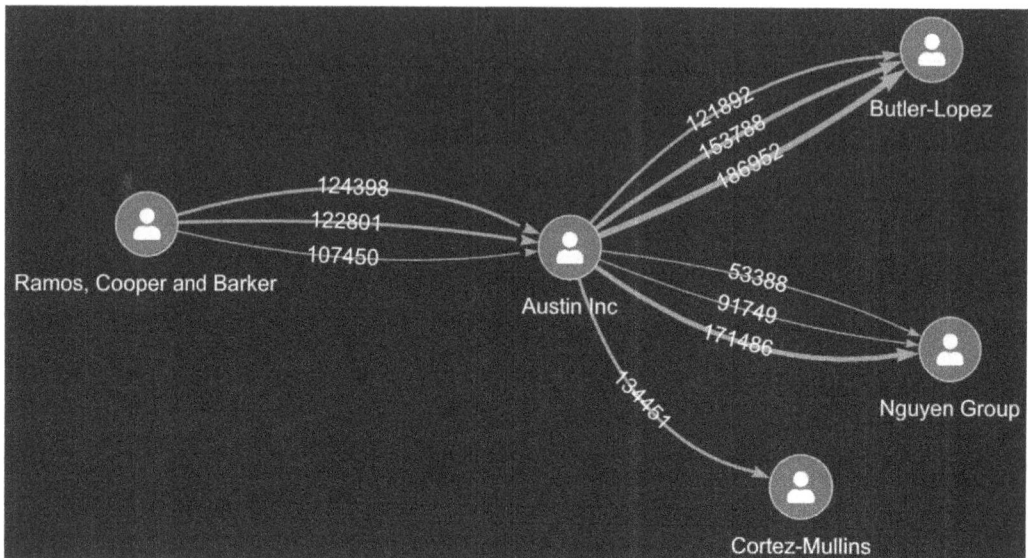

Figure 12.17: Two-hop paths from account14i excluding loops

With the `MATCH` statement, you can also perform aggregations.

For example, you could sum the total amount of all transactions from Ramos to other nodes:

```
GQL:
MATCH (ramos {name : "Ramos, Cooper and Barker"})
MATCH (ramos)-[t:Transfer]->()
RETURN sum(t.amount)
```

This query returns the total amount Ramos transferred.

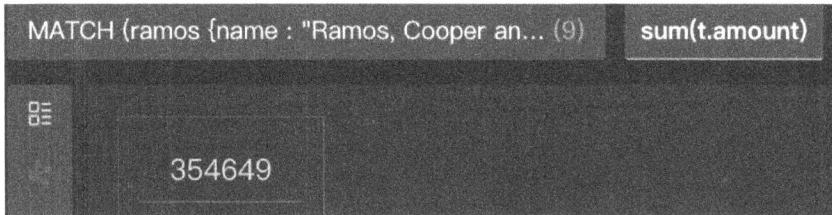

Figure 12.18: Total amount transferred out from ramos

Here, the filter is changed from an `_id` filter to a name filter, and node finding and path finding are split into two `MATCH` statements for readability. The first `MATCH` statement retrieves the node and stores it in the `ramos` variable. The second `MATCH` statement uses the `ramos` variable to execute pathfinding.

You can also combine the two `MATCH` statements into one. The following query gives the same result:

```GQL
MATCH (ramos {name : "Ramos, Cooper and Barker"})-[t:Transfer]->()
RETURN sum(t.amount)
```

To enhance query performance, let's create an index for account names:

```GQL
CREATE INDEX name ON NODE Account (name)
```

This query creates an index named `name` for the `Account` node on the `name` property, speeding up account name filtering.

Now that we can query nodes and edges, let's proceed to identify suspicious transactions in the graph.

Anti-fraud graph model

Before developing the anti-fraud graph model, it's essential to understand what constitutes fraudulent behavior. Fraudulent behavior typically involves illegal transactions that do not comply with regulatory requirements or directly harm other accounts.

In this case, we will identify and define the model to detect such non-compliant activities.

In the graph, we can identify certain sub-networks.

Let's use GQL to retrieve the entire graph again:

```
GQL:
MATCH p=()->() RETURN p
```

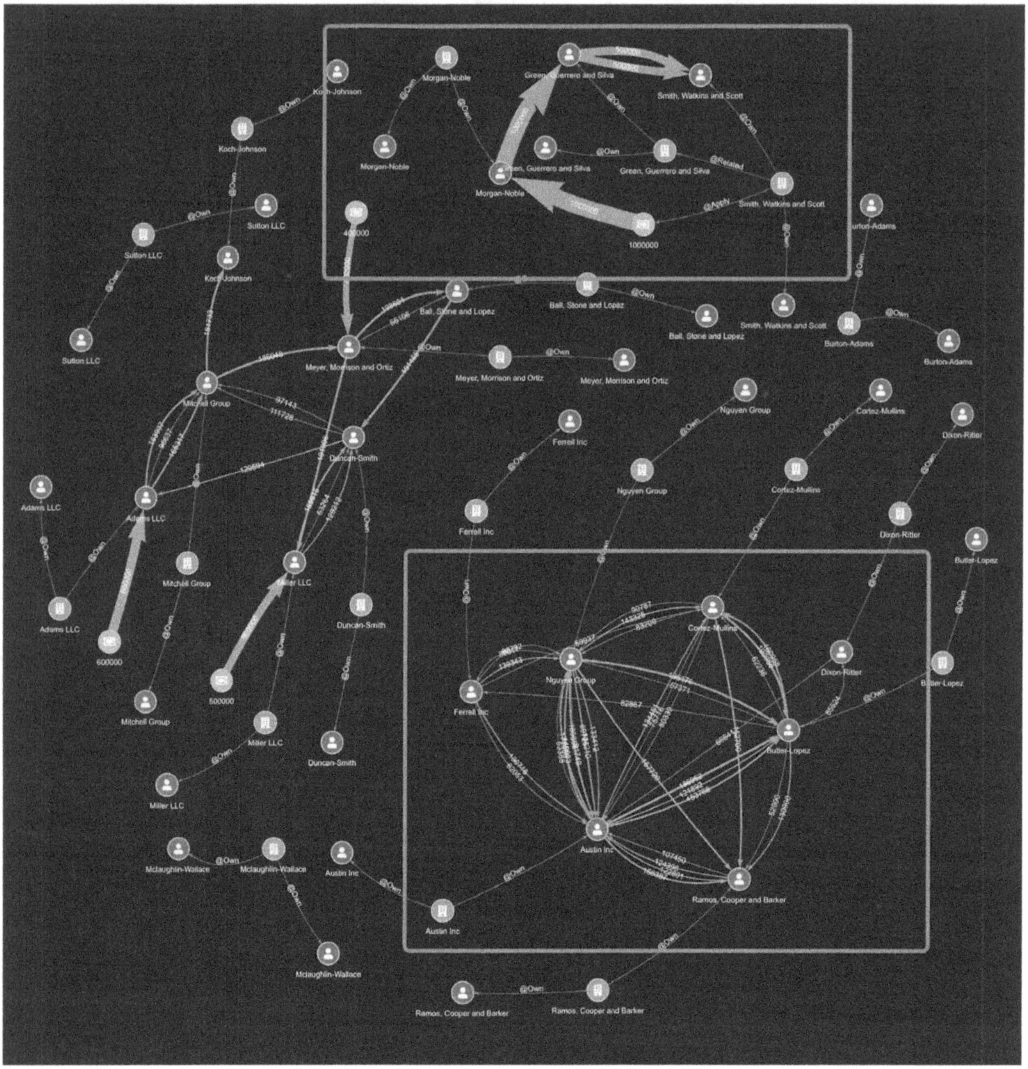

Figure 12.19: Transaction graph – highlighted subnets

Not all transaction networks are suspicious. Let's focus on the one located in the top area of *Figure 12.20* for further examination.

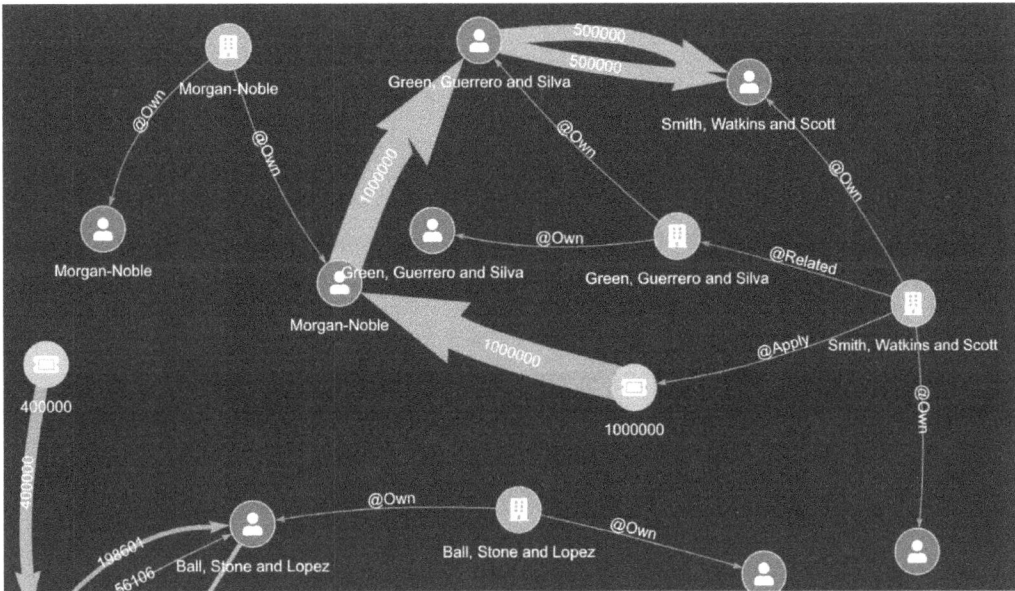

Figure 12.20: Transaction graph focused on suspicious subnet

Here is the description of the subgraph:

Corporation Smith, Waltkins, and Scott applied for a loan of $100,000 to pay Morgan-Noble. Morgan-Noble then transferred the money to Green, Guerrero, and Silva, who transferred the loan back to Smith, the original corporation. Each step involved the same amount of $100,000.

Additionally, it was found that Corporation Smith, Watkins, and Scott and Green, Guerrero, and Silva have a relationship, which could be considered as stock holding between the two companies. The loan request is illegal because this was intended for payment to a vendor, but the vendor transferred the money back to the company.

Alright, having identified the illegal transaction network, let's proceed to construct the query model. The objective of this model is to detect loans that are transferred back to the borrower through multiple steps.

The path query should be structured as follows:

```
<borrower> -> [multiple steps transactions] -> <borrower>
```

Here is the GQL:

```
GQL:
MATCH (loan:Loan)
MATCH p=(borrower:Corporation)->(loan)-[:Transfer]->{1,5}
        (:Account)<-(borrower)
RETURN p
```

This query identifies cyclic paths where the borrower transfers funds back to itself through transfer relations, with the initial transfer originating from a loan to an account. The quantifier {1,5} limits the number of -[:Transfer]-> with 1 to 5, meaning the path contains 1 to 5 transfer edges.

Figure 12.21 illustrates the result:

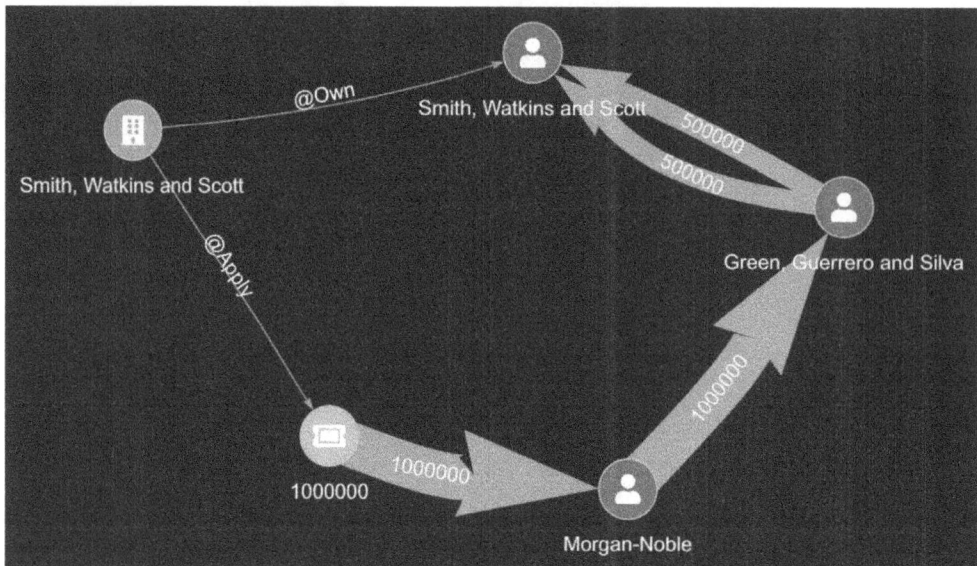

Figure 12.21: Cyclic paths from Loan

> You can explore the nodes in the resulting graph to uncover additional relationships among them.

However, auditors or regulators might prefer a straightforward report. To accommodate this, you can directly return the fraud nodes and the reason for suspicion.

```
GQL:
MATCH (loan:Loan)
```

```
MATCH p=(borrower:Corporation)->(loan)-[:Transfer]->{1,5}
        (:Account)<-(borrower)
LET Name = borrower.name, Reason = "Circular Loan Fraud"
RETURN DISTINCT table(Name, Reason)
```

This query returns a distinct table with the names of corporations involved in circular loan fraud and the reason for identifying them as such.

Name	Reason
Smith, Watkins and Scott	Circular Loan Fraud

Figure 12.22: Circular loan fraud result

Next, let's utilize graph algorithms to detect suspicious groups within the network.

GQL supports named procedures for extended operations. To employ algorithms in GQL Playground, you need to create an HDC graph and use the CALL function.

To create the HDC graph, you can use the following query:

```
GQL:
CREATE HDC GRAPH TransactionGraph ON "hdc-server"
OPTIONS {
    nodes: { "*" :["*"]},
    edges: { "*" :["*"]}
}
```

This query creates an HDC graph with the same name as the original graph, enabling advanced algorithmic operations.

You will use the Louvain algorithm to detect the communities from TransactionGraph.

The Louvain algorithm is a widely recognized and extensively used algorithm for community detection in graphs. It is named after the location of its authors – Vincent D. Blondel et al. from Université catholique de Louvain in Belgium. The primary objective of the algorithm is to maximize the modularity of the graph, and it has gained popularity due to its high efficiency and the quality of its results.

You will find a detailed introduction to Louvain algorithm by visiting https://www.ultipa.com/document/ultipa-graph-analytics-algorithms/louvain.

Let's execute the algorithm with the following query:

```GQL
GQL:
CALL algo.louvain.write("TransactionGraph", {
    params: {
        phase1_loop_num: 5,
        min_modularity_increase: 0.1
    },
    return_params: {
        db: { property: 'communityID' }
    }
})
```

This query runs the Louvain algorithm on the TransactionGraph HDC graph, setting the return type to write the results back to the database. The property parameter in return_params specifies that the results are written to the communityID property.

> Ultipa's HDC graph resides in the memory of a **High-Density Computing (HDC)** server and provides a high-performance computing engine capable of executing complex algorithms efficiently. By utilizing an HDC graph instead of the original graph, performance is boosted hundreds of times.

Once the algorithm completes, you can verify that the communityID property has been created:

```GQL
GQL:
SHOW NODE Account PROPERTY
```

name	type	lte	read	write	schema	description
_id	string	false	1	1	Account	system property
name	string	false	1	1	Account	
balance	double	false	1	1	Account	
communityID	uint32	false	1	1	Account	algo write back

Figure 12.23: Property list of the Account node

This command will display the properties, including communityID, for each node.

Use the following to view the nodes:

```GQL
GQL:
MATCH (n) RETURN n
```

@Account				
_id	_uuid	name	balance	communityID
account14o	72059793061184087	Ramos, Cooper an...	0	73
account10o	360290169212895...	Smith, Watkins and...	0	80
account18o	936750921516319316	Cortez–Mullins	0	76
account7o	172938445593352...	Sutton LLC	0	63
account3o	2017614832085238...	Meyer, Morrison an...	0	17
account3i	295436355457830...	Meyer, Morrison an...	69226	17
bank1	3026421148616229...	Standard Chartered...	0	6
account7i	324259393073001...	Sutton LLC	15042	63
account10i	3458766712843797...	Smith, Watkins and...	51743	80
account14i	374699708899550...	Ramos, Cooper an...	97331	30

Figure 12.24: Node list with communityID

This query will return all nodes, allowing you to see the newly assigned communityID for each one.

Let's find the top five largest community IDs:

```GQL
GQL:
MATCH (n)
let cid = n.communityID
RETURN cid, count(n) as total
GROUP BY cid
ORDER BY total DESC
LIMIT 5
```

This query returns the five largest community IDs based on the number of nodes.

Figure 12.25: Top 5 community IDs

Use the following to retrieve the community graph for the largest community ID:

```
GQL:
MATCH p=({communityID: 80})->({communityID: 80})
RETURN p
```

This query returns all the relationships within community 80, illustrated in *Figure 12.8*.

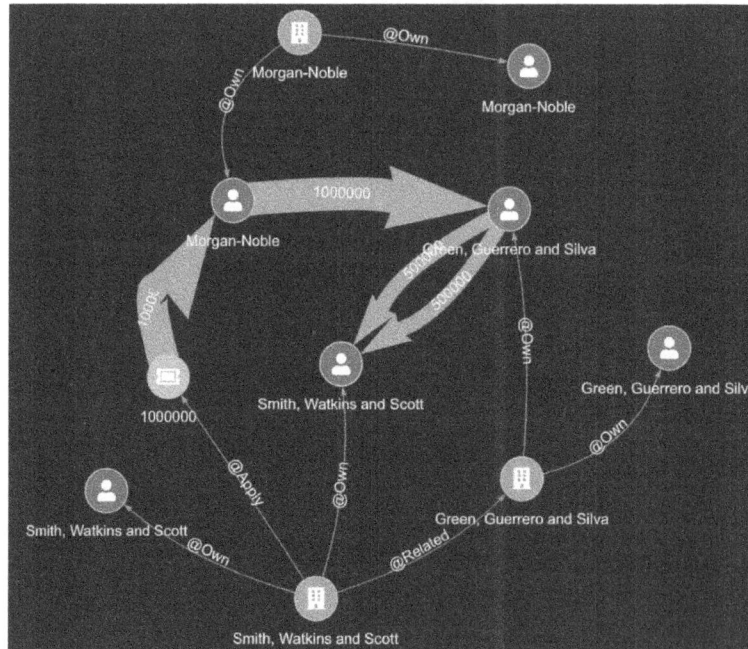

Figure 12.26: The largest community subgraph

You can combine the two queries into one:

```
GQL:
MATCH (n)
let cid = n.communityID
RETURN cid, count(n) as total
GROUP BY cid
ORDER BY total DESC
LIMIT 1
NEXT
MATCH p=({communityID: cid})->({communityID: cid})
RETURN p
```

This query retrieves the largest community and passes the community ID to the MATCH statement, returning the subgraph by the end.

This example demonstrates how to detect fraudulent subgraphs and communities. You can set flags on nodes to mark them as fraudulent and add time filtering for greater accuracy. Feel free to experiment with the graph to discover more intriguing models.

Summary

In this chapter, we used GQL to construct a comprehensive transaction graph. By leveraging GQL, we were able to perform a variety of queries that helped us uncover patterns indicative of fraudulent behaviors. These patterns were then translated into a GQL model, providing a robust framework for detecting and analyzing fraud.

Congratulations! You have successfully created a graph-based solution using ISO GQL. This achievement marks a significant milestone in your journey with GQL. As you continue to explore, you can increase the complexity of your graphs and develop more sophisticated queries and models. GQL Playground offers a plethora of algorithms that you can utilize to enhance your analysis.

Get This Book's PDF Version and Exclusive Extras

UNLOCK NOW

Scan the QR code (or go to packtpub.com/unlock). Search for this book by name, confirm the edition, and then follow the steps on the page.

Note: Keep your invoice handy. Purchases made directly from Packt don't require an invoice.

13

The Evolving Landscape of GQL

The world of database management and query languages is fast evolving, with new technologies reshaping how data is stored, processed, and queried. **Graph Query Language** (GQL) has emerged as one of the most promising advancements in this space. As data grows increasingly interconnected and complex, GQL promises to meet these challenges head-on.

This chapter explores the future trajectory of GQL, graph databases, and graph analytics, outlining emerging features, capabilities, challenges, and the opportunities that lie ahead.

Emerging features and capabilities

As the demand for more sophisticated data management systems grows, the features of GQL are expected to evolve in profound ways. The upcoming versions of GQL are poised to address the limitations of current query languages by offering enhanced flexibility, scalability, and power. Several key features will become central to GQL's ongoing development.

In *Chapter 11*, we outlined the GQL extensions that vendors such as Ultipa have already implemented. These extensions arise from the pressing need for a standardized approach to graph data management—one that GQL promises to fulfill. However, beyond the baseline functionality defined by the standard, graph **database administrators** (DBAs) today require advanced capabilities to effectively manage and optimize their systems. These include altering the GQL catalog, enhancing query performance, enforcing property constraints, implementing fine-grained access controls, and managing other administrative tasks. While GQL lays the foundation, it is essential that these extended features are accessible through a GQL-consistent syntax. This avoids the inefficiencies and complexity of relying on two separate query languages: one for standard operations and another for vendor-specific features. A unified, GQL-centric approach not only improves usability but also ensures portability and maintainability across different graph database platforms. We are confident that some of these capabilities will be addressed in the next version of GQL, though this is not yet guaranteed.

Advanced graph traversals

GQL is poised to become a more powerful (high-dimensional) database query language, if not just a superset of SQL, incorporating (and re-innovating) the powerful features of SQL while extending its capabilities to handle graph data more intuitively and efficiently. This evolution will not only enhance the functionality of GQL but also make it a more versatile tool for developers.

Graph traversal forms the backbone of graph databases. While current GQL versions offer powerful traversal mechanisms, future iterations are expected to introduce even more robust capabilities. These enhancements will allow for more efficient and deeper traversals of complex data structures.

For example, future versions of GQL will likely include built-in support for the MATCH statement at scale. Recursive queries, which allow users to trace relationships across multiple levels, are critical for applications such as fraud detection, social network analysis, and recommendation engines. The next generation of GQL will aim to make these recursive queries both faster and more efficient, supporting real-time processing of vast datasets without compromising on performance.

For example, the following code snippet illustrates how inter-step filtering is realized using the prev_n and prev_e system (predefined and reserved keywords) aliases in path templates by allowing reference to the previous node or edge at each step.

The following is an example two-step outgoing transaction path between accounts with ascending time:

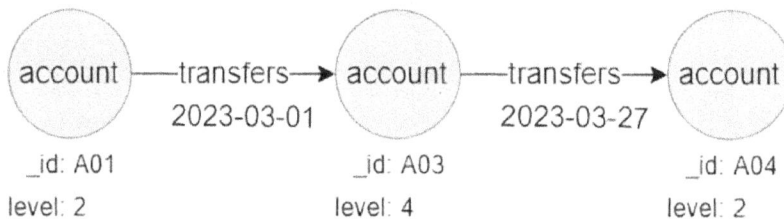

Figure 13.1: Accounts connected by a series of money transfers in a two-step transaction path

```
GQL:
MATCH p=(a)-[e1:transfers]->(b)-[e2:transfers]->(c)
WHERE e2.time > e1.time
RETURN p
```

This query returns a time-serialized path using edge filters.

```
UQL:
n().re({@transfers.time > prev_e.time})[2].n() as p
return p
```

This UQL query achieves the same result by using the prev_e reserved variable.

> ### GQL versus UQL
>
> The preceding two code snippets are in GQL and UQL, respectively. Note that UQL has built-in system-reserved keywords, such as prev_n and prev_e. This is due to the generalized yet unique graph design, which states that nodes and edges should be treated equally. If we were to recursively deep-traverse, it would be quite a hassle to write simple GQL code (see the following sample code). The reality is, however, that GQL borrows a lot from established players such as Neo4j, which put a lot of focus on node processing instead of edge processing—meaning GQL's current edge-oriented filtering capabilities are lagging well behind. Keep up to date with GQL developments to see whether they fill this gap.

It's not difficult to tell how cumbersome it can be to traverse 10+ hops in GQL now—of course, the following code snippet can be optimized and simplified using GQL's quantified path patterns, but there is still a lot of vendor-specific implementation logic to handle encapsulating and de-capsulating varied data points (i.e., nodes, edges, etc.):

```
GQL:
MATCH p = (n)-[e1:Invest]->(m1)-[e2:Invest]->(m2)-[e3:Invest]->(m3)-...-
[e10:Invest]->(m10)
WHERE e2.time > e1.time AND e3.time > e2.time AND ... AND e10.time >
e9.time
RETURN p
```

Named stored queries and functions

The introduction of named stored procedures is one of the most transformative capabilities in the evolving landscape of GQL. These procedures are expected to play a crucial role in the future of graph database systems, allowing for a more modular and flexible approach to query processing and application logic. Named stored procedures, defined within the GQL catalog, are procedures that encapsulate complex computations or operations that can be invoked with specific parameters.

In GQL, a **named procedure** is described through a **named procedure descriptor**, which includes the following key features:

- A list of mandatory and optional parameters, including their types, names, and default values
- The procedure result type, which specifies the kind of output that the procedure will return
- An indication of the side effects that the procedure can cause, such as modifying the catalog, altering data, or simply returning a result

Named procedures can be classified into three categories based on their side effects:

- **Catalog-modifying procedures**: These procedures may alter the structure of the graph catalog itself, adding new types, relationships, or entities.
- **Data-modifying procedures**: These procedures modify the actual data stored in the graph database, updating nodes, edges, or properties.
- **Query procedures**: These procedures do not cause any changes to the database. Instead, they simply retrieve information based on specific queries and return results without side effects.

One significant advantage of named procedures is their ability to **encapsulate complex logic** that can be reused across different queries or applications. By defining these procedures in the GQL catalog, developers can create modular components that are easy to maintain and update. This ability to call predefined procedures within queries not only improves code organization but also optimizes performance by reducing repetitive logic execution.

The procedural logic within GQL allows developers to perform operations on input arguments, manipulate data, and trigger actions based on the specific needs of the application. These procedures are executed within a defined execution context, and the parameters are validated against the procedure's descriptor, ensuring consistency and correctness.

Moreover, named procedures support optional parameters, where if any optional parameter is provided, the system expects arguments for all preceding optional parameters as well. This flexibility in parameter handling makes it possible to write dynamic and adaptable procedures that can handle various use cases effectively.

As **GQL evolves**, we can expect even more advanced features for procedures, such as the ability to handle **transactional consistency** and **error handling** within procedure logic, further solidifying GQL's role as the standard language for graph-based applications.

Integration with machine learning and AI

The integration of GQL with machine learning and AI technologies will open new avenues for data analysis and application development. There are a few areas where AI and graphs can mutually enhance each other, especially at the start and end of data-processing life cycles. Let's expand on that a little bit.

The following areas may see major integration of AI and graphs (GQL included):

- **First step—AI-augmented data ETL and modeling**: Automated data ETL, particularly extracting structured data from semi-structured or unstructured data, is often the first task that data engineers face. AI, specifically LLMs/GPTs, can greatly boost productivity and ease such tasks, by automagically (think of this as upgraded NLP technology) extracting structures, meaning entities and relationships, out of the original datasets. They can potentially even go the extra mile to allow graph data models to be constructed for DBAs to review and refine. AI can most likely help offload and accelerate these initial tasks.

- **AI-powered query construction and optimization**: This is another area pertaining to the hype or real breakthrough that we have witnessed with the rise of generative AI, where AI agents can help write code on programmers' behalf. The expectation here is for AI co-pilots to take natural-language instructions typed in by human users and auto-translate (generate) them to GQL queries that can be executed. This has seen some early success, such as in chatbots or graph-powered Q&A systems.

- **Last step—AI for report generation**: Again, in the last step, generative AI can be leveraged to specifically focus on generating reports, which is sought after by many compliance managers.

- **Graph RAG and beyond**: Graph **retrieval-augmented generation (RAG)** is just the beginning. The integration of AI with GQL will enable more intelligent querying and data manipulation, providing deeper insights and more powerful analytics. This will empower applications to perform complex network and connected data analysis with ease.

Enhanced performance and scalability

With the increasing demand for real-time data processing and deep analysis, GQL will see enhancements in performance and scalability. We anticipate multi-forked progress (and breakthroughs) in the following areas:

- **In-memory processing**: In-memory processing will allow GQL databases to store data in RAM, significantly reducing latency and improving query execution times. However, in-memory processing acceleration is often limited by large data volumes, which can be difficult (and costly) to process entirely in memory space. Careful architectural design, query optimization, and data-flow optimization are needed to truly make a breakthrough on this front.

- **Distributed computing**: Distributed computing techniques enable GQL databases to scale horizontally, distributing data and computational workloads across multiple nodes, enhancing the ability to handle large datasets and complex queries efficiently. The problem with horizontal scalable architecture design is that it's storage-friendly or metadata-friendly for shallow and wide queries only, but not so much for deep queries, or queries that span multiple shards, requiring recursive inter-shard network communications (meaning slow data shuffling). How to design a unified system that can handle both horizontal and vertical scalability, so as to handle both wide and deep queries, is an area that will likely experience significant breakthroughs in the next 10 years.

> **Unified graph storage and computing framework**
>
> The team at Ultipa has published multiple papers showcasing their unified graph system that's capable of horizontally scalable (and sharded) graph storage and elastic high-density graph computing. If you are interested in learning more, visit `https://www.ultipa.com/publications`.

Transition for SQL users

One of the guiding principles behind GQL's development is accessibility: ensuring that developers, particularly those experienced with traditional relational databases and SQL, can make a smooth transition into the graph paradigm. This next section explores how GQL has been intentionally shaped to be familiar and approachable for SQL users, providing a bridge between the established and the emerging.

Intuitive graph data modeling

The transition from SQL to GQL should be smooth and intuitive, especially for developers accustomed to working with relational databases. GQL was specifically designed to lower the barrier to entry for those familiar with SQL. In fact, many core principles of GQL align with SQL's foundational concepts, such as data modeling, querying, and relationship handling. These similarities allow SQL users to leverage their existing knowledge while adapting to graph-specific features, which is crucial for the widespread adoption of graph technologies.

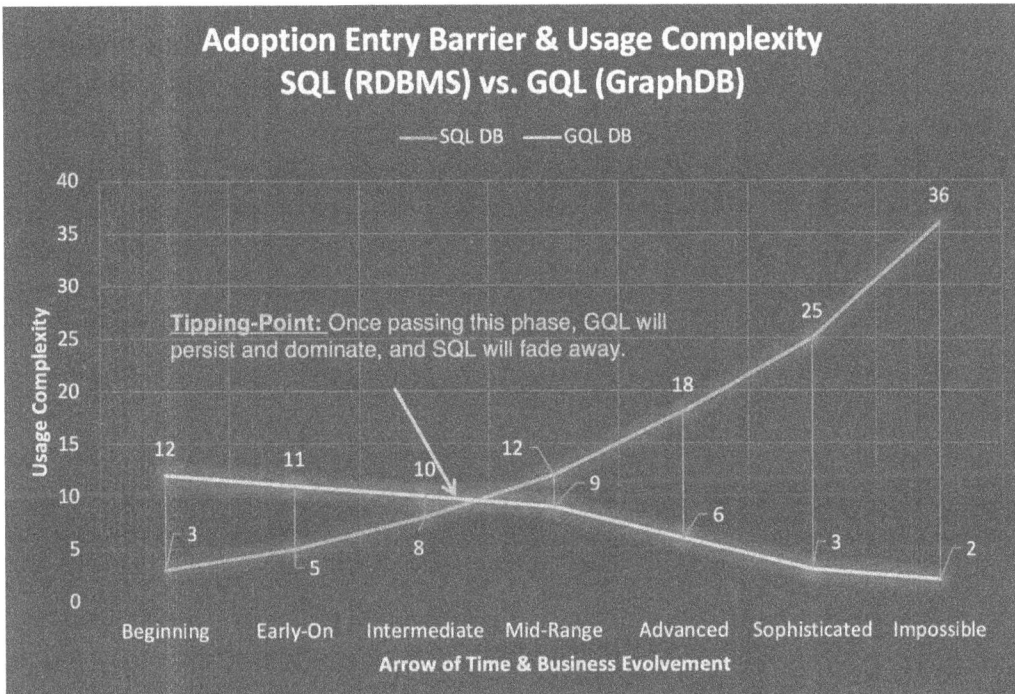

Figure 13.2: SQL versus GQL

For instance, just like SQL uses SELECT queries to retrieve data from tables, GQL employs MATCH queries to traverse graphs and retrieve nodes and edges based on their relationships. The syntax is designed to feel familiar yet extended, providing SQL users with an easy entry point into the world of graph data. Operations such as filtering and aggregation in GQL are similar to SQL, but the addition of graph-specific features such as pattern matching and path traversal unlocks new potential for handling complex, interconnected data.

Furthermore, GQL's flexibility in natively defining relationships among entities addresses some of the limitations inherent in SQL databases, especially in representing complex networks of data. In relational databases, joins are often cumbersome and inefficient for deep relationship queries. GQL simplifies this by allowing the natural, recursive traversal of graph structures, a feature that is easy to grasp for SQL developers but far more powerful in practice. A critical difference is that GQL allows relationships to be stored as data while SQL requires the query writer to include the relationships in the query.

The level of migration from SQL to GQL is expected to mirror that of many other paradigm shifts in technology. Initially, there might be a bit of a learning curve, sometimes even steep curves, especially as developers familiarize themselves with graph-specific concepts such as nodes, edges, and properties. However, once the basics are mastered, GQL offers a more flexible, performant, and scalable solution for managing complex data. *Figure 13.2* offers insights into how, in the long run, GQL and graph databases will potentially surpass SQL databases as graph technologies mature and businesses increasingly demand deeper insights from their interconnected data. Naturally, GQL is expected to provide at least the same core functionalities offered by traditional **relational database management systems (RDBMSs)**, such as triggers and views.

Challenges and opportunities

The continued evolution of GQL faces a range of challenges, particularly around technical and business aspects such as performance optimization and application transformation, as well as marketing and adoption hurdles. However, these challenges also present significant opportunities for growth, in terms of both expanding the capabilities of GQL and increasing its adoption across various industries.

Technical challenges

As GQL evolves, ensuring that it can scale to meet the growing demands of real-time data processing and complex analysis will be paramount. With each new feature, vendor-specific GQL implementations must strive to offer optimal performance while addressing important security concerns.

Performance optimization

One of the central challenges for any vendor-specific implementation will be ensuring that new features introduced into GQL do not degrade query performance. The complexity of graph data, especially as datasets grow in scale, means that GQL's query-processing algorithms and data storage mechanisms must evolve to keep pace. Optimizing traversal speeds, particularly for recursive queries and deep traversals, will be a crucial focus as future versions of GQL are developed.

It's not hard to imagine that some of today's most popular graph databases, with their known performance and scalability challenges, would be under immense pressure to upgrade their system architectures to avoid being considered non-adaptive to real-world data-centric requirements.

Security concerns

Addressing security concerns will be essential, including implementing robust authentication and authorization mechanisms, as well as ensuring data integrity and privacy. As the scope of GQL expands to support more complex operations and integrations with other technologies, such as blockchain or IoT, the need for secure authentication and authorization mechanisms will become even more critical. Protecting user data, ensuring data integrity, and safeguarding privacy will be ongoing priorities as the language matures.

It would be overambitious to expect GQL to handle all aspects of security. In many cases, customers may misplace the responsibility for security on the query language itself or on the graph database engine. However, in reality, critical security controls—including access management and data protection—should be implemented at the graph DBMS layer, or even further up in the stack, within the API/SDK or application layer.

An important caveat here is that overburdening GQL or the database core with security logic could have unintended consequences. It might introduce unnecessary complexity or degrade performance, ultimately defeating the purpose of adopting a lean, efficient query language designed for high-performance graph analytics.

Marketing and adoption challenges

While GQL offers powerful new capabilities, promoting its adoption will require overcoming marketing challenges and demonstrating its practical benefits. GQL's value proposition must be communicated effectively to the developer community, businesses, and organizations in various industries to drive widespread acceptance.

Educating the developer community

A key component of GQL's adoption will be the effort to educate developers about its features and advantages. This will involve creating comprehensive resources such as detailed documentation, tutorials, and workshops, designed to help developers transition from SQL-based approaches to graph-based thinking. Ensuring that developers understand how GQL can simplify complex relationships and provide more intuitive querying mechanisms will be essential to its success.

While a lot of people believe open source is the only way to build developer communities, there are other ways, such as providing a playground or sandbox environment or free to low-cost graph database instances for developers to get their hands dirty with GQL.

Demonstrating practical advantages

Equally important will be demonstrating how GQL solves real-world problems. Case studies and success stories will be valuable in showing GQL's potential to streamline complex workflows and improve performance in data-driven applications. Performance benchmarks and practical examples will help to bridge the gap between the theoretical advantages of GQL and its practical applications in industries such as finance, healthcare, and social media.

We also need to point out that most of today's GQL or graph database implementation showcases are heavily concentrated in the fraud detection domain. This has caused a lot of people to narrowly define and view graph databases and GQL as only suitable for that use case. This is a clear misunderstanding of the broad-spectrum capabilities of GQL. We can come up with a general rule of thumb that, as long as data is connected, GQL can be suitable for any use cases. There are amazing use cases leveraging graph databases for decision-making, root cause analysis, supply chain management, attribution analysis, digital twins, asset liability management, auditing, compliance and reporting, and more. From a very broad and visionary perspective, GQL is growing to be a superset of SQL, even for disconnected data. GQL is still able to handle that (though that's not what it is designed for) from a backward-compatibility perspective.

```
--Store Procedure queryChildrenInfo(Starting ID, # of level of explore)
CREATE DEFINER='root'@'%' PROCEDURE 'queryChildrenInfo' (startId INT,levelnum INT)
BEGIN
    DECLARE i INT;
    SET i = 0;
    create temporary table if not exists mytmpA(data varchar(200),level Int)  ENGINE = MEMORY;
    create temporary table if not exists mytmpB(data varchar(200),level Int)  ENGINE = MEMORY;
    INSERT INTO mytmpA values(CAST(startId AS CHAR),0);
    WHILE i < levelnum DO
        delete from mytmpB;
            insert into mytmpB select * from mytmpA;
        delete from mytmpA;
        insert into mytmpA select concat_ws(',',b.data,inv.companyID),i+1 from InvestRelation inv inner join (select data,func_splitStringLast(data,',') as id from mytmpB) b on inv.InvestorID=b.id;
        SET i = i + 1;
    END WHILE;
    select * from mytmpA;
    DROP TEMPORARY TABLE IF EXISTS mytmpA;
    DROP TEMPORARY TABLE IF EXISTS mytmpB;
END

-- Execute stored procedure, explore 5 levels against enterprise no. 12
CALL 'queryChildrenInfo'(12,5);
```

Figure 13.3: SQL-centric UBO

Taking **UBO** (which stands for **ultimate beneficiary ownership**, which is a common scenario as part of the anti-fraud or know-your-customer process) penetration and identification as an example, writing a solution using SQL/RDBMS would be both complex and time-consuming. *Figure 13.2* illustrates a MySQL-flavored core SQL code snippet to identify the UBOs, which may be hidden five hops (layers) away from the starting entity (to be penetrated or investigated). Achieving the same using GQL is just a matter of a single line of code:

```
MATCH p = (n:startID)<-[:Invest]-{1,5}(m)
RETURN p
```

With a real-time-capable graph database, the preceding GQL takes only single-digit milliseconds to run on a table equivalent of 10,000 rows of data points, while SQL would take around 3 dozen seconds. There is a speed-up of over 30,000 times.

Opportunities for growth

Despite the real or speculative challenges, GQL's evolving landscape presents numerous opportunities for growth, particularly in industries that rely heavily on interconnected data. As GQL and GQL implementations evolve, its advanced features will open new doors for application development and real-time data analysis.

Industry applications

GQL's ability to efficiently handle complex relationships and dynamic data structures will make it an indispensable tool across many industries:

- In finance, GQL can be used to identify fraud patterns and optimize risk management, as well as empowering decision-making and generating smart recommendations or compliance reporting

- Healthcare applications can benefit from graph-based data modeling for patient tracking and personalized treatment plans

- E-commerce platforms can leverage a graph database for enhanced customer experience and boosted ARPU

- Social media platforms can enhance user engagement through targeted content recommendations and community analysis

- Manufacturers and plants can benefit from graph-augmented maintenance and support planning to reduce TCO and benefit from an optimized supply chain network

- Supply chain enterprises (and customs offices) will gain more insights into the merchandise and trade network, which will help reduce trade friction and accelerate network optimization

- Governments around the world are collecting more and more data; to avoid dealing with this data in the old, siloed fashion, graphs are a smart way to go

- Utilities such as power transmission and distribution systems, water systems, sewage systems, and networks are all inherently graphs and so can be represented using graph technology

Academic and research opportunities

The evolution of GQL will also create opportunities for academic research and innovation. Researchers can explore new algorithms, data structures, and applications of GQL, contributing to the advancement of graph database technology.

Comparing it to SQL/RDMBS, today's GQL adoption rate is less than 1% of the former. From an academic education and career training perspective, there are tons of opportunities to broaden and deepen the reach of GQL and graph database management systems.

Collaboration and partnerships

To propel GQL forward, collaboration with technology providers, academic institutions, and industry leaders is paramount. By forming partnerships, the GQL community can foster innovation, ensuring that GQL evolves in alignment with real-world needs. These alliances can be pivotal in developing cutting-edge tools and frameworks that enhance GQL's usability, performance, and integration with various systems. Through collaboration, GQL can also benefit from the wealth of knowledge and expertise that these diverse sectors bring. For instance, academic collaborations can introduce new research findings that lead to algorithmic improvements, while partnerships with technology providers can integrate the best practices and new tools that streamline GQL adoption.

In addition, partnerships across industries can help GQL better address domain-specific challenges. In sectors such as finance, healthcare, and e-commerce, where data complexity and real-time processing are key factors, tailored solutions powered by GQL and graph algorithms can revolutionize business processes. Collaborative efforts will allow for the development of new features that support specific business needs, driving the widespread adoption of GQL. Moreover, joint initiatives can help bridge the knowledge gap by providing educational resources, workshops, and certifications, which will support the next generation of GQL developers. The collaborative approach will ensure that GQL's growth is driven by both technical advancements and the practical, real-world applications demanded by the market.

The future of GQL

Looking ahead, the future of GQL is exceptionally promising. As data continues to grow in complexity, GQL is poised to be a central player in data management and analysis. Over the next several years, GQL will likely evolve to integrate even more seamlessly with emerging technologies, dramatically enhancing its capabilities and expanding its applications across various industries.

Integration with emerging technologies

As the digital landscape becomes increasingly interconnected, GQL will play a key role in supporting cutting-edge technologies such as blockchain, the **Internet of Things** (**IoT**), and edge computing. These advancements will present new opportunities for GQL to manage and process complex relationships between data in real time. For instance, in the realm of blockchain, GQL can facilitate the analysis of distributed ledger data, tracing relationships and transactions across multiple networks. In IoT, GQL will empower the aggregation and analysis of massive datasets from a variety of interconnected devices, while edge computing will leverage GQL's speed and flexibility to enable data processing closer to the source, reducing latency and enhancing decision-making.

Moreover, GQL's ability to handle dynamic, multi-dimensional data structures will make it an ideal language for these next-generation technologies. As new use cases emerge, the language will adapt to support more complex queries and integrate more sophisticated data sources, driving innovation in industries ranging from finance and healthcare to smart cities and autonomous systems.

Standardization and interoperability

One of the key milestones in GQL's future will be its continued standardization. As the language matures, a unified, globally recognized standard will enable interoperability across different graph database systems. This will empower organizations to adopt GQL with greater ease, knowing they can integrate it into their existing technology stacks without concerns about compatibility. Standardization will also foster a stronger ecosystem of tools, frameworks, and resources, accelerating the adoption of GQL across industries.

Moreover, interoperability with other data management paradigms, such as relational databases and NoSQL systems, will help bridge the gap between legacy and modern technologies. This will allow GQL to function as a versatile, multi-functional tool that can work alongside other technologies, offering a flexible solution for organizations transitioning to graph-based data management.

Continuous innovation

The GQL community will continue to drive rapid innovation. The collaborative nature of the open source community, coupled with contributions from developers, academia, and industry leaders, will ensure that GQL remains at the forefront of graph database technology. As new challenges arise, such as the need for faster query processing and more complex graph analytics, GQL will evolve to meet these demands.

While the language specification itself is not responsible for performance optimization, GQL implementations play a crucial role in delivering the efficient execution of graph queries. As graph database vendors compete and collaborate, we can expect ongoing improvements in the performance, scalability, and visualization capabilities of GQL-powered systems. These innovations will help organizations better leverage GQL for real-time decision-making, automation, and next-generation analytics.

The missing protocol: How GQL could expand its reach through standardized access

RDF databases have experienced significant growth, driven by standards. One of the most influential among these is SPARQL, a powerful query language designed specifically for querying RDF data, an official, formal standard developed and maintained by the **World Wide Web Consortium (W3C)**. The recursive acronym **SPARQL** stands for **SPARQL Protocol And RDF Query Language**. Interestingly, the name SPARQL includes a "P" for "Protocol," highlighting its capability not only as a query language but also as a standardized method for accessing distributed data across different systems. This protocol supports querying over HTTP in a federated manner, enabling users to retrieve and combine information from multiple, disparate data sources seamlessly. This approach is revolutionary because it allows access to distributed databases provided by different vendors, fostering the creation of public ontologies and knowledge graphs. These publicly accessible datasets can be integrated with private RDF databases, encouraging data reuse and accelerating innovation.

With the emergence of GQL, the potential for graph data utilization is even more significant. GQL defines only a query language, focusing on a flexible and expressive syntax for querying graph structures. This minimalist approach is powerful, as it provides a universal language for interacting with graph databases, irrespective of the underlying implementation. However, introducing a standardized protocol for accessing GQL-compliant databases—similar to the federated querying approach of SPARQL—could significantly accelerate its adoption. This would enable users to query distributed GQL-ready datasets, for example, using the HTTP protocol, through a unified, standardized method. Such a capability would not only promote interoperability between different GQL implementations but also encourage the proliferation of public graph datasets that can be integrated seamlessly with private graph data sources. This vision of a standardized, federated access protocol for GQL could be a game-changer, driving the growth of the GQL community and enhancing the value of graph database technologies worldwide.

Furthermore, adopting additional features that have made RDF databases particularly successful could enhance GQL's adoption and potentially facilitate a convergence of the two data models, at least from a functional perspective. One such feature is the use of **Uniform Resource Identifiers (URIs)** for uniquely identifying nodes and relationships, which improves data interoperability and linkage across datasets. Another powerful feature is **Shapes Constraint Language (SHACL)**, used in RDF databases for validating graph data against a set of constraints. SHACL is another standard, formally adopted as a W3C recommendation on July 20, 2017. Implementing a similar validation system for GQL is technically feasible, although it would require adaptations to fit GQL's property graph model.

A tailored graph validation language—let's call it **GQL shapes**—could be designed following principles similar to SHACL but optimized for property graphs. This system would need to include the following:

- **Node structure validation**: Constraints on node labels, required and optional properties, and property value types
- **Relationship validation**: Specifications for valid relationship types between specific node labels, cardinality constraints, and property requirements for relationships

- **Path-based constraints**: Analogous to SHACL's path expressions but adapted to GQL's path syntax

- **Custom validators**: The ability to define custom constraint functions using GQL itself

These ideas are ambitious for a standard that is still being established, but we believe that leveraging the best features of alternative technologies can only enhance the validity and acceptance of the new standard. By capitalizing on proven concepts such as URIs for unique identification and SHACL-like validation systems, GQL can inherit the strengths that have contributed to the success of RDF databases. This strategic adoption would not only improve GQL's functionality and flexibility but also foster interoperability between different graph data models. Ultimately, embracing the best of both worlds can accelerate GQL's adoption and solidify its position as a leading standard in the graph database landscape.

Final reflections: A unified future with GQL

As we arrive at the conclusion of this book, it becomes clear that the evolution of database technologies has brought us to a pivotal juncture—one defined by the growing demand for handling interconnected data at scale, in real time, and with ever-increasing complexity. GQL emerges not as a mere addition to the pantheon of query languages, but as a transformative leap forward—shaped by decades of experience with SQL, inspired by advances in graph theory, and driven by real-world data needs.

Throughout this book, we've traced the historical trajectory of database query languages, from the foundational ideas of Codd and the rise of SQL, through the fragmentation and innovation of NoSQL, to the birth of GQL as the industry's first ISO-standard graph query language. We've examined core concepts such as pattern matching, path expressions, schema design, data modeling, and real-time analytics—all underpinned by the shift from tabular to graph-based thinking. Whether through theoretical models or practical use cases, each chapter has built toward a deeper appreciation of how GQL redefines the language of data.

Looking ahead, GQL's journey is far from complete. Standardization will broaden interoperability; named procedures and quantified paths will streamline programmability; integration with AI, machine learning, and Web3 (and a lot more trendy areas if you will) will expand capabilities; and new ideas—such as protocol layers, validation schemas, and unified frameworks—may shape what's next. But one thing is certain: GQL has already established itself as the most forward-looking query language for a world where data is no longer just relational, but richly connected.

By learning GQL, we're not just adapting to a new syntax. We're adopting a new paradigm for expressing relationships, traversing complexity, and unlocking insight. In this sense, GQL is not just the future of query languages—it is the language of the future.

Get This Book's PDF Version and Exclusive Extras

UNLOCK NOW

Scan the QR code (or go to packtpub.com/unlock). Search for this book by name, confirm the edition, and then follow the steps on the page.

Note: Keep your invoice handy. Purchases made directly from Packt don't require an invoice.

14

Glossary and Resources

Glossary

Term	Definition
4Vs	The four key challenges of big data: Volume (amount of data), Velocity (speed of data generation), Variety (different forms of data), and Veracity (uncertainty of data quality).
ACID	An acronym for Atomicity, Consistency, Isolation, and Durability – the set of properties that guarantee database transactions are processed reliably, even in the event of errors or system failures.
Aggregation	A function that performs a calculation on multiple values to return a single value, such as COUNT, SUM, AVG, MIN, or MAX in graph queries.
Anti-Fraud	Applications of graph databases to detect patterns indicative of fraudulent activities by analyzing connections and relationships between entities.
AQL	ArangoDB Query Language – the native query language for ArangoDB, designed to query documents, graphs, and key-value pairs.
ArangoDB	An open source, multi-model database system that supports graphs, documents, and key-value data models.
ASC	Ascending order specification, used in query result ordering.

Term	Definition
Async	Short for asynchronous, referring to operations that don't occur at the same time or in a synchronized manner, allowing the system to continue processing without waiting for an operation to complete.
Binary	A representation system using only two symbols (typically 0 and 1), or a data type representing such values.
Binding Table	A structure that maps variables to values in a query execution context.
Boolean	A logical data type with two possible values: true or false.
Canonical Composition	The process of reducing a character sequence to a standardized form according to normalization rules.
Cardinality	The number of elements in a set. In graph databases, it can refer to the total number of nodes and edges in a path.
Centrality Analysis	A method used in network theory and graph analytics to identify the most important or influential nodes within a graph. Common centrality measures include degree centrality, betweenness centrality, closeness centrality, and eigenvector centrality.
CET	Central European Time – a time zone used in many European countries.
CHAR	A data type representing a fixed-length string of characters.
ChatGPT	A large language model developed by OpenAI, capable of natural language processing and generation.
Clause	A distinct section of a query statement that performs a specific function.
Close Record	A record type that doesn't allow for additional properties beyond those defined in its schema.
Constraint	A rule that restricts the data that can be stored in a database, ensuring data integrity.
Constructor	A function or expression that creates a new value or object.
Context	The environment or scope in which a query or operation is executed.
CPU	Central Processing Unit – the primary component of a computer that executes instructions.
CRC32	A hash function that produces a 32-bit hash value.

Term	Definition
Cypher	A declarative graph query language originally developed by Neo4j, now part of the openCypher project.
DAY TO SECOND	An interval data type that represents a duration specified in days, hours, minutes, and seconds.
DBaaS	Database as a Service – a cloud computing service model allowing users to access and use a database without setting up hardware, installing software, or managing the database.
DBMS	Database Management System – software for creating, retrieving, updating, and managing data in a database.
DCL	Data Control Language – a subset of SQL used to control access to data within a database.
DDL	Data Definition Language – a subset of SQL used to define data structures in a database.
Degree	The number of edges connected to a node in a graph. It can be out/in degree and can be calculated by a specific edge property value.
DESC	Descending order specification, used in query result ordering.
Detach Delete	An operation that deletes a node and all its relationships without requiring explicit deletion of the relationships.
DGraph	An open source, distributed graph database designed for production environments.
DML	Data Manipulation Language – a subset of SQL used to manipulate data within database objects.
DQL	Data Query Language – a subset of SQL used to retrieve data from a database.
DST	Daylight Saving Time – the practice of advancing clocks during summer months.
Edge	A connection between two nodes in a graph, representing a relationship.
Edge Pattern	A specification that describes properties and characteristics of edges to be matched in a query.

Term	Definition
Edge Schema	A definition of the structure, constraints, and properties of edges in a graph database.
Elastic Search	A distributed, RESTful search and analytics engine capable of storing and processing graph-related data.
Endpoint	The node at the end of a path or edge in a graph.
ENIAC	Electronic Numerical Integrator and Computer – one of the first general-purpose electronic computers.
Euler Path	A path in a graph that visits every edge exactly once.
FPGA	Field-Programmable Gate Array – an integrated circuit designed to be configured after manufacturing.
Full-Text	A type of search that examines all the words in stored documents or textual properties of graph elements.
Gartner	A global research and advisory firm providing insights, advice, and tools for business leaders.
GDBMS	Graph Database Management System – a system designed to store, manage, and query graph data.
GFS	Google File System – a scalable distributed file system for large, distributed data-intensive applications.
GitHub	A web-based platform for version control and collaboration for software development projects.
GPM/GPML	Graph Pattern Matching/Graph Pattern Matching Language – languages or techniques used to find patterns within graph data.
GPU	Graphics Processing Unit – a specialized electronic circuit designed to rapidly manipulate and alter memory to accelerate graphics rendering, increasingly used for graph processing.
GQL	Graph Query Language – a proposed standard query language for property graphs.
GQL Catalog	A container for schemas and other GQL objects within a database system.

Term	Definition
GQL Directory	A repository containing information about available catalogs, schemas, and other GQL resources.
GQL Playground	An interactive environment for writing, testing, and debugging GQL queries provided by Ultipa Graph. URL: `https://www.ultipa.com/gql-playground`
GQL Program	A collection of GQL statements to be executed as a unit.
GQL Schema	A specification that can only contain graphs, graph types, binding tables, and procedures.
GQL Server	A server implementation that processes GQL queries and manages graph data.
GQL Session	A context or environment used to process GQL statements with maintained state.
GQL Transaction	A sequence of operations performed as a single logical unit of work in GQL.
GQLClient	A software component or tool that connects to and interacts with a GQL server.
Graph	A data structure consisting of vertices (nodes) and edges (relationships) that connect these vertices.
Graph Database	A database that uses graph structures with nodes, edges, and properties to represent and store data.
Gremlin	A graph traversal language developed by Apache TinkerPop for graph databases.
GSQL	Graph SQL – TigerGraph's query language, designed for high-performance graph analytics.
Hadoop	An open source framework for distributed storage and processing of large datasets.
Hamiltonian Path	A path in a graph that visits each vertex exactly once.
HDC	High Density Computing – a computing architecture founded by Ultipa for efficient graph processing.

Term	Definition
HDC Graph	High Density Computing Graph – a high-performance graph stored in HDC Server.
HDC Server	A server designed to store high-performance HDC graphs and execute HDC GQL/UQL queries or graph algorithms on an HDC graph database.
HTAP	Hybrid Transactional/Analytical Processing – database systems capable of performing both transaction processing and analytics workloads.
Hyperbolic Trigonometric	Functions involving hyperbolic sine, cosine, and so on, sometimes used in graph algorithms for embedding graphs in hyperbolic spaces.
IEC	International Electrotechnical Commission – an organization that publishes international standards for electrical, electronic, and related technologies.
Immaterial	A value that is not null, indicating the presence of a value even if its specific content is not yet determined.
Implementation-Dependent	Behavior or features that may vary across different implementations of the same specification.
Index	A data structure that improves the speed of data retrieval operations on a database.
Integer	A data type representing whole numbers without fractional components.
ISO	International Organization for Standardization – an independent, non-governmental organization that develops and publishes international standards.
JOIN Operations	Query operations that combine records from two or more database tables or graphs.
K-Hop	An algorithm that identifies all nodes that are exactly K steps (edges) away from a starting node in a graph.

Labeled Property Graph (LPG)	A graph model where edges and nodes have labels indicating their types and key-value pairs as properties.
LLM	Large Language Model – a type of artificial intelligence model trained on vast amounts of text data, capable of understanding and generating human-like text.
Loan	A financial scenario commonly used in graph database examples, representing lending relationships between banks and customers.
Louvain	A community detection algorithm for large networks, identifying communities by optimizing modularity.
MapReduce	A programming model for processing and generating large datasets with a parallel, distributed algorithm.
MATCH	A GQL query statement used to match patterns in a graph.
MemGraph	An in-memory graph database platform optimized for real-time applications.
Mixed Graph	A graph that includes both directed and undirected edges.
Money Laundering	The process of making illegally obtained money appear legal by disguising its source through complex financial transactions and networks. Graph databases excel at detecting these patterns by analyzing relationships between entities (people, accounts, companies), tracking transaction flows across networks, identifying circular transaction patterns, and revealing hidden beneficiaries in organizational structures.
MongoDB	A document database that stores JSON-like documents with dynamic schemas.
MultiGraph	A graph that allows multiple edges between the same pair of nodes.
MVCC	Multi-Version Concurrency Control – a technique used to provide concurrent access to a database without locking by keeping multiple versions of data.
Named Procedure	A stored procedure that can be called by name to perform a specific operation on a graph.
NLP	Natural Language Processing – a field of AI focused on enabling computers to understand, interpret, and generate human language.

Node	An element in a graph representing an entity. It's also referred to as a vertex.
Node Schema	A definition of the structure, constraints, and properties of nodes in a graph database.
Normalize	The process used for standardizing string values to ensure consistent representation and comparison.
NoSQL	A category of database management systems that don't use the traditional relational database structure; includes document stores, key-value stores, and column-family stores, but graph databases are typically considered a separate category.
nQL	The native query language of Nebula Graph, designed for querying and manipulating graph data.
NULL	A special marker used to indicate that a value is missing or unknown.
Numeric	A data type representing numbers, including integers and floating-point values.
Octets	Groups of 8 bits, commonly used in representing binary data.
OLAP	Online Analytical Processing – a technology used to organize large business databases for complex analysis.
OLTP	Online Transaction Processing – a category of data processing focused on transaction-oriented tasks.
Open Record	A record type that allows for additional properties beyond those defined in its schema.
OpenAI	A research laboratory focusing on artificial intelligence development.
openCypher	An open source implementation of the Cypher query language for property graphs.
Operators	Symbols or keywords that represent operations in queries or expressions.
Orientation	The direction assigned to edges in a directed graph.
PageRank	An algorithm used to rank web pages and, by extension, nodes in a graph based on their importance.
Path	A sequence of alternating vertices and edges in a graph.
Path Elements	The components (nodes and edges) that make up a path in a graph.

Path Pattern	A specification describing a path to be matched in a graph query.
Periodic	Occurring at regular intervals, often used in time-series or temporal graphs.
Property	A key-value pair associated with a node or edge in a property graph.
Property Graph (PG)	A graph model where both nodes and edges can have properties in the form of key-value pairs.
Quantified Path Pattern	A path pattern with quantifiers specifying how many times a subpattern can be repeated.
RAM	Random Access Memory – volatile computer memory used for the temporary storage of data and program code.
RDF	Resource Description Framework – a standard model for data interchange on the web, often used for representing knowledge graphs.
Record	A collection of related data items, typically representing a row in a table or a structured entity in a graph.
Redis	An in-memory data structure store that can be used as a database, cache, or message broker with graph capabilities.
Repository	A central location where data, metadata, or code is stored and maintained.
Shards	Partitions of a database distributed across multiple servers to improve performance and scalability.
Similarity	A measure of how alike two entities are, often used in recommendation systems and graph analytics.
Simple Graph	A graph with no self-loops or multiple edges between the same pair of vertices.
SNS	Social Network Service – platforms that focus on building social networks or relationships among people.
Spark	An open source unified analytics engine for large-scale data processing.
Spark GraphX	A component of Apache Spark for graphs and graph-parallel computation.
SPARQL	SPARQL Protocol and RDF Query Language – a semantic query language for databases, able to retrieve and manipulate data stored in RDF format.

SQL	Structured Query Language – a domain-specific language used for managing relational databases.
SQL Server	A relational database management system developed by Microsoft.
SQL/PGQ	SQL for Property Graph Queries – an extension to SQL for querying property graphs.
SSD	Solid-State Drive – a storage device using integrated circuit assemblies to store data persistently.
SSO	Single Sign-On – an authentication scheme that allows a user to log in with a single ID to multiple related systems.
Standard Deviation (STDDEV)	A statistical measure of the amount of variation or dispersion in a set of values.
Statement	A unit of execution in a query language.
Status Code	A numerical or symbolic code returned by the GQL engine in response to a query or command, indicating the outcome of the operation. Status codes are used to represent success, failure, or specific errors.
Stream	A continuous flow of data that can be processed incrementally.
Sync	Short for synchronous, referring to operations that occur at the same time or in a coordinated manner.
Syntax	The set of rules that defines the combinations of symbols considered correctly structured statements in a language.
Temporal	Relating to time; in databases, often referring to time-aware data models or queries.
TigerGraph	A graph database platform designed for high-performance data processing.
Timezone	A region where the same standard time is used.
Token	The smallest lexical unit of a programming language or query language.
Truncate	To cut off or remove a part of something; in databases, often referring to removing all records from a table or collection.
Truth Table	A mathematical table used in logic to determine whether a compound statement is true for all possible values of its components.

UBO	Ultimate Beneficial Owner – the person who ultimately benefits from or controls an entity, often used in anti-money laundering applications of graph databases.
Ultipa Graph	A high-performance, scalable graph database and analytics platform for TP and AP requirements.
Unicode	A computing industry standard for the consistent encoding, representation, and handling of text.
UNIVAC	Universal Automatic Computer – one of the first commercial computers produced in the United States.
Unsigned Number	A number that is always zero or positive, having no sign bit.
UQL	Ultipa Query Language – a native graph query language developed by Ultipa.
UTC	Coordinated Universal Time – the primary time standard by which the world regulates clocks and time.
UUID	Universally Unique Identifier – a 128-bit number used to identify information in computer systems.
Value Expression	An expression that results in a value when evaluated.
Vector Index	A specialized index structure optimized for similarity search in vector spaces, often used for graph embeddings.
Vertex	A node in a graph, representing an entity.
W3C	World Wide Web Consortium – the main international standards organization for the World Wide Web.
YEAR TO MONTH	An interval data type that represents a duration specified in years and months.
YIELD	A clause in graph query languages, used to specify which values to return from a query.

Resources

Optional features – GQL conformance

	Feature ID	Feature Name	Description
1	G002	Different Edges match mode	The DIFFERENT EDGES match mode.
2	G003	Explicit REPEATABLE ELEMENTS keyword	The REPEATABLE ELEMENTS match mode.
3	G004	Path variables	Path variable declaration in a path pattern.
4	G005	Path search prefix in a path pattern	Also see features G007 and G014 to G020.
5	G006	Graph pattern KEEP clause: path mode prefix	Apply a path mode prefix in the KEEP clause for all path patterns in a graph pattern.
6	G007	Graph pattern KEEP clause: path search prefix	Applies a path search prefix in the KEEP clause for all path patterns in a graph pattern.
7	G010	Explicit WALK keyword	The WALK path mode.
8	G011	Advanced path modes: TRAIL	The TRAIL path mode.
9	G012	Advanced path modes: SIMPLE	The SIMPLE path mode.
10	G013	Advanced path modes: ACYCLIC	The ACYCLIC path mode.
11	G014	Explicit PATH/PATHS keywords	Include the PATH or PATHS keyword in the path pattern prefix, such as ANY SIMPLE PATH.
12	G015	All path search: explicit ALL keyword	The ALL path search prefix.
13	G016	Any path search	The ANY [<k>] path search prefix.
14	G017	All shortest path search	The ALL SHORTEST path search prefix.
15	G018	Any shortest path search	The ANY SHORTEST path search prefix.

	Feature ID	Feature Name	Description
16	**G019**	Counted shortest path search	The SHORTEST <k> path search prefix.
17	**G020**	Counted shortest group search	The SHORTEST [<k>] GROUP path search prefix.
18	**G030**	Path multiset alternation	Combines path terms using the |+| operator.
19	**G031**	Path multiset alternation: variable-length path operands	An operand of a path multiset alternation can be a variable-length path pattern.
20	**G032**	Path pattern union	Combines path terms using the | operator.
21	**G033**	Path pattern union: variable-length path operands	An operand of a path pattern union can be a fixed variable path pattern.
22	**G035**	Quantified paths	Affix a quantifier to a parenthesized path pattern.
23	**G036**	Quantified edges	Affix a quantifier to an edge pattern.
24	G037	Questioned paths	Affix a question mark to an element pattern, a parenthesized path pattern expression, or a simplified path pattern expression.
25	**G038**	Parenthesized path pattern expression	Enclose a path pattern expression in ( ). Also see features G048 to G051.
26	G039	Simplified path pattern expression: full defaulting	Express a path pattern as a regular expression of edge labels, with directionality options including left, undirected, right, left or undirected, undirected or right, left or right, and any direction. Also see features G080 to G082.
27	G041	Non-local element pattern predicates	The element pattern WHERE clause can reference an element variable that is not declared in the element pattern.

	Feature ID	Feature Name	Description
28	**G043**	Complete full edge patterns	Complete full edge patterns include directionality options left, undirected, right, undirected, undirected or right, left or right, and any direction.
29	**G044**	Basic abbreviated edge patterns	Basic abbreviated edge patterns include directionality options left, right, and any direction.
30	**G045**	Complete abbreviated edge patterns	Complete abbreviated edge patterns include directionality options left, undirected, right, undirected, undirected or right, left or right, and any direction.
31	**G046**	Relaxed topological consistency: adjacent vertex patterns	Two node patterns can be juxtaposed in a path pattern.
32	**G047**	Relaxed topological consistency: concise edge patterns	Two edge patterns can be juxtaposed in a path pattern.
33	**G048**	Parenthesized path pattern: subpath variable declaration	Declare a variable for a parenthesized path pattern.
34	**G049**	Parenthesized path pattern: path mode prefix	Apply a path mode prefix to a parenthesized path pattern.
35	**G050**	Parenthesized path pattern: WHERE clause	Apply a WHERE clause to a parenthesized path pattern.
36	**G051**	Parenthesized path pattern: non-local predicates	A parenthesized path pattern WHERE clause can reference an element variable that is not declared in the parenthesized path pattern.
37	**G060**	Bounded graph pattern quantifiers	The quantifier has an upper bound.
38	**G061**	Unbounded graph pattern quantifiers	The quantifier does not have an upper bound.

	Feature ID	Feature Name	Description
39	**G074**	Label expression: wild-card label	Use the % symbol in a label expression to match a non-empty label set.
40	**G080**	Simplified path pattern expression: basic defaulting	Similar to feature G039, with directionality options only including left, right, and any direction.
41	**G081**	Simplified path pattern expression: full overrides	Similar to feature G039, with the option to override the specified directionality as left, undirected, right, left or undirected, undirected or right, left or right, and any direction.
42	**G082**	Simplified path pattern expression: basic overrides	Similar to feature G039, with the option to override the specified directionality as left, right, or any direction.
43	**G100**	ELEMENT_ID function	The ELEMENT_ID function.
44	**G110**	IS DIRECTED predicate	The IS DIRECTED predicate.
45	**G111**	IS LABELED predicate	The IS LABELED predicate.
46	**G112**	IS SOURCE and IS DESTINATION predicate	The IS SOURCE and IS DESTINATION predicates.
47	**G113**	ALL_DIFFERENT predicate	The ALL_DIFFERENT predicate.
48	**G114**	SAME predicate	The SAME predicate.
49	**G115**	PROPERTY_EXISTS predicate	The PROPERTY_EXISTS predicate.
50	**GA01**	IEEE 754 floating point operations	Handle approximate numeric types following the IEEE Std 754:2019 standard.
51	**GA03**	Explicit ordering of nulls	Apply NULLS FIRST or NULLS LAST when ordering a binding table.
52	**GA04**	Universal comparison	The declared types of the operands of an equality operation can be non-comparable essentially.

	Feature ID	Feature Name	Description
53	**GA05**	Cast specification	Specify a data conversion by CAST().
54	**GA06**	Value type predicate	Specify a value type test by IS [NOT] TYPED.
55	**GA07**	Ordering by discarded binding variables	The ORDER BY clause in a primitive result statement or a SELECT statement may contain a sort key that contains a binding variable reference that is not equivalent to a return or select item alias.
56	**GA08**	GQL-status objects with diagnostic records	GQL-status objects contain diagnostic records with diagnostic information.
57	**GA09**	Comparison of paths	The declared types of the operands of an equality operation may contain path types.
58	**GB01**	Long identifiers	The length in characters of the representative form of a non-delimited identifier or a delimited identifier may be more than 127.
59	**GB02**	Double minus sign comments	Simple comment introducer --.
60	**GB03**	Double solidus comments	Simple comment introducer //.
61	**GC01**	Graph schema management	Creates or drops a GQL schema.
62	**GC02**	Graph schema management: IF [NOT] EXISTS	Include IF [NOT] EXISTS when creating or dropping a GQL schema.
63	**GC03**	Graph type: IF [NOT] EXISTS	Include IF [NOT] EXISTS when creating or dropping a graph type.
64	**GC04**	Graph management	Create or drop a graph.
65	**GC05**	Graph management: IF [NOT] EXISTS	Include IF [NOT] EXISTS when creating or dropping a graph.

	Feature ID	Feature Name	Description
65	GC05	Graph management: IF [NOT] EXISTS	Include IF [NOT] EXISTS when creating or dropping a graph.
66	GD01	Updatable graphs	The INSERT, SET, REMOVE, and DELETE statements.
67	GD02	Graph label set changes	Sets the label set of graph elements using the SET statement.
68	GD03	DELETE statement: subquery support	A delete item in the DELETE statement may contain a procedure body.
69	GD04	DELETE statement: simple expression support	A delete item in the DELETE statement may contain a value expression that is not a binding variable reference.
70	GE01	Graph reference value expressions	A value expression may contain a binding graph reference value expression.
71	GE02	Binding table reference value expressions	A value expression may contain a binding table reference value expression.
72	GE03	Let-binding of variables in expressions	The LET value expression.
73	GE04	Graph parameters	Specify a dynamic parameter for a value of a supertype of a graph reference value type.
74	GE05	Binding table parameters	Specify a dynamic parameter for a value of a supertype of a binding table reference value type.
75	GE06	Path value construction	Concatenate path values with ||.
76	GE07	Boolean XOR	A Boolean value expression may contain XOR.
77	GE08	Reference parameters	Specify a reference parameter for a catalog reference.
78	GE09	Horizontal aggregation	Apply an aggregate function to a group variable.

	Feature ID	Feature Name	Description
79	**GF01**	Enhanced numeric functions	The ABS, MOD, FLOOR, CEIL, and SQRT functions.
80	**GF02**	Trigonometric functions	The SIN, COS, TAN, COT, SINH, COSH, TANH, ASIN, ACOS, ATAN, DEGREES, and RADIANS functions.
81	**GF03**	Logarithmic functions	The LOG, LOG10, LN, EXP, and POWER functions.
82	**GF04**	Enhanced path functions	The ELEMENTS and PATH_LENGTH functions.
83	**GF05**	Multi-character TRIM function	The BTRIM, LTRIM, and RTRIM functions.
84	**GF06**	Explicit TRIM function	The TRIM function for single-character trim.
85	**GF07**	Byte string TRIM function	The TRIM function for byte string trim.
86	**GF10**	Advanced aggregate functions: general set functions	The COLLECT_LIST, STDDEV_SAMP, and STDDEV_POP functions.
87	**GF11**	Advanced aggregate functions: binary set functions	The PERCENTILE_CONT and PERCENTILE_DISC functions.
88	**GF12**	CARDINALITY function	The CARDINALITY function.
89	**GF13**	SIZE function	The SIZE function.
90	**GF20**	Aggregate functions in sort keys	The value expression contained in a sort key may contain an aggregate function.
91	**GG01**	Graph with an open graph type	Create a graph with an open graph type.
92	**GG02**	Graph with a closed graph type	Create a graph with a closed graph type.
93	**GG03**	Graph type inline specification	Create a closed graph with a nested graph type specification.

	Feature ID	Feature Name	Description
94	**GG04**	Graph type like a graph	Create a closed graph with the graph type specified by LIKE.
95	**GG05**	Graph from a graph source	Create a closed graph with the graph type specified by AS COPY OF.
96	**GG20**	Explicit element type names	Specify the node or edge type name in an element type specification.
97	**GG21**	Explicit element type key label sets	Specify the key label set in an element type specification.
98	**GG22**	Element type key label set inference	In a graph type specification, if the key label set of a node (or edge) type is omitted, then its effective label set includes all labels that are in its implied label set but not in the label sets of all other node (or edge) types.
99	**GG23**	Optional element type key label sets	An element type specification may omit specifying a key label set.
100	**GG24**	Relaxed structural consistency	Without this feature, for every two property name-sharing element type specifications ET1 and ET2 of a graph type specification, and every property name PN in the intersection of the property names of ET1 and ET2, it holds that a hypothetical application of the graph-type specific combination of property value types with the set comprising the value types of the property types of ET1 and ET2 whose name is PN as DTSET would succeed.
101	**GG25**	Relaxed key label set uniqueness for edge types	A graph type may contain two edge types whose effective key label sets are the same but are not omitted.

	Feature ID	Feature Name	Description
102	**GG26**	Relaxed property value type consistency	Property types with the same name are not required to have the same value type.
103	**GH01**	External object references	Identify a GQL object with a URI.
104	**GH02**	Undirected edge patterns	Insert an undirected edge.
105	**GL01**	Hexadecimal literals	The unsigned hexadecimal integer values – for example, 0xFF (255).
106	**GL02**	Octal literals	The unsigned octal integer values – for example, 0o17 (15).
107	**GL03**	Binary literals	The unsigned binary integer values – for example, 0b10000000 (128).
108	**GL04**	Exact number in common notation without suffix	Support the unsigned decimal in common notation – for example, 10.5, .3.
109	**GL05**	Exact number in common notation or as decimal integer with suffix	An exact numeric literal that is an unsigned decimal in common notation, followed by an exact number suffix or an unsigned decimal integer followed by an exact number suffix – for example, 12.3M (12).
110	**GL06**	Exact number in scientific notation with suffix	An exact numeric literal that is an unsigned decimal in scientific notation followed by an exact number suffix – for example, 1.23E3 (1230).
111	**GL07**	Approximate number in common notation or as a decimal integer with a suffix	An approximate numeric literal that is an unsigned decimal in common notation, followed by an approximate number suffix or an unsigned decimal integer followed by an approximate number suffix – for example, 3.14F (3.14 as a FLOAT value), 1D (1 as a DOUBLE value).

	Feature ID	Feature Name	Description
112	**GL08**	Approximate number in scientific notation with suffix	An approximate numeric literal that is an unsigned decimal in scientific notation followed by an approximate number suffix – for example, 1.23e3F (1230 as a FLOAT value).
113	**GL09**	Optional float number suffix	The approximate number suffix F.
114	**GL10**	Optional double number suffix	The approximate number suffix D.
115	**GL11**	Opt-out character escaping	The no escape symbol @ for a character string literal.
116	**GL12**	SQL datetime and interval formats	SQL-datetime literal and SQL-interval literal.
117	**GP01**	Inline procedure	The inline procedure call.
118	**GP02**	Inline procedure with implicit nested variable scope	An inline procedure call can omit the variable scope clause.
119	**GP03**	Inline procedure with explicit nested variable scope	An inline procedure call may contain a variable scope clause.
120	**GP04**	Named procedure calls	The named procedure call.
121	**GP05**	Procedure-local value variable definitions	A binding variable definition in a procedure body may contain a value variable definition.
122	**GP06**	Procedure-local value variable definitions: value variables based on simple expressions	A value variable definition may contain a value expression that does not conform to the value specification.

	Feature ID	Feature Name	Description
123	**GP07**	Procedure-local value variable definitions: value variable based on subqueries	Support a value variable definition that contains a procedure body.
124	**GP08**	Procedure-local binding table variable definitions	A binding variable definition may contain a binding table variable definition; a binding variable reference can be a supertype of a binding table reference value type.
125	**GP09**	Procedure-local binding table variable definitions: binding table variables based on simple expressions or references	Support a binding table variable definition that contains a binding table expression that does not conform to the value specification or is a binding table reference.
126	**GP10**	Procedure-local binding table variable definitions: binding table variables based on subqueries	Support a binding table variable definition that contains a procedure body.
127	**GP11**	Procedure-local graph variable definitions	A binding variable definition may contain a graph variable definition; a binding variable reference can be a supertype of a graph reference value type.
128	**GP12**	Procedure-local graph variable definitions: graph variables based on simple expressions or references	Support a graph variable definition that contains a procedure body.
129	**GP13**	Procedure-local graph variable definitions: graph variables based on subqueries	Support a graph variable definition that contains a graph expression that does not conform to the value specification or is a graph reference.

	Feature ID	Feature Name	Description
130	**GP14**	Binding tables as procedure arguments	The declared type of a value expression immediately contained in a procedure argument can be a supertype of a binding table reference value type.
131	**GP15**	Graphs as procedure arguments	The declared type of a value expression immediately contained in a procedure argument can be a supertype of a graph reference value type.
132	**GP16**	AT schema clause	A procedure body may contain an AT SCHEMA clause.
133	**GP17**	Binding variable definition block	A procedure body may contain a binding variable definition block.
134	**GP18**	Catalog and data statement mixing	A procedure specification may contain a data-modifying procedure specification or a catalog-modifying procedure specification.
135	**GQ01**	USE graph clause	The USE graph clause.
136	**GQ02**	Composite query: OTHERWISE	The OTHERWISE query conjunction.
137	**GQ03**	Composite query: UNION	The UNION query conjunction.
138	**GQ04**	Composite query: EXCEPT DISTINCT	The EXCEPT DISTINCT query conjunction.
139	**GQ05**	Composite query: EXCEPT ALL	The EXCEPT ALL query conjunction.
140	**GQ06**	Composite query: INTERSECT DISTINCT	The INTERSECT DISTINCT query conjunction.
141	**GQ07**	Composite query: INTERSECT ALL	The INTERSECT ALL query conjunction.
142	**GQ08**	FILTER statement	The FILTER statement.
143	**GQ09**	LET statement	The LET statement.

	Feature ID	Feature Name	Description
144	**GQ10**	FOR statement: list value support	The FOR statement may contain a list value expression.
145	**GQ11**	FOR statement: WITH ORDINALITY	The FOR statement may contain WITH ORDINALITY.
146	**GQ12**	ORDER BY and page statement: OFFSET clause	An order by and page statement may contain an OFFSET clause.
147	**GQ13**	ORDER BY and page statement: LIMIT clause	An order by and page statement may contain a LIMIT clause.
148	**GQ14**	Complex expressions in sort keys	Without this feature, a sort key shall be a binding variable reference.
149	**GQ15**	GROUP BY clause	The GROUP BY clause.
150	**GQ16**	Pre-projection aliases in sort keys	A sort key may contain a binding variable reference that is not a return item alias in the preceding RETURN statement.
151	**GQ17**	Element-wise group variable operations	Evaluate a value expression that contains references to exactly one variable whose type is a group list value type.
152	**GQ18**	Scalar subqueries	Specify a scalar value derived from a nested query specification.
153	**GQ19**	Graph pattern YIELD clause	A graph pattern binding table may contain a graph pattern YIELD clause.
154	**GQ20**	Advanced linear composition with NEXT	A procedure body may contain a NEXT statement.
155	**GQ21**	OPTIONAL: Multiple MATCH statements	An optional MATCH statement may contain a MATCH statement block.

	Feature ID	Feature Name	Description
156	**GQ22**	EXISTS predicate: multiple MATCH statements	An EXISTS may directly contain a MATCH statement block.
157	**GQ23**	FOR statement: binding table support	The FOR statement may contain a binding table reference.
158	**GQ24**	FOR statement: WITH OFFSET	The FOR statement may contain WITH OFFSET.
159	**GS01**	SESSION SET command: session-local graph parameters	The SESSION SET command may contain a session set graph parameter clause.
160	**GS02**	SESSION SET command: session-local binding table parameters	The SESSION SET command may contain a session set binding table parameter clause.
161	**GS03**	SESSION SET command: session-local value parameters	The SESSION SET command may contain a session set value parameter clause.
162	**GS04**	SESSION RESET command: reset all characteristics	The SESSION RESET command may contain a session reset argument.
163	**GS05**	SESSION RESET command: reset session schema	The SESSION RESET command may contain SESSION RESET SCHEMA.
164	**GS06**	SESSION RESET command: reset session graph	The SESSION RESET command may contain SESSION RESET PROPERTY GRAPH or SESSION RESET GRAPH.
165	**GS07**	SESSION RESET command: reset time zone displacement	The SESSION RESET command may contain SESSION RESET TIME ZONE.
166	**GS08**	SESSION RESET command: reset all session parameters	The SESSION RESET command may contain SESSION RESET ALL PARAMETERS or SESSION RESET PARAMETER.

	Feature ID	Feature Name	Description
167	**GS10**	SESSION SET command: session-local binding table parameters based on subqueries	The SESSION SET command may contain a session set binding table parameter clause that contains a procedure body.
168	**GS11**	SESSION SET command: session-local value parameters based on subqueries	The SESSION SET command may contain a session set value parameter clause that contains a procedure body.
169	**GS12**	SESSION SET command: session-local graph parameters based on simple expressions or references	The SESSION SET command may contain a session set graph parameter clause that contains a graph expression that does not conform to the value specification or is a graph reference.
170	**GS13**	SESSION SET command: session-local binding table parameters based on simple expressions or references	The SESSION SET command may contain a session set binding table parameter clause that contains a binding table expression that does not conform

to the value specification or is a binding table reference. |
171	**GS14**	SESSION SET command: session-local value parameters based on simple expressions	The SESSION SET command may contain a session set value parameter clause that contains a value expression that does not conform to the value specification.
172	**GS15**	SESSION SET command: set time zone displacement	The SESSION SET command may contain a session set time zone clause.
173	**GS16**	SESSION RESET command: reset individual session parameters	The SESSION RESET command may contain a session reset argument that immediately contains a parameter name.

	Feature ID	Feature Name	Description
174	**GT01**	Explicit transaction commands	The START TRANSACTION and the END TRANSACTION commands.
175	**GT02**	Specified transaction characteristics	The START TRANSACTION command may contain transaction characteristics.
176	**GT03**	Use of multiple graphs in a transaction	A GQL transaction may contain two USE graph clauses that have different graph expressions.
177	**GV01**	8-bit unsigned integer numbers	The UNSIGNED INTEGER8 or UINT8 value type.
178	**GV02**	8-bit signed integer numbers	The SIGNED INTEGER8, INTEGER8, or INT8 value type.
179	**GV03**	16-bit unsigned integer numbers	The UNSIGNED INTEGER16 or UINT16 value type.
180	**GV04**	16-bit signed integer numbers	The SIGNED INTEGER16, INTEGER16, or INT16 value type.
181	**GV05**	Small unsigned integer numbers	The USMALLINT value type.
182	**GV06**	32-bit unsigned integer numbers	The UNSIGNED INTEGER32 or UINT32 value type.
183	**GV07**	32-bit signed integer numbers	The SIGNED INTEGER32, INTEGER32, or INT32 value type.
184	**GV08**	Regular unsigned integer numbers	The UINT value type.
185	**GV09**	Specified integer number precision	A signed binary exact numeric type that contains a precision or a scale.
186	**GV10**	Big unsigned integer numbers	The UBINGINT value type.
187	**GV11**	64-bit unsigned integer numbers	The UNSIGNED INTEGER64 or UINT64 value type.

	Feature ID	Feature Name	Description
188	**GV12**	64-bit signed integer numbers	The `SIGNED INTEGER64`, `INTEGER64`, or `INT64` value type.
189	**GV13**	128-bit unsigned integer numbers	The `UNSIGNED INTEGER128` or `UINT128` value type.
190	**GV14**	128-bit signed integer numbers	The `SIGNED INTEGER128`, `INTEGER128`, or `INT128` value type.
191	**GV15**	256-bit unsigned integer numbers	The `UNSIGNED INTEGER256` or `UINT256` value type.
192	**GV16**	256-bit signed integer numbers	The `SIGNED INTEGER256`, `INTEGER256`, or `INT256` value type.
193	**GV17**	Decimal numbers	The `DECIMAL` or `DEC` value type.
194	**GV18**	Small signed integer numbers	The `SMALLINT` value type.
195	**GV19**	Big signed integer numbers	The `BIGINT` value type.
196	**GV20**	16-bit floating-point numbers	The `FLOAT16` value type.
197	**GV21**	32-bit floating-point numbers	The `FLOAT32` value type.
198	**GV22**	Specified floating-point number precision	An approximate numeric type that contains a precision or a scale.
199	**GV23**	Floating-point type name synonyms	The `REAL` or `DOUBLE` value type.
200	**GV24**	64-bit floating-point numbers	The `FLOAT64` value type.
201	**GV25**	128-bit floating-point numbers	The `FLOAT128` value type.

	Feature ID	Feature Name	Description
202	**GV26**	256-bit floating-point numbers	The FLOAT256 value type.
203	**GV30**	Specified character string minimum length	A character string type that contains a min length.
204	**GV31**	Specified character string maximum length	A character string type that contains a max length.
205	**GV32**	Specified character string fixed length	A character string type that contains a fixed length.
206	**GV35**	Byte string types	The BYTES, BINARY, or VARBINARY value type.
207	**GV36**	Specified byte string minimum length	A byte string type that contains a min length.
208	**GV37**	Specified byte string maximum length	A byte string type that contains a max length.
209	**GV38**	Specified byte string fixed length	Contains a byte string type that contains a fixed length.
210	**GV39**	Temporal types: date, local datetime, and local time support	Temporal instant type: LOCAL DATETIME, TIMESTAMP, DATE, LOCAL TIME, TIME WITHOUT TIME ZONE.
211	**GV40**	Temporal types: zoned datetime and zoned time support	Temporal instant type: ZONED DATETIME, TIMESTAMP WITH TIME ZONE, ZONED TIME, TIME WITH TIME ZONE.
212	**GV41**	Temporal types: duration support	Temporal duration type: DURATION.
213	**GV45**	Record types	Contain at least one of feature GV46 and feature GV47.
214	**GV46**	Closed record types	The RECORD value type containing a field types specification.
215	**GV47**	Open record types	The RECORD value type not containing a field types specification.

	Feature ID	Feature Name	Description
216	**GV48**	Nested record types	The RECORD value type containing a field types that contains a RECORD type.
217	**GV50**	List value types	The LIST value type.
218	**GV55**	Path value types	The PATH value type.
219	**GV60**	Graph reference value types	The GRAPH value type.
220	**GV61**	Binding table reference value types	The BINDING TABLE value type.
221	**GV65**	Dynamic union types	Contain at least one of feature GV66 and feature GV67.
222	**GV66**	Open dynamic union types	The ANY or a LIST value type that does not contain a value type.
223	**GV67**	Closed dynamic union types	The ANY<> value type.
224	**GV68**	Dynamic property value types	The ANY PROPERTY VALUE value type.
225	**GV70**	Immaterial value types	The NULL or NOTHING value type.
226	**GV71**	Immaterial value types: null type support	The NULL value type.
227	**GV72**	Immaterial value types: empty type support	The NULL or NOTHING value type.
228	**GV90**	Explicit value type nullability	The NOT NULL type.

Implementation-defined elements — GQL conformance

	Fea- ture ID	Feature Name
1	IA001	Whether the declared type of a regular result of a successful outcome of a GQL request is exposed to the GQL client.
2	IA002	The extent to which further GQL status objects are chained.
3	IA003	The result of any operation other than a normalize function or a normalized predicate on an unnormalized character string.
4	IA004	The rules for determining the actual value of an approximate numeric type from its apparent value.
5	IA005	Whether rounding or truncating occurs when the least significant digits are lost on assignment.
6	IA006	The choice of value selected when there is more than one approximation for a numeric type that conforms to the criteria for each supported type of numeric value.
7	IA007	Which supported numeric values, other than exact numeric types, also have approximations.
8	IA010	The boundaries within which the normal rules of arithmetic apply.
9	IA011	Whether rounding or truncating is used for division with an approximate mathematical result.
10	IA012	Whether a GQL Flagger flags implementation-defined features.
11	IA013	Whether the general rules of evaluation of a selective path pattern are terminated if an exception condition is raised.
12	IA014	Whether an exception condition is raised when the declared type of NULL cannot be determined contextually.
13	IA015	Whether to pad character strings for comparison, or not.
14	IA016	Whether to treat byte strings differing only in right-most X'00' bytes as equal or not.
15	IA017	Whether or not an exception condition is raised or an arbitrary value is chosen when multiple assignments to a graph element property are specified.

	Fea-ture ID	Feature Name
16	IA019	Whether bidirectional control characters are permitted in string literals.
17	IA020	Whether characters of the Unicode General Category class "Co" are permitted to be contained in the representative form of an identifier.
18	IA021	Whether an exception condition is raised, or truncation or rounding occurs, when an assignment of some number would result in a loss of its least significant digits.
19	IA023	The character (code) interpreted as newline.
20	IA025	The effect that additional values resulting from the support of feature GA01, "IEEE 754 floating-point operations," have on the processing of a GQL request.
21	IA026	Whether a GQL implementation supports leap seconds or discontinuities in calendars, and the consequences of such support for temporal arithmetic.
22	ID001	The object (principal) that represents a user within a GQL implementation.
23	ID002	The association between a principal and its home schema and home graph.
24	ID003	The set of privileges identified by an authorization identifier.
25	ID004	The value types of inner elements of constructed values when no concrete value is specified.
26	ID005	The declared type of an <elements function>.
27	ID006	The default transaction characteristics.
28	ID016	The translations of condition texts.
29	ID017	The map of diagnostic information, if provided.
30	ID022	The default collation.
31	ID023	The preferred name of a string type, for each supported kind of string type.
32	ID028	The effective binary precision of each supported integer type.
33	ID034	The effective decimal precision of each decimal type.
34	ID037	The effective binary precision and scale of each supported approximate numeric type.
35	ID048	The default time zone displacement.

	Fea-ture ID	Feature Name
36	ID049	The default session parameters.
37	ID057	The exact numeric type with scale 0 (zero) of list element ordinal positions.
38	ID058	The exact numeric type with scale 0 (zero) of list element position offsets.
39	ID059	The exact numeric declared type of the results of the COUNT function.
40	ID061	The declared type of SESSION_USER.
41	ID062	The exact numeric declared type of a non-negative integer specification.
42	ID063	The numeric declared type of the result of a dyadic arithmetic operator when either operand is an approximate numeric.
43	ID064	The numeric declared type of the result of a dyadic arithmetic operator when both operands are exact numeric.
44	ID065	The precision of the result of the addition and subtraction of exact numeric types.
45	ID066	The precision of the result of the multiplication of exact numeric types.
46	ID067	The precision and scale of the result of the division of exact numeric types.
47	ID068	The exact numeric declared type of result length expressions.
48	ID069	The numeric declared types of results of trigonometric functions, general logarithm functions, natural logarithms, exponential functions, and power functions.
49	ID070	The declared type of the result of a cardinality expression.
50	ID074	The precision of an exact numeric result of a numeric value expression.
51	ID075	The precision of an approximate numeric result of a numeric value expression.
52	ID076	The declared type of results of the ELEMENT_ID function.
53	ID079	The declared type of an approximate numeric literal.
54	ID085	The nullable declared type of NULL if its declared type cannot be determined contextually.
55	ID086	The default graph pattern match mode.

	Fea-ture ID	Feature Name
56	**ID089**	The use of GRAPH or PROPERTY GRAPH in the preferred name of graph types and graph reference value types.
57	**ID090**	The use of NODE or VERTEX in the preferred name of node types, node reference value types, and their base types.
58	**ID091**	The use of EDGE or RELATIONSHIP in the preferred name of edge types, edge reference value types, and their base types.
59	**ID095**	The exact numeric declared types of the results of the SUM function.
60	**ID096**	The exact numeric declared types of the results of the AVG function.
61	**ID097**	The approximate numeric declared types of the results of the SUM and AVG functions.
62	**ID098**	The approximate numeric declared types of the results of the STDDEV_POP and STDDEV_SAMP functions.
63	**ID099**	The approximate numeric declared types of the results of binary set functions.
64	**IE001**	The object, resource, or value identified by a URI or a URL.
65	**IE002**	The levels of transaction isolation, their interactions, their granularity of application, and the format and syntax rules for <implementation-defined access mode> used to select them.
66	**IE003**	The UAX31-R1-1 profile, if used.
67	**IE004**	Relaxations of the assumption of serializable transactional behavior, if any.
68	**IE005**	The treatment of language that does not conform to the formats and syntax rules.
69	**IE006**	Additional restrictions, requirements, and conditions imposed on mixed-mode transactions.
70	**IE007**	The conditions raised when the requirements on mixed-mode transactions are violated.
71	**IE008**	Additional conditions for which a completion condition warning (01000) is raised.
72	**IE009**	Additional informational conditions raised.

	Fea-ture ID	Feature Name
73	IE010	The subclasses providing information of a non-cautionary nature when the completion condition is successful completion.
74	IL001	The minimum and maximum cardinalities of label sets for each kind of graph element.
75	IL002	The maximum cardinalities of property sets for each kind of graph element.
76	IL003	The minimum and maximum cardinalities of key label sets for each kind of graph element.
77	IL009	The minimum length of a string resulting from the string concatenation of strings of variable-length string types for each supported string type.
78	IL010	The maximum number of digits permitted in an unsigned integer literal.
79	IL011	The maximum precision and scale of numbers of numeric types for each supported kind of number.
80	IL013	The maximum lengths of string values of string types for each supported string type.
81	IL015	The maximum cardinality of constructed values for each supported constructed value type.
82	IL018	The maximum value of the upper bound of a general qualifier.
83	IL020	The maximum depth of nesting of GQL directories.
84	IL023	The minimum and maximum values of the exponent for an approximate numeric type.
85	IL024	The maximum value of fractional seconds precision for a temporal instant or a temporal duration.
86	IS001	The implicit ordering of NULLs.
87	IV001	The character repertoire of GQL source text.
88	IV002	The result of an inequality comparison between operands that are essentially comparable values when not otherwise specified.
89	IV003	The choice of the normal form of each supported kind of GQL object type with a defined normal form.

	Fea-ture ID	Feature Name
90	IV008	The choice of the normal form of each supported kind of value type with a defined normal form.
91	IV010	The result of a comparison between two operands that are universally comparable values.
92	IV011	The dynamic union type chosen as the dynamic property value type.
93	IV012	The set of component types of the open dynamic union type.
94	IV014	The set of value types that includes at least one supertype of every static value type supported by the GQL implementation.
95	IV015	The valid syntactic representation of an authorization identifier.
96	IV016	The description of any additional text provided about conditions.
97	IV023	The set of characters included in truncating whitespace.
98	IW001	The mechanism for instructing a GQL client to create and destroy GQL sessions to GQL servers, and to submit GQL requests to them.
99	IW002	The mechanism for creating and destroying authorization identifiers and their mapping to principals.
100	IW003	The mechanism for determining when the last request has been received.
101	IW004	The alternative mechanism for starting and terminating transactions.
102	IW005	The mechanism by which termination success or failure statuses are made available to the GQL agent or administrator.
103	IW006	The mechanism for determining the dictionary of GQL request parameters.
104	IW007	The manner in which GQL status objects are presented to a GQL client.
105	IW010	The manner in which external procedures are provided.
106	IW011	The mechanism for determining the reference value type of an element variable declared by a graph pattern.
107	IW012	The mechanism for determining the reference value type of an element variable declared by the insert node pattern.

	Feature ID	Feature Name
108	IW014	The mechanism used to determine if two character strings are visually confusable with each other.
109	IW015	The manner, if it so chooses, in which a GQL implementation automatically creates and populates a GQL directory.
110	IW016	The manner, if it so chooses, in which a GQL implementation automatically populates a GQL schema upon its creation.
111	IW017	The manner in which the result of the concatenation of non-normalized character strings is determined.
112	IW018	The manner in which lax casts (and supporting type tests) are generated and included in the syntax transforms for the dynamic generation of strict casts.
113	IW019	The mechanism for determining a common supertype of a set of value types of the same primary static base type.
114	IW021	The mechanism for determining a permutation of all value types of a set of value types that adheres to type precedence rules.
115	IW022	The mechanism for determining if the null value is not actually going to be assigned to a site.
116	IW023	The mechanism for determining the canonical name form of a <delimited identifier> or <non-delimited identifier>.
117	IW025	The mechanism for determining which and how many catalog-modifying procedures are under transaction control, and which catalog-modifying procedures can be contained in a single transaction.

Implementation-dependent elements — GQL conformance

	Feature ID	Feature Name
1	UA001	The interaction between multiple GQL environments within the constraints of GQL transaction semantics.
2	UA002	Whether or not diagnostic information pertaining to more than one condition is made available.
3	UA004	Whether or not that exception condition is actually raised when the evaluation of an inessential part of an expression or search condition would cause an exception to be raised.
4	UA005	Which path bindings are retained in an any path search if the number of candidates exceeds the required number.
5	UA006	Which additional path bindings are actually probed to establish whether they might also raise an exception when the GQL implementation has terminated the evaluation of a selective path pattern.
6	UA007	Whether or not a rollback is forced when a GQL transaction becomes blocked, cannot complete without causing semantic inconsistency, or the resources required to continue its execution become unavailable.
7	US001	The sequence of records in an unordered binding table.
8	US005	The order of path bindings that have the same number of edges.
9	US006	The relative ordering of peers in a sort.
10	US007	The relative ordering of items in a sort whose comparison is unknown.
11	US008	The actual order of expression evaluation.
12	US009	The point in time at which the request timestamp is set.
13	UV001	The value of an object identifier.
14	UV003	The <value expression> whose evaluation raises the exception condition: data exception — invalid value type (22G12).
15	UV004	The value returned by an evaluation of the ELEMENT_ID function.
16	UV005	The physical representation of an instance of a data type.

	Feature ID	Feature Name
17	UV007	The declared type of a site that contains an intermediate result.
18	UV009	Which arbitrary value is chosen when multiple assignments to a graph element property are specified.
19	UV014	The start datetime used for converting intervals to scalars for subtraction purposes.
20	UW001	The mechanism for determining which exception condition is to be returned as the primary GQL-status object of an execution outcome from a set of raised exception conditions.

15

Unlock Your Exclusive Benefits

Your copy of this book includes the following exclusive benefits:

- ⟲ Next-gen Packt Reader
- 🗎 DRM-free PDF/ePub downloads

Follow the guide below to unlock them. The process takes only a few minutes and needs to be completed once.

Unlock this Book's Free Benefits in 3 Easy Steps

Step 1

Keep your purchase invoice ready for *Step 3*. If you have a physical copy, scan it using your phone and save it as a PDF, JPG, or PNG.

For more help on finding your invoice, visit https://www.packtpub.com/unlock-benefits/help.

> **Note:** If you bought this book directly from Packt, no invoice is required. After *Step 2*, you can access your exclusive content right away.

Step 2

Scan the QR code or go to `packtpub.com/unlock`.

On the page that opens (similar to *Figure 15.1* on desktop), search for this book by name and select the correct edition.

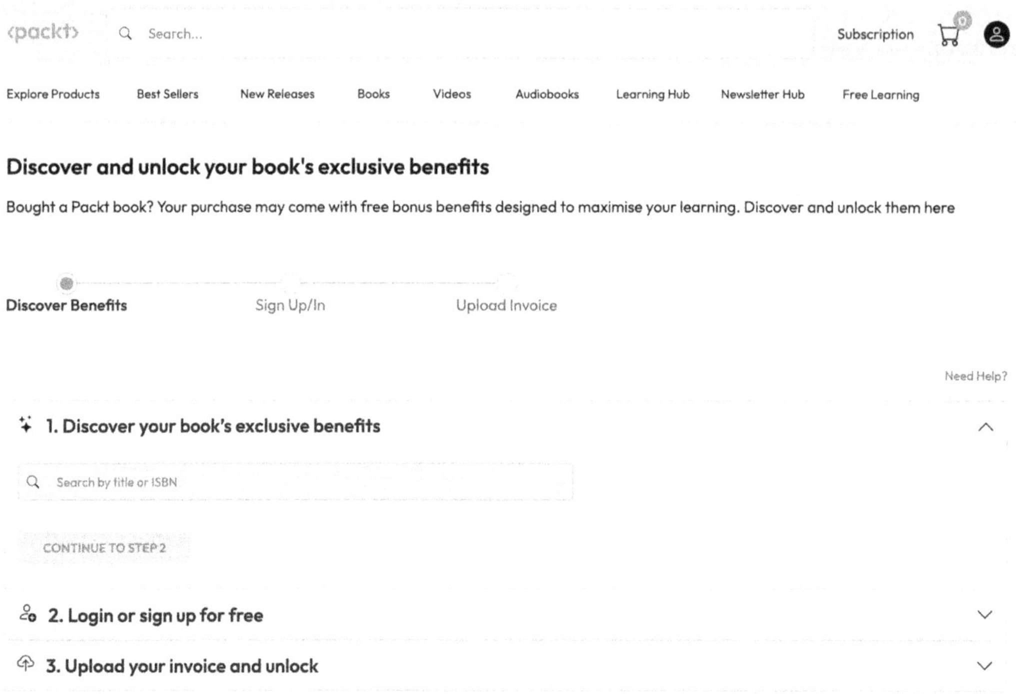

⟨packt⟩   🔍 Search...   Subscription 🛒 👤

Explore Products   Best Sellers   New Releases   Books   Videos   Audiobooks   Learning Hub   Newsletter Hub   Free Learning

Discover and unlock your book's exclusive benefits

Bought a Packt book? Your purchase may come with free bonus benefits designed to maximise your learning. Discover and unlock them here

Discover Benefits   Sign Up/In   Upload Invoice

Need Help?

✦ **1. Discover your book's exclusive benefits**   ⌃

🔍 Search by title or ISBN

CONTINUE TO STEP 2

👥 **2. Login or sign up for free**   ⌄

☁ **3. Upload your invoice and unlock**   ⌄

Figure 15.1: Packt unlock landing page on desktop

Step 3

After selecting your book, sign in to your Packt account or create one for free. Then upload your invoice (PDF, PNG, or JPG, up to 10 MB). Follow the on-screen instructions to finish the process.

Need help?

If you get stuck and need help, visit `https://www.packtpub.com/unlock-benefits/help` for a detailed FAQ on how to find your invoices and more. This QR code will take you to the help page.

> **Note:** If you are still facing issues, reach out to `customercare@packt.com`.

‹packt›

Subscribe to our online digital library for full access to over 7,000 books and videos, as well as industry leading tools to help you plan your personal development and advance your career. For more information, please visit our website.

Why subscribe?

- Spend less time learning and more time coding with practical eBooks and Videos from over 4,000 industry professionals
- Improve your learning with Skill Plans built especially for you
- Get a free eBook or video every month
- Fully searchable for easy access to vital information
- Copy and paste, print, and bookmark content

At www.packtpub.com, you can also read a collection of free technical articles, sign up for a range of free newsletters, and receive exclusive discounts and offers on Packt books and eBooks.

Other Books You May Enjoy

If you enjoyed this book, you may be interested in these other books by Packt:

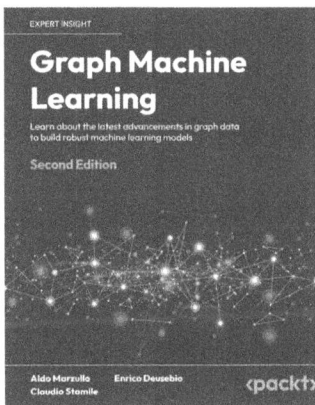

Graph Machine Learning, Second Edition

Aldo Marzullo, Enrico Deusebio, Claudio Stamile

ISBN: 978-1-80324-806-6

- Implement graph ML algorithms with examples in StellarGraph, PyTorch Geometric, and DGL
- Apply graph analysis to dynamic datasets using temporal graph ML
- Enhance NLP and text analytics with graph-based techniques
- Solve complex real-world problems with graph machine learning
- Build and scale graph-powered ML applications effectively
- Deploy and scale your application seamlessly

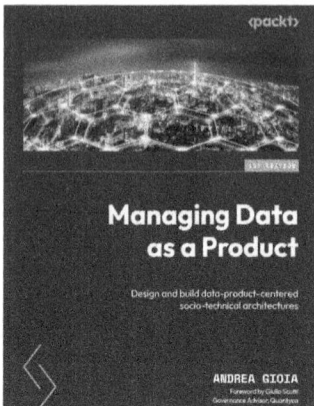

Managing Data as a Product

Andrea Gioia

ISBN: 978-1-83546-853-1

- Overcome the challenges in scaling monolithic data platforms, including cognitive load, tech debt, and maintenance costs
- Discover the benefits of adopting a data-as-a-product approach for scalability and sustainability
- Navigate the complete data product lifecycle, from inception to decommissioning
- Automate data product lifecycle management using a self-serve platform
- Implement an incremental, value-driven strategy for transitioning to data-product-centric architectures
- Optimize data modeling in distributed environments to enhance GenAI-based use cases

Packt is searching for authors like you

If you're interested in becoming an author for Packt, please visit authors.packt.com and apply today. We have worked with thousands of developers and tech professionals, just like you, to help them share their insight with the global tech community. You can make a general application, apply for a specific hot topic that we are recruiting an author for, or submit your own idea.

Share your thoughts

Now you've finished *Getting Started with the Graph Query Language (GQL)*, we'd love to hear your thoughts! Scan the QR code below to go straight to the Amazon review page for this book and share your feedback or leave a review on the site that you purchased it from.

https://packt.link/r/1836204019

Your review is important to us and the tech community and will help us make sure we're delivering excellent quality content.

Index

www.ingramcontent.com/pod-product-compliance
Lightning Source LLC
Chambersburg PA
CBHW081044220326
41598CB00038B/6981